for Molly,
with love,
Sheila, 28.3.15

# A SECOND BOOK OF BOOKSELLERS

SHEILA MARKHAM

A Second Book of

# BOOKSELLERS

*Conversations with the*
*Antiquarian Book Trade*

———

with an introduction by
NICOLAS BARKER

Sheila Markham *Rare Books*

MMXIV

ISBN 978-0-9547997-2-4

Edition limited to 500 copies

Designed and typeset in 10pt Minion by Kirsty Anderson
Printed by Berforts Information Press, King's Lynn

Sheila Markham Rare Books
15 The Priory
Blackheath
London SE3 9XA
United Kingdom

In Memory of
Michael Silverman
1949 – 2011

# Acknowledgements

I am deeply grateful to my colleagues whose cooperation has enabled me to publish another volume of conversations with the antiquarian book trade. I would also like to thank Kirsty Anderson for once again looking after its design and production. Intended as a sequel to *A Book of Booksellers*, published in 2004 in a limited edition and co-published in 2007 with Oak Knoll Press, the present work follows the same editorial methods and format. The interviews were conducted between 2007 and 2013, and are arranged in chronological order. The exact date is given in the index to this volume.

I owe special thanks to Michael Berry who succeeded Barry Shaw as editor of *Bookdealer* and invited me to continue the magazine's series of interviews which had begun in 1991. The first twenty interviews in this volume were commissioned by Michael Berry and, in the case of Alan Mitchell's and John Windle's interviews, by the late Richard Sawyer.

The article in the Appendix was first published in *Bookdealer* in 1991 as a contribution to the 1000th edition of the magazine. The Epilogue appeared in the newsletter of the Antiquarian Booksellers Association in July 2011.

Shortly after *Bookdealer* ceased publication, I was invited by Nicolas Barker to start a new series of conversations with the antiquarian book trade for *The Book Collector*. The last ten interviews in this volume were first published there, and I am most grateful to Nicolas Barker for permission to reprint them, and to James Fergusson for his editorial rigour.

My sincere thanks for valuable help and advice are also due to Robert Bartfield, Charles Brand, John Critchley, Clive Farahar, Emily Fotheringham, Marianne Harwood, Thomas Hudson, Bill Kuhn, Brian Lake, Nicolette Le Pelley, Michael Meredith, Carol Murphy, James Shurmer, John Saumarez Smith, James Sprague, Thomas Sutherland and John Wells. I would also like to thank Christopher Phipps for kindly agreeing to compile the index, and Susan Palmer for reading the proofs.

Finally it is my pleasure to thank Ian Jackson for his unstinting support and encouragement, and for the generosity with which he shares his extraordinary learning.

# Contents

# INTRODUCTION

The book trade has changed in many ways over the last fifty or sixty years, and it is customary to say that there aren't so many characters in it as there used to be. By this they mean that there are fewer people who look like Ronald Searle's 'Slightly Foxed'. That was, of course, not a character, but a caricature. What gave it point was the need to distinguish the bookseller from some faceless functionary speaking or writing on behalf of a firm, 'per pro', as business letters used to end. Firms had multiple employees, any one of whom might represent, even be the firm in some way or other. The post clerk who took in and despatched the mail would be the firm, as far as the postman was concerned. To its more important customers, at a more exalted level, the directors would be the firm. It was these different facets that gave the singular entity that was the firm its character. So when people say there aren't so many characters around, what they really mean is that there are fewer people who diverge from the image of the firm as the sum of its parts. Those who diverged, whether because they looked or spoke or dressed in some way different were by definition eccentric, slightly foxed, at least. Now they are less conspicuous, because there is no norm to diverge from. There are fewer firms now, in the old sense of the word, and more individuals in the book trade than ever before; the boss and the packer are often the same person.

These reflections are prompted by a tendency that seems to me to distinguish Sheila Markham's second anthology of character studies from her first. Some (by no means all) of those whose memoirs made up the first volume had at least grown up within the framework where the firm predominated over the individual. The majority (I think) of those in the second have, one way or another, found their way into and around the trade on their own, as individuals, whether they have many or no colleagues. Edward Bayntun-Coward was born to the purple, inheriting the direction of a long-established business, to which he has given his own personal direction. Sabrina Izzard had no expectation of becoming a bookseller at all. It was only the accident of being picked by Elizabeth Blackwell to assist her at Hall's Bookshop, and Elizabeth's untimely death that pitchforked her into becoming the owner of the business. Both these experiences are in their different ways typical of the life-stories and reflections on the trade in the other vignettes. Both had exceptional advantages that coloured and supported their first steps: one had parental memory and the Rivière stock, the other the constant help for three years of the previous owner of Hall's, Harry Pratley, the kindest and most generous of men. He too it was who set Tim d'Arch Smith on the primrose path by inviting him to do the publicity for the antiquarian book fair.

Such influences, and chance encounters, loom large in these narratives. In the absence of any formal training in bookselling, other kinds of education are a matter of absorbing interest. Tony Cox got the best of beginnings from his father, Claude Cox, and he was taught by Arnold Muirhead. Tony was at York University, as was Brian Lake of Jarndyce and Peter Miller of Ken Spelman; so was John Fuggles, not to mention Tony Blair (not, in the event, a secondhand bookseller) – what was it about York? Larry Ilott learned bookselling in the public library service, whose downfall (not his) makes pitiful reading. The unforgettable Jack Joseph taught Chris Kohler. Richard Hatchwell absorbed all that Tom Thorp and Walter Harris could pass on, but was truly self-taught by the books and manuscripts that he bought. Many a bookseller owes a debt, not always recorded, to wife or partner. Mary Hatchwell had a second career as a paper- and book-conservator. Peter Budek found himself giving an attractive young woman increasingly high discounts, and then, reckoning it would come cheaper to marry her, did so. He has the last word on education: 'having a bookshop,' he says, 'is the best university in the world'. Perhaps Elizabeth Strong has the first as well as last word on the choice of bookselling as a career. 'I began', she says, 'to buy books faster than I could read them – a tell-tale sign of a bookseller.'

Some of the impressions and beliefs are inevitably similar – why should they not be? – but some are different. Peter Scupham is a poet as well as a bookseller, with a sharp eye for the eccentricities of both métiers. 'Poets are vain animals', he says. 'When they start to worry about their reputations, I always say to myself, "the ammonites are laughing". They have lasted millions of years. As a poet, you're lucky if your reputation lasts twenty or thirty years.' The same thought must have occurred to all the booksellers present here. It is a sobering experience to turn the pages of a seventeenth-century book and reflect that it has been around for four or five times as long as you have, and will most likely outlive you. This habit of mind can make a bookseller short-tempered with those who stray into the shop visibly bent on not buying. 'Tyre-kickers' is a good word for them, those who come in and ask for a particular book and then say, if you produce it, 'You can't want as much as that for it'. Or, 'Isn't it wonderful', they gasp, looking round, 'I could spend all day in here', and, having said it, promptly walk out. You can see why so many booksellers think of customers as an obstacle to the more serious business of selling books.

Bookshops are magical places, where who knows what adventures may not start. It may be this sense that makes a lot of customers doubt if they are really businesses at all. 'I am frequently asked if I inherited it, or if it is a hobby, or a museum.' Well, it can be all these things and still a bookshop. Cal Hyland has a sharp eye for what really makes a good bookseller, remembering Harold Landry, who 'loved packing and was very good at it', or Bob Gilbert who 'can spot an Irish book at fifty feet', quite an achievement if only the spine is showing. But it is Ian Marr who puts the book trade in perspective, or rather the auction house caterer he asked if there was any pattern in sales of refreshments to different types of dealer. 'Without hesitation, she replied that she sold chocolate cake at fine arts sales, lemon cake at picture sales, sausage rolls to dealers in general junk, and book dealers always ate rock cakes – nothing fancy.'

Nothing fancy, not here the hype that makes the headlines, but – science books, Spanish maps, the copy of *La Cifra* that Borges forgot to sign, ANC pamphlets packed beneath a false bottom in boxes of books shipped to Apartheid South Africa, a blind man cataloguing the great sixteenth-century editions of the classics from braille-read descriptions backed by a capacious memory – no one can say it's a boring business. *A Second Book of Booksellers* is just as full of the rich loam of character that made the first such capital reading, and now that *Bookdealer* has sadly ceased publication, I look forward to a third, drawn from future pages of *The Book Collector.*

Nicolas Barker

# The Mechanics of Bookselling ∾ John Loska

My father was a Pole who escaped to this country during the Second World War. He was blinded and lost an arm in 1945 while serving with the Eighth Army. On my mother's side I'm descended from Sir Charles Waterton, a great eccentric and pioneer in many fields, best known to booksellers as the author of *Wanderings in South America*. My interest in books began as a child when I started to read my mother's books, and discovered Sir Walter Scott whom I enjoy to this day. My interest in literature awakened, I began to explore and greatly enjoy authors from the seventeenth to the nineteenth centuries.

I started collecting books while I was reading Mathematics at the University of Sussex. I'm Brighton born and bred and it suited me to go to my local university and live at home with all my creature comforts – I should add that Sussex did have at the time one of the best maths departments in the country. This was in the 1970s and the age of comparatively generous student grants, which enabled me to start buying books, spending twenty quid here and there. That was a week's money to live on, but it was also enough to buy a rather good book – for example, a first edition of Dickens in original cloth. You could buy eighteenth-century books for a pound, when maths text books were costing ten or fifteen pounds.

By the time I got my degree in 1980, I had become very interested in books and book collecting. I decided to take a year off, having saved enough money to do so, and stayed at home reading for twelve hours a day. As you read one book, so it leads you to another. It was fantastic, just reading entirely for my own pleasure. Some might regard my taste as a bit dry – seventeenth-century poets, eighteenth- century novelists. But the mainstream authors – Fielding, Smollett, Sterne – are all worth reading.

By the end of the year my parents were getting on my back, and quite rightly so. It happened that Colin Page, from whom I had been buying books, was looking for someone to put his stock on to a computer he had just installed. Colin believed that computers were the way forward for the trade and had bought one as early as 1979 and taught himself to program it. He wanted to produce tailor-made lists to match customers' interests and, in due course, was able to advertise this service in the pages of the *Bookdealer*. The machine cost several thousand pounds and was constantly crashing. It used seven-inch floppy discs which could only store 300 entries. Although I had a maths degree, I had never encountered a computer at university. It was intended to be a six-week project, but inevitably the job took longer. Meanwhile we were getting on very well, and Colin offered me a permanent position which I accepted and loved from my first day.

In 1900 Colin Page's grandfather had founded the first garage in Brighton. Colin began his working life as a mechanic, but neither he nor his brother Brian enjoyed life in the family firm. In 1969 they set up together in a shop in Lewes dealing in secondhand books and oriental antiques, later moving to the present shop in Brighton opposite Holleyman & Treacher.

George Holleyman had dominated bookselling in Brighton since the war. When Colin opened in the same street, George treated him very well, telling him the various points about books and paying him fair money. At the time John Kite was still working for Holleyman's. He was a lovely old boy, the spitting image of John Betjeman in appearance and manner. When the firm went out of business, Colin Page inherited many of their customers, some of whom had wonderful collections.

There were also a number of back street bookshops, notably Ben Hutchinson's. Ben is perhaps best known for selling an enormous collection of Tauchnitz editions to Chris Johnson, who sold it to the University of Texas, where it was consulted by the great American husband-and-wife team, William B. Todd and Ann Bowden in the preparation of their monumental bibliography of *Tauchnitz International Editions in English*. It's curious to think that it all started in a shop behind Brighton railway station.

Colin Page had a great eye for antiquarian books and, by the time I joined him, the shop had an interesting and varied stock of books at all levels, although it was not nearly as large as it is now. Colin taught me the mechanics of the booktrade. A bookseller needs to have skills relating to buying and selling. A market trader would probably make a better bookseller than an academic. I was learning from him all the time, going on house calls and to auctions. I remember seeing my first Arthur Rackham book and being surprised that there was a market for it – let alone a very good market. For me books were about words, not pictures.

Colin taught me to treat people fairly, whether buying from or selling to them. I like to think that we pay more and charge less for our books than many other dealers. It pays off in the long run as books gravitate to us, at least from private sources. I became a partner in the business in the late 1980s and, when Colin retired in 1999, I bought him out fully. Just as I was about to make the biggest transaction of my life, I was diagnosed with cancer. I had an operation and I've been fine ever since. I'm delighted that I went through with the deal, but it caused me an enormous amount of stress at the time.

Today my wife and I are equal partners in the shop, although Jill doesn't work in the business. She did, however, have the interesting experience of working briefly for Peter Eaton in the early 1970s, and remembers some of the amazing books he was able to buy from totters or rag-and-bone men. Our two sons are in their twenties and neither will be following us into the trade. They are both carving their careers in the theatre and we take great pleasure in watching them perform.

My twin brother, Stephen, joined the business in 1983 and is on the road quite a bit, doing a lot of the auctions and house calls. Michael Hearne and two part-time assistants look after the shop, and I do a bit of everything. As in most small businesses, there's no strict division of labour, but I like to do most of the pricing. Every book is individual, and the price depends to a certain extent on how I feel about a copy at a particular moment.

I like the social contact of having a shop. It would drive me mad to work in a room on my own. I don't have the skill to write flowing phrases about books, and have the greatest admiration for people who can catalogue a book well, acquire in-depth knowledge of their subject and carve a niche for themselves. I have never cultivated the institutional market, although I occasionally sell something to the British Library – for example, John Betjeman's collection of thirty-two Ordnance Survey maps with his annotations and doodles, which I picked up very cheaply in a Cambridge auction. A local journalist saw them in my shop and asked if he could write an article for *The Times,* where it was spotted by someone at the BL.

Mine is a more old-fashioned niche; it's a jack of all trades style of general bookselling. We are very unusual nowadays and, as more secondhand bookshops close, it puts us in a stronger position. I must be almost the only bookseller in the south of England who still rents his premises in the centre of an expensive town. My rates went up 40 per cent last year. It's all right as long as we keep doing the turnover to match it, but you have to keep your eye on the ball. If I ever feel short of money, it's because I'm buying lots of books. It's not the overheads that knock you for six.

The trade buys 80 per cent of my books. We meet a lot of Continental and American dealers at book fairs, and I'm always impressed by the high quality of the books they buy. Some years ago I was diagnosed with a propensity for blood clotting, and told to avoid long flights. As a result I have never been to America, which I naively regard as the golden land of book collectors. Bookselling is probably just as tough there as it is here, but there's no question where the more valuable books end up.

Mr Howlett, the king of runners, used to buy a lot of books from us and then sell them to the West End dealers. Then there was 'Bicycle' Tony who died recently. In Brighton one meets a lot of characters. 'Peg Leg' Mick and 'Fast' Eddie are both suppliers. There was an extraordinary incident in the early 1980s when the entire stock of a Brighton bookseller turned up at a Sunday market. Runners were coming into our shop with colour-plate books, signed copies of Rackham and other wonderful books. It turned out that he had kept his stock in various storage depots in Brighton and, when he failed to pay the rent, the books had been sold in lieu of payment. Nowadays there are very few runners left, and those who are still active tend to buy from charity shops, boot sales and markets in which Brighton abounds.

I get my biggest buzz from bookselling when I buy collections. It's a wonderful feeling when you leave a house with a carload of good books, perhaps having spent more money than you can afford. The transitory ownership can be great fun. I bought Raymond Smith's private library in January this year. Booksellers always have interesting books in their homes, and Raymond was no exception. Our friendship dated from when I walked into his shop in Eastbourne wearing the same tweed jacket. He found that very amusing. Actually I must have been something of a fuddy duddy to be wearing the same jacket as a man forty years my senior. When Raymond retired in the early 1990s, I introduced him to Alan Gibbard who bought his shop in Eastbourne. Raymond had indicated that he would like me to buy his private library, which I did against two independent valuations. He had been collecting for over 60 years, and I came away from his home in Eastbourne with twelve carloads of good quality books.

I'm one of the very few booksellers who doesn't put his books on the internet. I believe this makes my shop more interesting for customers. At book fairs I have occasionally put up a sign saying 'internet free'. It began as a joke, but has become a selling point. It seems to work; my two annual fairs, Chelsea and Olympia, are always very fruitful. Everyone likes the idea of fresh books that haven't been touted on the internet. I like to put a book on the shelf and let someone discover it. It's all about the thrill of the chase.

Bookselling has become tougher in the last seven or eight years and the internet has contributed to this. The 'four-quidders' are much harder to sell – that is, the secondhand hardback book that is not intrinsically collectable, but which may nevertheless make a significant contribution to its subject. There are tens of millions of them on the internet, and we certainly don't sell as many in the shop as we used to. Labour and storage are both expensive, and there may come a time when it's no longer economical to stock cheap books. But it would be a very sad day for bookselling. I believe that people should buy all classes of books in their subject. The 'four-quidder' can be just as valid in its way as a book that costs £400.

Internet bookselling requires a very different style; it's all about cataloguing, packing and posting, which can make the price more expensive than a bookshop. I disagreed with Paul Minet on this subject in the *Daily Telegraph* recently. Paul stated that people will find a book in a shop, and then buy a cheaper copy on the internet. Paul is a bookseller for whom I have the greatest respect, but actually I believe that it works the other way round – ordinary books are nearly always cheaper in shops.

The general public use the internet as a crude valuation tool. But the price is only half the equation. I buy up to 70 per cent of my stock privately and it can be very difficult to convince the vendor that just because they have seen a copy of their book priced at $x$ on the internet, I can only charge $y$ for it in my shop. I consider the hammer price at auction to be a fairer gauge of the value of a book.

It's not just the public who use ABE as a pricing tool. Many of the newcomers to the trade don't seem to spend money on reference books; they get their information from the wonderful descriptions by the best booksellers freely available on ABE. This is having an effect on the market for Bibliography. I recently bought Chris Kohler's reference library, accumulated over forty years of selling literary and author-based collections. The books weren't as commercially valuable as they would have been before the internet. Pure 'information' books have become much harder to sell. But there's no question that you can still score if you have the right reference book, and access to that tiny nugget of information that can result in a wonderful profit.

Highlight collecting is more prevalent than author collecting today – perhaps due to the influence of *Printing and the Mind of Man*. Although it is a wonderful catalogue, it turned the greatest books in western civilisation into a self-contained subject. But there is far more to books than that – I like to go after the obscure little pamphlet that fits into the subject and boosts the collection.

Very few members of the trade like the concept of buying books for investment. It's an artificial form of collecting, keeping books too expensive for more genuine collectors. You should buy a book because you like it and, over the years as you become familiar with the field, you will probably also buy quite astutely. There are many undervalued areas of book collecting. Apart from the obvious high spots, seventeenth-century English Literature is still ludicrously cheap. I also think that English Topography is undervalued, if you consider that some of the great county histories in multiple volumes are available for a few hundred pounds.

Book collecting is very much a male activity. Most of my collectors are men in their 50s and 60s. There are various factors why young people are not collecting books. If you can't afford somewhere to live, you're unlikely to be collecting anything much. Also the younger generation turns to the internet for its primary source of information, where we would have consulted a book. I notice this with my two sons. There are great cultural changes at work.

There will always be a living to be made out of buying and selling books. We all do our bookselling in a slightly different way. It's this ability to perceive books differently that enables us to buy and sell from each other. Booksellers are very individual and that is the glory of the trade.

# Gamekeeper turned Poacher ❧ Larry Ilott

I was born in South London at the tail end of the war. My mother was a singer and my father was what would today be called a graphic designer. There was a lot of interest in the arts in my childhood home, but not specifically in books. I had polio when I was five years old. I can only describe it as character forming; something you give in to or you fight. It made me a very determined person. I went to school at Alleyn's in Dulwich, where the Head of English was an exceptionally good teacher. The school had a historic connection with the Jacobean theatre, and endowed me with a lasting interest in language and literature.

I wasn't necessarily the ideal pupil – in fact, something of a sixties drop-out. But I was already buying books, mainly from Dillon's in Malet Street, and reading hugely. My health was still indifferent and I couldn't quite see how a conventional university education would benefit me in terms of a career. I might end up teaching English to another bunch of layabouts like myself, and didn't find the prospect very attractive. The Head of English wrote in my final report that he had no idea if I would pass my A-Level as I hadn't done any written work during the entire course. He was kind enough to add that he would buy my beer for the evening if I passed, which in due course he did.

After school I drifted into working in public libraries, first of all in what became the London Borough of Southwark. It turned into a career and I spent thirty years as a librarian, not that I was particularly cut out to be a local government officer. I did my training in what was then the North Western Polytechnic in Camden Town, where I was fortunate to be taught by some excellent lecturers, including John Morris who became Curator of Rare Books at the National Library of Scotland, and Stan Brett who became a leading light in the PBFA. The academic training formalised my interest in books and book collecting which had existed from an early age. I found the study of historical bibliography absolutely fascinating, in particular the transmission of text and the development of bookbinding styles.

In due course I was given the job of running the cataloguing department in Lewisham, where I spent ten years. Lewisham still had its own bindery, and it was part of my job to order materials and liaise with the foreman. He also did a bit of private work and rebound some of the books in my own collection. He would ask my advice about binding styles and gradually became a good restorer. Meanwhile I spent a lot of time watching him work on the bench, and picked up the ability to do a certain amount myself. When we went to Hewit's to buy leather, John would introduce me as the oldest apprentice in the trade.

Although one didn't realise it, the 1960s and 1970s were the golden age of public libraries in London – in terms of funding, public awareness and general good will towards the service. This situation came about with the creation of the London boroughs in 1965, when a huge amount of funding was made available to cope with such a major upheaval in local government structure.

Contrary to popular belief, librarians are quite good at managing change, and made the most of the extra funding at their disposal. Things had never been better and very rapidly got worse. By the late seventies, much of local government funding began to depend on central government. Where the finance lies, there the power lies. As a Borough Librarian put it to me, 'There're a lot of votes in dustbins, but not a lot of votes in books'.

In 1985 I became Collections Manager for the library service in Kent, with its stock of around three and a half million books. It gave me the opportunity to handle a great many early books which was of great benefit to me in my later bookselling career. There was a formal working relationship between the County Council and the Dean and Chapter of Canterbury Cathedral and on one memorable occasion, I was asked to collaborate with their librarian on a valuation for the ecclesiastical insurers. I shall always remember her opening remark, 'We don't have any Caxtons, but we've eighty or ninety incunabula. Shall we start with those?'

By 1990 there had been a massive restructuring in the library service, which involved taking out a whole tier of management. I was offered the one job I said I would never do; they wanted me to asset-strip the collections. I was the only person on the staff who knew more or less what there was, and had some idea of its monetary value and contacts with the book trade. I was forty-five at the time and had already made up my mind that I wanted to become a bookseller. I needed to hang on for five more years for the good of my pension. I declined to take the job, which I considered the professional equivalent of putting King Herod in charge of the crèche. After being a spare part for a few months, it was agreed that I should do anything I could to generate income for the department – short of selling books.

I turned to the idea of increasing the libraries' revenue from greetings cards, and spent the next five years learning skills which ultimately helped me to run my own business. The libraries were carrying all the overheads of production and storage, and weren't particularly good at identifying and concentrating on the saleable images. In effect, I set myself up as a wholesaler, sourcing good material from commercial companies and marketing it through the libraries. Kent had 127 branch libraries, which I treated as 127 retail outlets. I tried very deliberately not to compete with local tradesmen to avoid any political fall-out. The cards were displayed near the issue desk, which was good for impulse buying, while people were queuing with their books.

Within eighteen months, I was turning over something like £180,000 a year, and was able to generate more income by selling myself as a consultant to other local authorities who wanted to do the same thing. At any time an external auditor could have come in and shut down the whole commercial operation. We were relying on certain paragraphs in the Local Government Finance regulations never having been tested in the courts. Politically it was expedient for everyone to turn a blind eye as the local authorities needed the money.

A few weeks after my 50th birthday in 1995, I walked into my director's office and suggested that it would be easier to balance the budget if he made me redundant. An offer was put on the table. I accepted it and left local government service at the end of the financial year. My bookselling business was up and running on the following Monday. I was very lucky to have been in the right place at the right time, and to have been able to make a five-year plan.

Thirty or forty years ago one might have advised newcomers to the secondhand book trade to work for a big firm like Blackwell's, Maggs or Sotheran's by way of serving an apprenticeship. Today there are fewer and fewer of these houses available to newcomers. What I lacked when I first started was a knowledge of the trade itself, although I had already been doing local book fairs, and subscribing to the *Bookdealer*. The obvious lesson that all booksellers learn is to buy at the right price and sell at the right price – and to be prepared to be flexible on both. Like everybody else in trade, I bought my experience.

Within six months of opening the business, I decided to move my stock into an antiques centre in Westerham, where I spent a couple of years. In due course I set myself up on the internet, and managed to slide under the little bit of lease left on the antiques centre and start working from home. I sold my landlord all the stock that I wanted to leave behind, and my wife and I crowded everything else into Cobnar, our home in Wateringbury.

I spent the next five years saying to myself, 'Sell ten books and buy one', as a means of disposing of the shop stock, and trading up in quality. If you can afford to do that without borrowing money, it's the soundest way to conduct business. I now have something like 1,300 books of which around half would be termed antiquarian.

I joined the PBFA in 1997 and had my arm twisted into becoming South East Regional Chairman about five years later. It had reached the stage in the evolution of every organisation when the founding fathers have moved on, and a fresh start is needed. It requires drive, vision and the will to change to make the PBFA fit for purpose for another ten to fifteen years, and at the moment this is not much in evidence. At one Committee meeting, I suggested that the income stream could be greatly improved by using the PBFA website (*not* books@pbfa) to host online book auctions, initially just for members. This was before eBay was a force in the land. In fact, there were very few online auctions at all. By taking a smaller commission than the mainstream auction houses, the PBFA might find a ready market for its online auctions. However nothing came of it. Perhaps it was too radical, or the time just wasn't right.

To combat the dominance of the internet, it is more essential than ever to build up one-to-one relationships with collectors. This is one of the advantages of book fairs. Although fairs in general seem to be declining as a way of trading, they do provide the opportunity for personal contact. Yorkshire is a good place to meet top quality private collectors – perhaps it's something to do with the concentration of four major universities within a relatively small radius. I always exhibit at the PBFA fairs in York and Harrogate, and enjoy my chats with collectors and academics from whom I always learn something. Whereas greetings cards are just a commodity, books are life-style. I probably learn something from every book I buy – even if it's only never to pay that much again.

There's a specialised form of bibliographical madness which is an interest in English provincial printing. When I became Collections Manager for Kent, I found in my in-tray a letter from Richard Goulden who was working for the ESTC project at the British Library. It was an invitation to our staff to catalogue locally printed material for the ESTC. I took this letter round the cataloguing department, but there was no interest. So I pursued it myself and it led to a long and fruitful connection with the British Library, which I have continued in my bookselling career. I was able to contribute around 180 unique records to ESTC when I discovered two eighteenth-century printers' day books, belonging to one of the first Maidstone printers, dismembered and housed in various files in Maidstone Museum. Ultimately Richard and I obtained a conservation grant for the material, which was described on the application form as being of national importance.

The British Library has big gaps in its collection of English provincial printing, and I quickly saw a little niche there for a bookseller – not that I was the first to do so by any means. Every one of us has to find their own own market. If you have acquired some specialist knowledge from a previous professional background, it will give you a head start as far as familiarity with the literature and target customers are concerned. I always e-mail a draft of my catalogue to the British Library, who have been very helpful to me. In general, I target libraries shamelessly, partly because I still have some good contacts, and also because I've controlled library budgets and know that if you don't spend it, you lose it. You might say that I regard it as my bounden duty to help out my former colleagues.

My catalogues have never been very regular but, for a bookseller with my sort of stock and institutional customers, this good old-fashioned approach still has a lot of mileage in it. Acquisitions librarians and academics like to have a piece of paper in their hand – something they can read on the train, or scribble notes on when they're online. It's difficult to browse a website in the same way. Catalogues and the internet complement rather than replace each other. A sensible bookseller makes full use of both.

It's going to be increasingly difficult for booksellers to combat the availability of complete texts on the internet. Although the publication of new novels electronically doesn't seem to have caught on yet, the principle threatens to short-circuit the whole world of publishing and the book trade as we know it. My personal route ahead, apart from concentrating on my established business of selling topography, antiquarian books and provincial printing to libraries and a few private customers, is to think more in terms of the book as art object, and to be able to talk knowledgeably to customers about binding, printing and paper-making. At a book fair recently a member of the public asked me how to become an antiquarian bookseller. He was in his thirties, a doctor at King's College Hospital in South London with a serious interest in dealing specifically in sixteenth-century Italian books. Now there's someone who thinks there's a future in bookselling.

According to my accountant, booksellers do everything the wrong way round. They carry big stocks with slow turn-over, and still achieve quite large profit margins. We justify those margins by putting in added value. I spend a long time looking for the right material, and then I research it, put my own money up front, and spend time describing it before finally offering it to perhaps the one person in the whole wide world who actually wants it. The combination of risk, time and knowledge represents the added value, and that, I am told, is the text book answer.

# The Evolution of a Collection ∾ Chris Kohler

I was lucky to come into contact with the world of secondhand books at a very impressionable age. I was fifteen and had just started smoking. As this was frowned upon at my boarding school in York, I needed to find somewhere with a little more privacy. In due course I drifted into the bookshops of York and found that, not only could I smoke, but the books were quite interesting. My English master had introduced me to Laurence Sterne, who intrigued me as his reputation rested on two books, and he had lived in York. On my last day of school in the summer of 1960, I spent some prize money on an eighteenth-century edition of *Tristram Shandy*. It had 'six volumes only' pencilled in the first volume and was priced accordingly. This discovery gave me enormous pleasure as I knew that, although Sterne's book had originally come out in nine volumes, my copy of a slightly later reprint was complete in six volumes. I left the bookshop clutching my prize with glee.

My father was an accountant in London and it was decided that I should work for him while I thought of what to do with my life. Every lunch hour I would gravitate towards secondhand bookshops and, by December 1960, I had decided that I wanted to work for a bookseller. My parents were very supportive and, early in the New Year, I began looking for a job and getting nowhere because of my lack of experience. I tried Joseph's and they said no and sent me to Foyles who said no so I proceeded to Maggs and Quaritch, two more noes, before I finally reached Bertram Rota where I burst into tears of frustration. They didn't have a job, but told me exactly what to do: I was to go back to Joseph's and tell Sam that I was desperate to become a bookseller and wouldn't be wasting his time. So I went back, with some misgivings, and had to brave big surly Sam Joseph who, after a bit of huffing and puffing, took me through to the back room to meet his brother. I repeated what I had been told to say, and Jack gave me a job, starting the following Monday on £6 a week. It was February 1961 and I was eighteen years old.

I loved everything about the job from my first day. The work was hard, the repartee was sharp and the outcome was an obsession with secondhand bookselling. The Josephs tended to be rather abrupt with customers, but their favourites were ushered through the shop into the office, or taken down to the warehouse in Great Newport Street. Dealers came from all over the world and we also had a lot of show business visitors – acquaintances from Sam Joseph's previous life when he had been married to Binnie Barnes, a Hollywood actress. Walt Disney and Sophie Tucker used to visit the shop.

Jack would take me to the London auctions and pick out a book and tell me what was important about it. After the sale, dealers would come back to the shop for the knock-out, which Jack would conduct in the back office. At some point, the buzzer would sound which was my signal to come in and take orders for tea and coffee. When I returned with a tray from Lyons tea shop, I would be let in to the smoke-filled room and Jack would peel a pound note off the top of the pile of cash on the table and give it to me as a tip. As I have commented elsewhere on the ring in London, it was made up of 'Joseph's, Marks, Thomas Thorp (London), Francis Edwards, Frank Hammond, Charles Traylen and Dawson's', (*Out of Print and Into Profit*, edited by Giles Mandelbrote, 2006).

Meanwhile I discovered that I would inherit £1000 from my grandmother on my twenty-first birthday, and decided this sum was enough to start my own business. Jack had been very generous with his knowledge and was sorry to lose me just as I was beginning to earn my wages. But he understood the give-and-take of the apprenticeship system, having been sent in his youth to work for a German bookseller. I was living with my parents in Dorking, and set off with my cheque book on my first book buying trip around the country. Many of the books I had handled at Joseph's were to be found considerably cheaper in the provinces, and I thought to myself, 'this is the life'.

The next stage was to buy a secondhand typewriter and duplicating machine and issue my first catalogue, putting together a mailing list based on reference books in Dorking Public Library, and an advertisement in the *Times Literary Supplement*. The catalogue did fairly badly, but I learnt a valuable lesson – an unknown pipsqueak working out of his bedroom in the provinces cannot hope to achieve the same price for a book as a top West End dealer.

At some stage it dawned on me that it was silly to try to ape the big boys in London. I needed to specialise in something and I chose English Literature. The mid-1960s coincided with the great expansion of university libraries in North America, and I began to receive an increasing number of institutional orders. At about the same time, I became aware of Robin Alston and his Scolar Press's *English Linguistics 1500-1800*, a series of 365 facsimile reprints of major texts for the study of the English language. Robin had invented the Prismascope, a device which enabled an early printed book to be photographed without opening it more than 45 degrees. This development helped to allay the fears of rare book librarians about the risk of damage to fragile originals.

As a respected academic, Robin had an entrée into scholarly libraries where the original editions were to be found. I thought the reprint programme was a fantastic idea and went up to Leeds to meet Robin and to offer my services as an unofficial salesman and, ultimately, I sold a major part of the print run. An entire set of reprints sold for £2600 over a period of a few years. I received a 25 per cent discount and eventually sold 125 sets. Several new titles would be published once a month for which I had to invoice and pack 125 orders. For a few years I almost gave up secondhand bookselling to concentrate on the Scolar Press reprints. The cash flow was amazing, and I was making contact with institutional libraries all over the world.

A turning point came in 1967 when I bought a collection of uniformly bound early Socialist pamphlets. It struck me as a bit of fun, and I bought them for £200 in a sale at Hodgson's. I sent a catalogue of the collection, priced at £700, to some libraries on my mailing list and received seventeen firm orders. That changed my life. Collections were the thing. I was soon trading successfully, and moved into offices in Dorking High Street. I was employing staff by that stage and, while we continued to sell individual rare books, the emphasis was on collections.

By the late 1960s, my accountant father was keen to think of ways to reduce my tax bill. We explored the idea of setting up business in a tax haven, and for a few years I ran my original business in Dorking and a second business called Guernsey Books in the Channel Islands. My colleague Lyn Elliott looked after the business in Guernsey, and I came over once a month to rubber-stamp decisions in order to comply with company law. When the Chancellor of the day closed a relevant tax loophole in the early 1970s, we closed down Guernsey Books and moved the stock back to Dorking. It coincided with the death of Lyn's husband and her returning to Surrey where she was able to continue to work for us in Dorking.

Although Lyn did a fantastic job cataloguing the collections, we always invited a respected academic to write an introduction to give it the seal of approval. In 1972 my future wife, Michèle, responded to one of my advertisements in the *TLS* for someone to write an introduction to a catalogue of eighteenth-century books. She was American and a newly minted PhD but, as I was looking for an established scholar, she didn't get the job. However, she had an interesting CV, and I invited her to contact me if she ever came to England, and that is how we eventually met and married. Within a year, she started working in the business and, since Lyn's departure about fifteen years ago, she has been responsible for all the cataloguing.

The concept of a collection bookseller is a largely twentieth-century phenomenon. Collections of books and manuscripts were traditionally assembled by private collectors and passed into institutional ownership by gift or sale. The earliest examples of dealer-assembled book collections were offered for sale at the end of the nineteenth century by J. Pearson, a company founded in the 1860s. To be a collection bookseller, you need an idea, the patience to pursue it, and not least the confidence to throw money at it. The gamble is always the same – will the collection as a whole be greater than the sum of its parts? A key to success for smaller collections is that they have to be repeatable. You need to have a secure source of supply so that you can go out and build the collection again.

When we received multiple orders, we would offer to put together another collection within about six weeks. It suits institutional libraries to acquire ready-made subject collections, and a number of booksellers – notably Noel Bolingbroke-Kent and later Kennys in Ireland – were making a living supplying this seemingly insatiable market, particularly in Japan. The composition of each of our collections on a specific subject might not be exactly the same every time. But we would ensure that the important authors were always represented. Typically we would be working on three types of collection at the same time – our small standard collections of about 200 titles; large-size collections, such as British Poetry of the Romantic Period and a John Milton collection; and mega projects such as the Kohler Darwin collection. The profits from the sale of standard collections would help to fund large-size collections and so on. We aimed for a selling price of two to three-and-a-half times cost, and sometimes more for standard collections. This is a very capital intensive business, and we have at most times been heavily indebted to the bank.

Our standard collections were put together predominantly from within the trade. First of all I would identify a subject and learn about the key books, sometimes including new books, particularly on a subject of topical interest where you need to have the latest thinking represented. For our ecology and environmental crisis collections I would go to Hay-on-Wye where I knew where to find what I needed and then to London to buy the relevant new books. Other good subjects for our standard collections included British business histories, the history and development of newspapers in Britain, women's health, and two series of university histories – American and European. The title of a collection is very important. When we found that women's health wasn't selling, we re-branded it sex and society, and it flew off the shelf.

I went to Japan for the first time in 1978, a year after we had started selling collections to the Japanese. There were already a few Dutch booksellers there, but I was one of the first British dealers to do the rounds of Yushodo, Maruzen, Kinokuniya and Far Eastern. A lot of my colleagues got into the habit of visiting Japan annually, but I preferred to build up our relationship by fax and letter and, in the early days, by telex. I have always been more comfortable selling at one remove, and we prided ourselves on the high standard of our catalogues with their scholarly introductions. Sales of collections are usually made by sending catalogues to Japanese booksellers who then sell to institutional libraries. We used the scatter shot approach, sending catalogues to twenty or so Japanese booksellers at the same time. Usually we would wait until the catalogue had been out for three weeks before reserving a collection, although we came to learn which dealers were most likely to convert reservations into orders.

The big firms had their own salesmen who went around the universities with our catalogues, to which they usually added a few preliminary leaves and a Japanese translation of the introduction. They loved statistics, and for really big collections it was always a selling point to be able to compare the collection favourably with, say, the holdings of the Bodleian or the British Library. The academics were incredibly powerful within their institutions and, while the librarian made out the purchase order, it was always the professor who made the decision.

By allocating ISBNs to our best catalogues, they found their way into copyright libraries and were accessible to anyone who wanted them. We did this with the catalogue of a collection of John Milton; it was one of our best collections and Kinokuniya sold it to a Japanese library. The Bodleian came to hear about it and was very excited about a number of items in it. They asked to be put in touch with the Japanese buyer on a purely scholarly basis to exchange bibliographical information. I put their request to Kinokuniya and there was complete silence. In my experience the western tradition of scholarly cooperation does not exist in Japan. Their institutional libraries have accumulated some vitally important material and it is important that this should be made available on a friendly basis to the scholarly world at large.

The peak of the Japanese market was in the mid-1980s when it was possible to build up and sell collections on a specific theme repeatedly, averaging between thirty to forty sales a year. This figure dropped to zero by the end of the 1990s when the Japanese economic bubble burst. The disappearance of Japan from the market didn't particularly affect me as a businessman, because we had been investing all the profits from the glory days into the making of a great Darwin collection. All booksellers need fuel to stoke the furnace, books to keep the production line going. I remember wandering into the Guildhall Bookshop in Kingston-upon-Thames in 1985, and standing in front of a section labelled 'Evolution', and asking myself if it had the makings of a collection – no big deal, just another string to our bow. I bought 74 books for £95, and this was the origin of the Kohler Darwin collection on which we were to spend the next twenty years.

The Guildhall Bookshop was followed by visits to Graham Weiner, Brian Lake, Sotheran's and the Harringtons where I bought the first of our 470 editions of the *Origin of Species*. By mid-1986 we had accumulated 300 volumes at a cost of £4000. A visit to Eric Korn, the Darwin specialist, transformed the collection and took it on to a new level. By 1987 we were on our way to building one of our most important antiquarian collections, but we still had no inkling of the massive project into which it would develop.

Our original plan was to sell it in America, where we did actually trail the collection in the late 1980s. By the early 1990s, we decided to withdraw it from the market and to go ahead with our ambition to build the biggest Darwin collection in the world, investing profits from our other activities and borrowing ever more money. A number of the best items in the collection came from the Jeremy Norman sale at Sotheby's on 11 December 1992. Jeremy had started to collect Darwin, and books on the  history of evolution in the late 1960s, and the 400-lot sale of his property remains the greatest ever auction of such material.

Our collection was made up of three sections – every edition of every book in every language by Charles Darwin; books about Darwin and evolution, including the works of the pre-evolutionists, and the evolutionary biologists after Darwin; and, thirdly, 152 autograph letters relating to the above. As regards the first section, Darwin made many revisions to the text of the *Origin of Species*, and every edition needs therefore to be represented. Darwin was keen to have his book translated into foreign languages and he corresponded at length with translators. Eight different translators worked on the German editions of the *Origin* from 1860 to the present day and they are all represented in the collection. As to the second section, we decided to include the writings of Creationists and anti-Darwinians in general, mostly because such material was not represented in most academic libraries and deserved a place in the debate as a whole.

Michèle began to catalogue the collection around the year 2000, by which time the internet had arrived in full force. It enabled us to fill very quickly a large number of the gaps in our section of books about Darwin. It also helped us to identify numerous minute variants in common editions of the *Origin of Species*. As one cannot always rely on a bookseller to describe his copy of a very common edition in the necessary detail, it was simpler to order every copy of *Origin* on the internet for under ten dollars and sort it all out in our warehouse. We probably only added about half these purchases to the collection, but the process greatly increased our bibliographical knowledge.

For many years, the University of Toronto possessed the biggest Darwin collection in the world, which had come from Richard Freeman, Darwin's bibliographer. This was followed in size by the collection of Warren Mohr whose books are now in the Huntington Library in California. We knew exactly what had to be done to overtake them. By about 2002 the price of our collection had gone over £1 million and we were beginning to lose our nerve. As we had no experience of selling at this level, we asked Quaritch, Maggs, and Heritage Book Shop in Los

Angeles if they would be interested in taking over a joint and several agency for the selling of the Kohler Darwin collection. We appointed them agents for one year, and their names appear on the title-page of the first edition of the catalogue, for which the introduction was written by Michael Ruse, the great Darwin scholar. Japan was excluded from the arrangement, where we had a separate agreement with Yushodo and Bunsei Shoin.

Quaritch started the ball rolling by offering the collection to Cambridge University Library. As Darwin's alma mater, Cambridge would have been a good home for the collection but CUL declined the offer. David Brass at Heritage Book Shop had a go at selling the collection in the States, but nothing much came of it there or in Japan. After a year the agreement with our colleagues came to an end and we were happy to take back control of the collection.

Our next thought was to approach the Natural History Museum in South Kensington. We had no contacts in the library, and our first step was to establish the quantity and condition of their Darwin holdings. We spent three days in the reading room, and later discovered that the staff had raised the alarm about a 'suspicious elderly couple', who, they thought, might to be book thieves. Meanwhile we had satisfied ourselves that the NHM's copies of the expensive Darwin books were generally in poor condition and no threat to our collection. Our next step was to approach Dr George Beccaloni, curator of orthopteroid insects in the Museum's Department of Entomology.

We already knew George through his interest in Alfred Russel Wallace. In 2002 he had acquired for the Museum important Wallace manuscripts, books and Lepidoptera specimens from the scientist's surviving family. George kindly agreed to approach the NHM library on our behalf. We made it a condition of sale that the Museum buy all the "By Darwin" material and all the autograph letters, but we allowed them to buy only those items from the "About Darwin" section that they needed as they already had a good half of this material. The price was £985,000.

The Museum's Board of Trustees soon gave unanimous approval to proceed to try and get the collection. We agreed to reserve it for a year, during which the development office of the Museum mounted an appeal to raise funds for the most expensive acquisition in its 125-year history. A successful application was made to the National Heritage Memorial Fund for a grant of £712,000 and the development office did a brilliant job in raising the balance, inviting current members of the Darwin family and major benefactors of the Museum to attend private views of highlights from the collection. The deal was signed, sealed and delivered in April 2006.

Hitherto the library of the Natural History Museum had primarily existed for the use of their in-house scientists. The purchase of the Kohler Darwin collection will enable it to attract the interest of the wider academic community, not only as the ultimate Darwin resource, but also as one of the greatest collections of nineteenth-century science in the world.

After selling the Darwin collection, Michèle and I wanted to retire. We sold our warehouse, John Loska bought our reference library, and most of our residual stock went to Dominic Winter Book Auctions. Now we are left with three collections with very few gaps to be filled – nineteenth-century pamphlets on social and political history, English literature published outside England, and the history of publishing and bookselling in Britain. We can continue to work on them, or simply put them into auction. It's Michèle's decision as she does all the cataloguing. My idea of retirement is to sit in the garden and read a book at half past ten in the morning and not feel guilty about it.

# Spanish Inquisition ⌇ Paul Orssich

My father was brought up in Vienna and came to England just before the war. He trained horses for dressage and polo, including the Duke of Edinburgh's polo ponies, and was a founder member of the Windsor Horse Show. He was also a close friend of the late Joseph Allen of The Horseman's Bookshop, whom you interviewed some years ago. I enjoyed a privileged childhood and, after university in France, I went into the world of advertising and fashion photography. It was an immensely lucrative occupation, and I would be very pleased to earn, as a bookseller today, the rate I was earning as a photographer in the late 1960s. I was working on big corporate jobs for the likes of BOAC, Coca Cola, Courtaulds, Dunlop and Volvo. In time it began to strike me as a most parasitic occupation with no real meaning in life, and at about the same time I fell in love with the island of Menorca. I invested some of the money I had earned from photography first of all in a catering business and then, quite by accident, in fruit farming.

I bought the fruit orchards with no thought of farming but simply because they were in a beautiful location where I wanted to build a house. I then decided to take an active part in fruit farming, and came to an arrangement with the original owner to stay on for a season and show me the ropes. He spoke nothing except the Menorcan dialect of Spanish, which I had to learn pretty rapidly. The local farmers no doubt viewed me as a soft Englishman who had entered their rather harsh world – until they shook hands with me. 'Ah', they said, 'so you are a man who works'. The skin on my hands is very dry and I only have to pick up an agricultural tool for my hands to become calloused. But I did work hard in the orchards, digging irrigation channels by hand. It was what I wanted to do at the time, and I had the money to be able to do it.

Then I found myself getting divorced and having to sell everything. I was making frequent trips from Menorca to London, and an antique dealer in Menorca asked me to look out for old maps for him. On my next trip to London I went straight to the Map House and spent £300 on maps of Menorca. I took them back to the dealer, who didn't even look at them, gave me a cheque for £300 plus the cost of my flight, with instructions to do the same again. It became a regular exercise, and enabled me to cover my travelling costs.

On one occasion I returned to Menorca, my maps rolled up under my arm, when I bumped into another dealer who asked to see them and immediately gave me a cheque for £600. I returned to the Map House to place my usual order for £300 worth of maps of Menorca only to be told that I had exhausted their stock.

The time had clearly come to look around and to expand my growing map business to include Mallorca, the Balearics, Valencia, Catalonia and gradually other parts of Spain. I speak almost perfect Spanish, and am fluent in the local dialect in which all business is conducted in the whole of Catalonia. This was an important factor in my being accepted in Balearic and Catalan business circles, and eventually becoming a buying agent for the Institut Cartogràfic de Catalunya.

There was a strong enthusiasm for old maps of Menorca, which is the best served of the Balearic Islands, cartographically speaking. Because of its strategic importance as a harbour where a large fleet could over-winter in perfect safety, Menorca received a lot of cartographic attention, not least from the British who occupied the island three times during the eighteenth century. For every map of Ibiza, there are ten of Mallorca, and for every ten of Mallorca, there are a hundred of Menorca.

When I came back to England in 1984 I continued to develop my map business, which had now expanded to include books, and published my first printed book catalogue. I'm entirely self-taught and modelled my catalogues on those of established dealers whom I admired. Early on in my map dealing I realised the importance of a good reference library – but only after making a costly mistake with a rather dull looking sea chart of Mexico, *El Seno Mexicano*. It turned out to be the first scientific mapping of the coast of Texas and of the greatest rarity. I had offered it all around the trade and eventually managed to sell it for £75; it later changed hands for £22,000. It was Clive Burden who alerted me to my mistake, and since that moment I have amassed a reference library of some 2,400 titles.

Fortunately from the very first day that I bought a map of Menorca, I retained a photocopy of it. I have now a research file with images of every single map of the Balearic Islands which has passed through my hands, including a lot of material which I haven't personally handled but seen in other collections, wherever possible recording prices, who bought it, where it went and other information privy to me. As a long-standing exhibitor at the monthly Bonnington Map Fair, I saw a large amount of material, and this has enabled me to compile a carto-bibliography of maps of the Balearic Islands which is almost complete.

I had the immense good fortune early on in my business to meet Juan Gili of the Dolphin Book Company just before he retired. A giant in his field, Juan was the most important Hispanic dealer outside Spain, a Catalan, immensely erudite and fiercely anti-Franco. When Franco forbade the speaking of Catalan in Spain, Gili published from England a Catalan grammar. I remember my visit to him at his home outside Oxford, and feeling humbled in his presence. I went with a friend of mine who was a private collector and always paid in cash. He chose a few books and I saw Gili's eyes light up as the pouch of cash was brought out. Then I put down the books I had chosen and very gently and graciously he suggested that I might not do very well with them as he had paid too much for them, and then guided me towards some pamphlets in a cupboard. I bought them and in due course sold them very well. I never knew if this was Gili's way of thanking me for bringing him a good client, or of helping a novice to avoid a commercial blunder; either way I was immensely grateful.

By 1989 I had a shop in Munster Road, Fulham, where there was then a concentration of dealers. Simon Finch, Christer von der Burg of Han-Shan Tang, Nicholas McConnell and Nicholas Bernstein were all in the area, which made for quite a bit of synergy. Collectors would come to Fulham, although it was not a good location for selling books on Hispanic Studies, but I sold enough prints through the shop window to pay the rent. It worked very well until the rents went up, and everyone started to leave the area. I closed my shop and bought my present house in Stockwell where I have worked ever since. If I had my life again, I'd do everything the same. Fruit farming was a wonderful experience and a true adventure; there was something about going back to nature, which I needed to get out of my system. But I've also loved the bookselling life, it's another kind of adventure, an intellectual one and the learning curve has never ceased.

It's a mistake to think of Spain as a single entity. In spite of the fact that General Franco did everything possible to make it one, Spain remains a federal union of provinces. This breeds tremendous regional chauvinism and accounts for the fact that Spanish collectors tend to focus on a specific province rather than a specific genre. In other words they will happily buy a book or a map, a painting or a print, as long as it relates to their region. I have found this willingness to collect both books and maps to be uncommon in other areas, but one can always play the regional card in Spain.

The nature of Spanish books is that they are rare. Spain has been subject to a succession of civil and natural upheavals, added to which books were produced in very short print runs until the 1930s. This is partly a reflection on the regional nature of the market. However, there are a very large number of English accounts of travels in Spain. When I catalogue a general book on the subject, I will always mention if there is, for example, a section on Catalonia or any other specific region. This will serve as the hook to draw in the regional collector who would very probably not be interested in a more general work on Spain.

The Spanish are very interested in foreigners' impressions of their country. In the eighteenth and nineteenth century these tended to be written by English and French travellers, and to be very uncomplimentary about the state of the roads, the hotels and the food – unless you took your own, or shot it on the way, it was likely to be appalling. Spain in the nineteenth century was not part of the standard Grand Tour, and it was considered quite adventurous to go there. However it was immensely popularised by the writings of Richard Ford and George Borrow, who wrote wonderful accounts dating from the 1840s and 1850s. They viewed Spain from totally different perspectives – Ford was an English gentleman with letters of introduction to the Spanish nobility; Borrow went to Spain to spread the New Testament in English, mixing with the underprivileged and working classes. I read *Gatherings from Spain*, the abridged version of Richard Ford's *Handbook for Travellers in Spain* while sitting on the balustrade of the terrace at my farm house in Menorca. I laughed so much, I nearly fell off – so little had changed since Ford was writing about Spain in 1845.

Once I felt that I had the Hispanic peninsula under my belt, I began to deal peripherally in books on the Pyrenees, Morocco, Gibraltar, Portugal, the Azores and the Canary Islands. I have always bought books on Latin America, mainly exploration – though these tend to be extremely pricey – and books on military history. The book market in Spain is largely dominated by three very important dealers, all based in Madrid, but the 'Godfather' of them is Luís Bardón, a third generation bookseller with an immense knowledge of Spanish books. He bought some very expensive books from me the other day and explained that he was capitalising his grandchildren's stock. Just as he was still selling books that his grandfather had bought for him, so Luís was buying for his grandchildren.

Travel books on Spain served as my Trojan horse into the world of Cervantes and the golden age of Spanish literature. As Shakespeare is to the English language, so Cervantes is to Spanish. *Don Quixote* is considered to be the first novel ever published in any language. It appeared in two parts, in 1605 and in 1615, and we are therefore in the middle of celebrations for the four hundredth anniversary of the first part, which took place in 2005 and was marked by any number of events and publications, and of the second part, in 2015. There is only one copy known in private hands of the first edition of both parts of *Don Quixote*, which was bought at Swann Galleries in New York about fifteen years ago for $1.6 million.

I caught the market just right in 2004, when I brought out a monothematic catalogue of editions of *Don Quixote*. A great number of Hispanic libraries were putting together exhibitions for the four hundredth anniversary, and my catalogue was almost a sell-out, in spite of being mainly composed of books that had failed to sell in previous catalogues. From an aesthetic point of view, the most desirable edition of *Don Quixote* is Don Joaquín Ibarra's of 1780, beautifully type-set and illustrated, and printed on lovely paper, the first of the editions sponsored by the

Real Academia Española. Most of the seventeenth-century editions were printed on poor quality paper and are not particularly attractive. The market for Cervantes doesn't particularly depend on the language – the London editions of J. and R.Tonson in 1738, and John Bowle in 1781, which is incidentally one of the first critical editions, are both much sought after.

At a time when English literature was flourishing in the nineteenth century, Spanish literature was rather weak and didn't really recover until the so-called 'Generación del 1927', as the Spanish refer to the plethora of poets and writers who emerged at the same time as Federico García Lorca. As regards Latin America, the market really takes off with Gabriel García Marquez and his contemporaries in 'El Boom' years of the 1960s and 1970s, the Hispanic equivalent of the modern first editions market, with high spots achieving the same enormous prices. But as the price goes up, so the market will shrink. I have seen this happen with old maps, where the market has shrunk dramatically as most collectors can no longer aspire to own the high spots. It's no fun being a collector if you can't afford to add to your collection.

However secondhand books have never been cheaper. If you want to build a collection of twentieth-century books, the internet is undoubtedly a wonderful tool. I'm putting together for my own fun a collection on the development of the tourist industry in Spain from 1950 to 1965. In my opinion mass tourism has single-handedly changed the face of Spain and massively contributed to its economic prosperity. I've accumulated around 4,000 items, many of which are of negligible financial value but serve to document the subject. What I would really like to find is an airline ticket for one of the first charter flights to Spain in 1950.

The coming of the internet has changed the market beyond belief. The days when one could drive around the country and buy books for £5 and sell them for £20 have long gone. The rule of thumb in those days was to add a fiver to the cost price and double it. There are currently 228 copies on the internet, priced as low as £2, of a book which I used to sell for £40. It's no longer possible to go to a book fair and buy something outside your field just following your nose, or even your head. You're sure to find several copies online at a fraction of the price you've just paid.

Nowadays one hears people say proudly, 'there's no copy on the internet', implying that it's very rare, but failing to take into account the number of dealers who don't put their stock online. The other day someone bought a copy against me at auction of Henry Swinburne's *Travels through Spain in the Years 1775 and 1776*. In conversation after the sale it emerged that he thought it was a very rare book as there was no copy on the internet. Actually I have eight copies in stock, and I know a dealer in Madrid has seven, so that's fifteen I can think of without really trying.

Auction prices can distort the true market value, as specialist dealers will try to ensure that books in their traditional patch don't sell too cheaply, or a newcomer loses his head.

If I put my Spanish books on the internet, after twenty-seven years in the Hispanic market, any savvy book buyer knows I haven't been able to sell them through my catalogues. Therefore the price is negotiable. You could say that anyone who puts a book on the internet hasn't got a client for it; they may even be 'fishing' for one. I have known people to put books on the internet which they don't possess, just to measure the level of interest. Which comes first – the client or the book? One of the internet databases tried to stop this practice by grading their sellers – a low star rating may indicate that you haven't fulfilled all the orders you have received. When my catalogues have been out for, say, three months, I put the unsold items on the internet, the results are poor but I do capture the odd client in that way.

I believe that ultimately the control of the secondhand book market will be dominated by a small number of very big dealers, with huge inventories and warehouses. If one can amass a sufficiently large stock and persuade one's customers to patronise your own website, then one avoids price comparisons and the high commission charges of some of the internet databases. The critical mass for the book trade seems to be around 30,000 titles, and a number of Spanish dealers that I know, who have that figure online, report good returns.

I have always placed an immense amount of trust in my clients, which is totally contrary to the methods of the new generation of internet booksellers. I do most of my business on a 'nod and a handshake.' There's very little written down. I've often sent a £1000 book to someone I don't know, and never had a bad debt. I have to remember that my clients can usually walk into the shop of one of my Spanish colleagues and hold the book in their hand, but I'm in London so I take great pains in cataloguing, noting any defects in minute detail, but it's not the same as walking into a shop. Sometimes I wonder what I'm doing in London trying to deal in Spanish books. Obviously it would make more sense to be in Madrid or Barcelona, but London's where I like to be.

# Some Lost Victorian Sunday  ❧ Richard Hatchwell

When I was thirteen I went to Dean Close in Cheltenham as a classical scholar. After spending a Christmas book token on a copy of Percy Muir's *Book-Collecting as a Hobby*, my interest was firmly established. But it was my House Master who set the seal on my future as a bookseller. The school was not far from Thirlestaine Hall, the former home of Sir Thomas Phillipps, and he advised me to get on my bicycle and go and have a look at the books. The caretaker let me in by the side door and allowed me to see one room – it was piled high with books, though most were already packed in boxes. I had no idea at the time that I was looking at the Phillipps collection. When I did make the connection some time later, it gave me a sort of proprietary interest in it, as I realised that I must have seen the great library a couple of years before the Robinson brothers bought it in 1946. Looking back it seems inevitable that I should become a bookseller.

I was born in the Swan Hotel in Alton in 1927. My mother came from a brewing and hotel-keeping family and she and my father managed The Swan in Alton where I was born in 1927. However, my father wanted to run his own business and, in 1931, he bought The Old Bell in Malmesbury where I grew up before going to school in Cheltenham. I didn't take Higher Certificate, but joined the Navy in 1944. After three years' service, I came out with not much idea of what I wanted to do, except that it had to be something with books. I answered an advertisement in the *TLS* for an assistant librarian in Reigate. Within a very short time, I decided it wasn't for me and began to cast around for alternative employment.

Reigate had an excellent new bookshop, the Ancient House, owned and run by Tom Langdon. Tom had also been in the Navy, and before the war he had been in charge of the rare book department at Foyles in Charing Cross Road. We became friends and spent many evenings together, usually hilariously, in one of the local pubs or hotels. Tom knew I was fed up with my job at the library and advised me to go into the rare book trade. He wrote introductions for me to Maggs, Quaritch, and Thomas Thorp who took me on in their small shop in Berkeley Street.

While I was working out my three months' notice at the library, I met another bookseller, John Ruston, who was running a bookshop in Redhill at the time. John became a life-long friend and was to play a great role in my future bookselling. After moving to Manchester for a while, he settled in Bournemouth where he bought Alan Thomas's shop, who had taken it over from Horace G. Commin.  It was John who put me in the atmosphere of rare bookselling.

When I joined Thorp's, the firm was about to move from Berkeley Street to larger premises in Albemarle Street, entailing much humping of boxes. A pair of young shoulders would obviously be useful – the other staff at Thorp's were Walter Harris the manager, and Ernest the packer, both in their sixties. Walter, whom I always called 'Mr Harris', was a bookseller of the old school and had been with Thorp's under Tom's father when the bushiness was in Bond Street. He was a specialist in nineteenth-century literature and could recite all the points of Dickens in original parts without looking at a reference book. A later addition was Margaret Montgomery who looked after the accounts after the move to Albemarle Street. She left in due course and opened a bookshop in Canterbury specialising in children's books. Tom Thorp himself was a curious character, short sighted to a degree, and consequently a rather shy man, but always kind and polite. His younger brother Hugh ran the bookshop in Guildford.

After only a few weeks, I was asked to compile a catalogue of eighteenth century books. Although a lot of the books had already been catalogued, quite a number hadn't. Guided by descriptions in previous catalogues, I began to teach myself and quickly discovered that I was in my element – handling the books, reading them, finding out what they were about. On one occasion, I came across what purported to be an early edition of Boccaccio. The paper didn't feel right and I was generally puzzled by it, until Walter pointed out that it was an eighteenth century facsimile. I was delighted to have had my suspicion confirmed. I was sitting at my desk one morning when the door opened and a fairly rough-looking tramp entered wearing an overcoat that reached to the ground. We had a box in the shop containing half-crowns for such visitations, but as I got up to give the man one, Walter walked across and shook hands with him, 'Good morning Mr Foyle'. That was my only contact with Willie Foyle.

This London life continued for about two years, until I became tired of living there. The opportunity came up for me to move to the Guildford shop in 1950. The former manager, Charles Traylen, had left some time before and set up shop in premises opposite Thorp's. The current manager was a rather fussy elderly man who probably resented my appearance, knowing that I was destined eventually to replace him, which I did on his retirement. The shop in Guildford was a veritable warren of books on several floors, not all of which were entirely safe. In fact several storeys were eventually put out of bounds to customers.

Hugh Thorp would arrive almost every morning with a carload of books of all kinds, the product of his previous day's buying. It was my job to sort them out, mark them off, and put them ready for cataloguing or immediate sale before the next carload arrived. It was an experience beyond price for a budding bookseller. In due course I began to attend sales, which in those days would take place on the actual premises, rather than in sale rooms. I had encountered the ring in London, when I was sent to bid at sales for the firm, and been obliged to take part in the settlement afterwards. This usually took place in Joseph's shop in Charing Cross Road, or in an upstairs room at Marks' shop further up the road. These occasions, though conducted in a most gentlemanly manner, often led to a degree of skulduggery that I found very difficult to take.

Charles Traylen and Frank Hammond ran the ring at country sales. I've known auctioneers get up at the end of a sale and say, 'Gentlemen, I've put a room at your disposal'. They knew perfectly well what was going on. The catalogues would often be prepared by the local bookseller who might not know much about old books, which would be bundled up in large mixed lots, and catalogued without estimates. Sometimes there might be rings within rings, when the little country booksellers were told to go away after the first settlement, the big boys staying on for the next round of the knock-out. Senior members of the trade were among the most assiduous in their participation in the ring. I told myself I would have nothing to do with the ring if I ever had my own business.

When my father died in August 1952, I gave in my notice to Hugh and went back to Malmesbury to live with my mother who was not in good health. She was living in accommodation in an antique shop which my father had bought during the war. The shop was at 52 Gloucester Street, right opposite The Old Bell. So there I was, aged twenty-five, with a shop-full of antiques that I knew little or nothing about. My mother agreed that, as she sold the antiques, I could replace them with books. I put what books of my own I had into the shop, and very slowly the word got around. Then just before Christmas my mother died. I had £200 in hand and the free use and eventual ownership of the premises in Gloucester Street. Prices of books may have been low by current standards, but £200 didn't last long.

One day I went to Lloyds Bank in Malmesbury to see the manager, a genial character called Marks, known in the town as Harpo. I was putting my problem to him when he cut me short, 'Mr Hatchwell. I have known your father, your mother and yourself for some ten or fifteen years. I shall honour whatever cheque you choose to write'. Some weeks later I was in the bank and Harpo came across to the counter and whispered in a very conspiratorial manner, 'people buy these books do they?' I assured him that they did and left. What a difference between Harpo and modern banking practice.

It was a lovely shop with a wonderful view at the back and a big basement where I stored most of my old books. I knew the local people wouldn't come into the shop if they saw a lot of old calf through the window. I kept nineteenth-century and later books in the shop, and there was a sixpenny shelf in the porch. But business was very slow to start with. The country was still recovering from the war, and books were not high on most people's list of priorities. A friend told me that the local people put a shop like mine on a par with Malmesbury Abbey: they might look around the porch, but they were frightened to go in.

However, it was a great asset for my business to be right opposite The Old Bell, and I did receive a lot of visits from well-known collectors and librarians and others who were staying there. Among them was Major J. R .Abbey who was amazed to find a shop full of eighteenth-century books in the country. After a brief look round the stock, he turned to me and said, 'This isn't your stock, is it?' I assured him that it was and offered to put him on my mailing list. 'Thank you. No', he replied, 'I get far too many catalogues already'. Siegfried Sassoon was another visitor, and often bought a book. I liked him; he was someone you could talk to.

John Betjeman would also come in after a good lunch at the The Old Bell. He was a tremendous collector, and very knowledgeable about local topography, and of course Swindon and its railway history. Bertrand Russell had been having lunch at The Old Bell when he saw a CND poster in my window. He came in to ask if local opinion was favourable; I had to tell him that on the whole it was not. Peter Wilson, the chairman of Sotheby's, called in one day and offered to take off my hands any library that I could not cope with. I declined, gracefully I hope, but rather wondered that Sotheby's should be touting for business from a small country bookseller.

Most auctions in the area were held by Bruton Knowles of Gloucester, where Arthur Negus was in charge of the Fine Art department. Arthur asked me to take over the cataloguing and valuation of books. This I did and, in the course of my long association with the firm, I valued well over a hundred libraries for them and catalogued many sales. Arthur and I became great friends and, shortly before he died, he entrusted me with the sale of two boxes of books. Among them was a lovely copy of the first edition of the *Annalia Dubrensia*, 1636, which Bent Juel-Jensen bought, and later contributed an introduction to the facsimile edition published in 1973. There was also a manuscript volume of farriery accounts, 1620-1621, for the Prince of Wales before he became King Charles I, which is now in the Royal Library Windsor.

There were also monthly sales at Ovens of Cirencester, always uncatalogued and, on one occasion, containing a copy of Thornton's *The Temple of Flora*. I used to attend these sales with G. V. M. Heap, an admired colleague and fierce opponent of the ring, who had been a classics don at Cambridge until he retired and opened a bookshop in Cirencester. Eventually he left Cirencester, claiming there were more bogus people living in and around the town than anywhere else to his knowledge. He opened a shop in Wells where he remained for a number of years before finally retiring from bookselling.

I was fortunate to be in at the tail-end of the dispersal of so many good libraries belonging to the rural clergy. Many of these had sufficient means to indulge their extra-clerical interests which were many and varied, with astronomy, botany, ornithology and gardening books in abundance. The disappearance of this type of rural clergy is to be regretted. Many of them may not have been perfect parish priests, but they were learned men, frequently antiquaries, and they made a great contribution to the life and history of the parish in other ways.

Being of an antiquarian turn of mind, I joined the Wiltshire Archaeological and Natural History Society (WANHS) soon after opening the shop. Over the years I have issued thirty or so catalogues on Wiltshire topography. It helped me to become very well known in Wiltshire, and certainly brought in a lot of libraries and customers. Topography isn't so fashionable these days but, in my experience, provincial booksellers could benefit from making more of it. I started collecting drawings and paintings of Malmesbury and Wiltshire when I spotted John Britton's watercolour of Malmesbury Market Cross in a sale at Christie's.

The collection steadily grew to almost unmanageable proportions and about ten years ago I sold most of it to the museum in Devizes, now the Wiltshire Heritage Museum, retaining only the Malmesbury and Stonehenge items. My catalogues of Wiltshire material helped to establish relations with the museum, where I eventually became the first Honorary Keeper of Prints and Drawings. This resulted in the publication in 2005 of *Art in Wiltshire*, my catalogue of the WANHS's superb collection of paintings, drawings, maps and prints.

My most important visitor to the shop however was Geoffrey Grigson who lived a few miles away and eventually became my brother-in-law. Jane Grigson was working at Thames & Hudson with her sister, Mary, and the two of us became the object of Geoffrey's match-making. Eva Neurath, wife of Walter who founded Thames & Hudson, had originally been married to an antiquarian bookseller, and said to Mary, 'Never marry one'. I'm glad to say that Mary ignored her advice and we were married in November 1956. Mary entered wholeheartedly into the life of antiquarian bookselling, first as secretary and then as collaborator in many other aspects of the business. In due course we decided that the shop in Gloucester Street would not be suitable for the family of four that we were planning.

While we were still living in Gloucester Street, the opportunity arose to buy the Old Rectory at Little Somerford. It was a wonderful house and ideal for our purposes. There were lots of rooms which I could fill with books, and the ceilings were high enough to accommodate the tall bookcases from our shop. We moved in at Easter 1960, and Mary's instinctive hospitality came into its own. She was a wonderful hostess and we got to know private and trade customers so much better over coffee, tea, a light lunch, or during a night's stay. David Low would turn up occasionally on a buying tour and we would return the visit some time after, with a good lunch to be had on both occasions. I first met David when I was working in London, and he had a shop at 17 Cecil Court. But I only got to know him well when he moved out to Emmington, a hamlet near Oxford. David wrote in his memoirs that 'bookshop' didn't quite fit my circumstances at the Old Rectory 'with its atmosphere of some lost Victorian Sunday. Maybe it is related to the lunch with the well-behaved children whom one has seen as babies, and to whom now, as great uncle bookseller, one brings boiled sweets?' (*With All Faults*, 1973).

I've always liked library furniture and tried to acquire interesting pieces to furnish our house. There's a marvellous library table in Autun, originally from a monastery and described as a 'table à pupitres mobiles', illustrated in André Masson's *Le Décor des Bibliothèques du Moyen Age à la Révolution*, 1972. I had it copied by Ian Heseltine, who also made for me a copy of a fifteenth-century Chinese scroll cabinet – a most ingenious design based on a series of interchangeable boxes. We replaced the Chinese characters on the doors of the original cabinet with early printers' devices, and I use it to store my personal books.

When the children began to leave home, Mary found she had the time to take up paper conservation. I had been giving her simple repairs to do, and she clearly had a flair for it. She found a tutor in London, and in due course became very expert indeed. I set up a laboratory for her in one room and from then on she never lacked work, either from me, from private owners, or from the trade – as far away as California.

Mary had spent part of her university career in Strasbourg, and we shared a great love of France. In 1962 we bought a small property about sixty miles south of Tours in very 'untouristy' but beautiful country. We used to go there for six weeks every summer, August being a rather dead month for bookselling, especially when we no longer had the shop. I got into the habit of making a tour of French provincial bookshops, and was a regular visitor at the Librairie Durance and the Librairie Bellanger in Nantes, which I had first visited on a walking holiday before I was married. At that time I don't think there was an available guide to French provincial bookshops, so I had to guess at the most suitable route for my purposes. I travelled via Rennes, Tours, Poitiers and Nantes and found that, except for one or two shops that David Low had visited, I was the first English bookseller in those parts.

In due course we had the opportunity of buying a bookshop in Tours, at the Cathedral end of the Rue de la Scellerie. It was very tempting, but I could foresee problems running two businesses in different countries. I was finally put off the idea by the sight of endless shelves of nineteenth- and twentieth-century books in wrappers, which form the major part of the stock in most French shops.

Perhaps my luckiest find in France was in a bookshop in St Estienne where my eye was caught by a very battered copy of *Recueil des Plus Beaux Vers de Messieurs de Malherbe, Racan, Maynard, &c*, Paris, 1638. I was about to put it back on the shelf when I noticed some writing in a rather faint hand on the verso of the title-page, 'This book was given me by Mr. Izaac Walton. August 22th 1668. Charles Cotton'. Needless to say it was added to my pile of purchases – a book illustrating the association of the two authors of *The Complete Angler* had to be of considerable interest. On closer inspection, it turned out to contain other notes in Cotton's hand. I showed the book to Peter Croft, who believed it to be the only known example of Cotton's hand, as he states in the introduction to his *Autograph Poetry in the English Language*, 1973. That information may of course be out of date by now. When I catalogued the book, I was very surprised not to sell it to an English library or collector. But it went to a safe home in the Osborn Collection at the Beinecke Library.

As a bookseller, I would like to be remembered for my catalogues. How long do personal memories last – perhaps one generation, but not much more? During the last fifty or so years, I have issued about 180 catalogues or lists on a number of very disparate subjects from *Stonehenge* to *Printing in Venice,* and *The Papacy* to *Books with Anglo-Saxon type.* The list of my catalogues might suggest a somewhat dilettante approach to bookselling. If Geoffrey Grigson wanted to make a damning comment on someone, he would call them a dilettante. I can only say that it has all been so interesting. In his book, *The Robinson Legend*, Martin Hamlyn relates how his colleague Eric Bligh described the nature of antiquarian bookselling in terms of adventure. He was of course right, as Martin goes on to say, 'selling old books offers us adventures in the world of ideas, controversy, poetry, imagination and the whole gamut of human emotions; with the possibility (extremely faint) of riches'. I would add that it requires a good memory, an inquiring mind and luck. I chose *Adventure* as the title of a booklet I prepared, in which I describe my bookselling life with Mary, who died in 1995. I have since married again and now live with my wife, also called Mary, just outside Malmesbury.

Three of our four children started their working lives in books. I think they saw what a nice life we had. My son Matthew worked for Swann Galleries in New York, before spending four or five years in the English Department at Bernard Quaritch. My daughter Lucy worked first for Stanley Crowe and then for Roy Davids at Sotheby's, and Emily worked for Hatchards before becoming a travel journalist. I asked all my children some years ago if they wanted to carry on my business, but they were all too happy and busy with their current occupations.

Five or six years ago we turned the business into a company in which my children became shareholders, and I was the director. When my health began to decline, I decided to close the company, and the remaining 2,500 or so books now belong to my children who are free to do as they please with them. I imagine the future of antiquarian (i.e. before 1850) bookselling belongs to firms like Maggs, Quaritch and one or two other, perhaps very specialist, dealers. I wouldn't encourage any of my eleven grandchildren to come into the trade. It's such a different world since my day. I'm told that when my name cropped up in conversation with a rather grand bookseller, I was referred to rather dismissively as 'that country bookseller'. Actually I've never wanted to be anything else.

# Talking Shop in Silent Street  ∾  Tony Cox

My father spent his career in the education branch of the Royal Air Force. He had been a book collector since his school days, when Arnold Muirhead was his Classics master. Perhaps inspired by Arnold's example of the collector-turned-bookseller, my father decided to do the same when he retired from the RAF. Arnold made his mark by issuing catalogues and trading from home, a style of bookselling which greatly appealed to my father. He had formed the idea of specialising in eighteenth-century literature which he had always enjoyed and which, in those days, wasn't much collected, apart from the obvious high spots.

Although Claude could live off his Air Force pension, he taught for a few years in local schools in Suffolk in order to earn money to buy books for his intended stock. He had been used to reading booksellers' catalogues from his collecting days, and always looked forward to anything from Peter Murray Hill, with whom Arnold Muirhead had served his apprenticeship, and also from Blackwell's and Quaritch. By 1975 he was ready to open Claude Cox, and to learn the business the way we all do – by going out there and parting with money.

My first scent of the world of antiquarian books had also come when I was still at school. Saturday afternoons would be spent in the many-storeyed dusty rooms of Thornton's in Oxford – not looking for anything in particular, but taking great pleasure in handling an eighteenth-century book, as a physical object as much as anything else. I was also involved in the printing society at Magdalen College School where we printed on an Arab treadle press. There was something very satisfactory about the bite of type into paper and producing something. We printed tickets, letterheads and other ephemeral items for the school, never with any great proficiency. I simply enjoyed handling type, and this early interest in the arts of the book was later to come out in my bookselling.

At York University I found myself just behind Brian Lake, Peter Miller, and Peter Allen of Robert Temple Books. Chris Johnson was also part of this 'kindergarten' of booksellers. Peter Allen and I worked on the student newspaper, which I edited and in due course handed over to Greg Dyke, who went on to slightly greater things. In due course I started my working life teaching English at Latymer Upper in Hammersmith. The school was convenient for lunchtime séjours at Bill Foster's bookshop in Chiswick. By some generous freak of time-tabling, in my first year, I had Thursday afternoons off, which coincided with sales at Hodgson's. My father was still accumulating stock for his business, and I was able to go to sales on his behalf. Fred Snelling, the auction clerk, had been a school mate of my father's, and he introduced me to Lord John Kerr. They were both very helpful to me in my rapid apprenticeship in the world of the auction house.

Meanwhile my wife, Sue, had started a second hand and remainder business with a colleague from her days at The Economist Bookshop. We issued a catalogue under the name of Badgers Books, for which Sue did most of the work. It contained 250 or so items, mainly modern literature, particularly women writers in whom Sue was interested – Dorothy Richardson, Anna Kavan, and of course Virginia Woolf. The catalogue also contained a lot of books that I had bought from Bill Foster, including a box of John Masefield, who was then just as unfashionable as he is now. But the box contained some real rarities, for example, a first edition of Salt-Water Ballads. Masefield's popularity in the 1930s coincided with the taste for vellum-bound, signed, limited editions, and so there were a number of 'artificial' scarcities, created for that first great modern first boom.

We advertised the catalogue in *Bookdealer*, having put together a mailing list from reference books at our local library. We received around 50 orders and were thrilled with this toe-in-the-water exercise. The catalogue came out towards the end of my three years' teaching in London, but our fledgling bookselling career came to an end when we moved up to Yorkshire and decided to start a family. I was teaching at Bradford Grammar School, but we were living on the edge of the Yorkshire dales, fulfilling our romantic aim of getting out into the country.

Meanwhile I was watching from the wings as my father built up his business – knowing that I didn't want to teach Macbeth for the next thirty years. By the time I joined the business, my father had got up to Catalogue 12. He had stopped making a loss, but wasn't really making a profit. The thought of my coming down to Suffolk, with a young family, and living off the firm absolutely terrified him. But it was a question of now or never: if I stayed on in teaching for a few more years, my salary would have gone up as I reached Head of Department level, and it would have been harder to bridge the income gap.

I joined the business in 1979, knowing that I would have to make a very specific contribution. I couldn't bring experience, skill or capital, but I could add a speciality to our catalogues and develop my interest in printing and the arts of the book. Soon after I joined the firm, we bought a large collection of books published by William Pickering, and/or printed by Charles Whittingham at the Chiswick Press. Pickering is a fascinating character; he took a great interest in reviving old texts, as well as publishing fairly esoteric nineteenth-century material alongside such mainstream writers as Coleridge. He also cared passionately about what his books looked like, and so it was quite reasonable to have a Pickering section in Catalogue 21, our first devoted entirely to printing and the arts of the book. The catalogue sold extremely well, and gave me the confidence to expand into the field of private press books.

Within three years of my joining the firm, we were offered Tom Cook's bookshop in Silent Street. Tom had run the shop in Ipswich since 1944 and had intended to die in harness, until his doctor persuaded him otherwise. My parents wanted a shop like a hole in the head, but I was convinced that it would transform the business. We took it on in 1982 and it became very much my baby. My parents were very supportive from the start and would man the shop as required. My mother did the book-keeping and a lot of the telephone work. She was very often the first point of contact that most of our customers had with the firm. Between the four of us – my parents and my wife – we developed a family firm. However, neither of my children will be joining the business – my daughter is a doctor and my son a journalist. I'm not disappointed about this as I don't see Claude Cox Books in dynastic terms. As I was almost in at the start, it didn't feel like joining the family firm. My father would not have minded my saying that he wasn't first and foremost a dealer. He greatly enjoyed the business, but I have tended to be a bit more hard-headed about it all.

By the mid-1980s, I had taken over most of the buying. When I'm at an auction, obviously I try to buy as cheaply as possible. The preoccupation with booksellers' settlements in the auction ring is to some extent misplaced. I quite understand that the ABA has to promote good practice, and can hardly turn a blind eye to the law of the land. But the notion that it's the purchaser's responsibility to make sure that the lot makes a good price is obviously ludicrous. It's the auctioneer's responsibility, and he's charging enough in commissions and premiums to have the necessary incentive to do so.

When I'm dealing with the public, I try to pay as much as I can. A lot of our best purchases have come by word of mouth, and a good reputation is enormously important. All my greatest moments in bookselling have begun with a door opening. Over the years I've been invited into a lot of homes, both humble and grand, and it's a huge privilege which I don't underestimate. I shall never forget walking into Loyd Haberley's studio in the attic of Stoney Down in Dorset, and finding everything more or less as he had left it when he returned to the States in 1937 to teach at Harvard. I was able to buy not only copies of all his books in sheets, but also wood blocks and notebooks.

Several very good collections have come to us through the shop, although of course there are people who think that any old book will do for the old bookshop in Silent Street. The charity bookshops have largely taken over the run-of-the-mill side of second hand bookselling, and it's impossible to compete with them. We do have regular customers who live locally and others who make a pilgrimage from further afield, whom we welcome with open arms. I'm very conscious of the second hand bookshop's function as a meeting place, and the shops that do well are often those where the customer is made to feel welcome. It's always a pleasure when young people come in and gaze in wonder at an odd volume of eighteenth-century literature, which might cost very little. They just get a kick out of handling something of that age which is also affordable. It might happen to no more than one in 10,000, but perhaps the antiquarian book trade doesn't need more than this percentage of the population for its survival.

The 'tyre kickers' are less welcome – a phrase I learnt from the Kendalls of Limestone Hills Bookshop in Texas, who came to this country every year and would spend two days combing the shop for stock. Tyre kickers are people who come into the shop and ask for some great rarity. When you produce it, they are horrified that anyone could be expected to spend more than a fiver on a book. They're not to be confused with people who come into a shop just to browse. What is the point of having a bookshop if you don't welcome browsers?

But basically the shop is here because it houses the stock. The printed catalogue is still our mainstay, and I try to produce one every other month. A lot of my cataloguing these days is fairly mundane, because one tends to plough a similar furrow and therefore to handle the same things. Ironically, I spend more time cataloguing these days, because of the wealth of information instantly accessible on the net. The coming of the internet had quite a significant impact on our business. A lot of our customers around the world are academics. When they need to buy a particular book, rather than waiting for a catalogue to arrive, they can go on to the net and spend their money.

It became clear that we had to respond in some way. Initially we uploaded on to ABE around 4,000 books which hadn't sold from the previous ten catalogues. The first upload was pretty dramatic and, within a month, we sold about half our back stock. The result was equivalent to issuing a couple of big and very successful catalogues. As every internet bookseller knows, you never repeat the success of that initial upload. Nowadays I have a routine of uploading what's left from a catalogue a month or so after it's been sent out. It provides a regular trickle of sales, mostly through ABE, but also the ILAB site, UKBookworld and our own very basic website, which enables you to read our last ten catalogues online.

The internet has made rarities more expensive, and common books cheaper. Scarce items are more expensive because if you've got to pay more, you've got to charge more. In the old days a lot of dealers made a living going round provincial bookshops and picking up on their mistakes, and also on books that were outside their field where, in both cases, there was still a profit to be made. Now everyone can check the price, and that pecking order has to some extent gone. Common books have dropped in price because, if there are already plenty on the net, your copy will only sell if it's the cheapest. However, this isn't always the case; there's also an element of the devil you know, and buying from a dealer, whose copy may not be the cheapest, but whose reputation you trust. ABE's star-rating system, which I believe is based on the successful fulfilment of orders, is not always the answer. I've managed to slip from five to three stars, because I've failed to keep my internet stock up-to-date, which happens very easily when you also sell books in the shop and through printed catalogues.

In the last fifteen years a lot of the new money in book collecting has gone into modern first editions and children's books. The high-spot antiquarian books have kept going up in price, but the middle ground has just trodden water. The easy answer is that modern firsts are easy to collect. In a word, it's all about condition. If you're going to pay a high price for something, there has to be a degree of scarcity and, in the field of modern firsts, this is likely to be a dust wrapper in pristine condition. You can learn a few points, but by and large it's not complicated and you can assemble a collection rapidly. The internet has made it possible to do a lifetime's browsing in seconds.

There will always be a place for the book as a work of art which reflects great craftsmanship and stimulates one to read a wonderful text. I exhibit at the Oxford Fine Press Book Fair, which includes fifteen or so specialist dealers and representatives from a large number of private presses. It's an opportunity to meet a lot of enthusiasts of all ages in a very buoyant area of book collecting. I'm never very convinced by the articles published from time to time predicting the death of the book. Apparently we will soon be reading novels on our mobile phones. To paraphrase Samuel Johnson, it's amazing that you can do this, but more amazing that you would want to.

# Current Thinking on Bookselling ❧ Peter Budek

As an undergraduate, I was able to indulge myself in the bookshops of Oxford, many of which are no longer there. Thornton's in Broad Street was an iconic secondhand bookshop, where I loved spending my spare time. I knew nothing about what made a book collectable; I just knew what I liked. I was reading Physics and Philosophy, and was generally interested in the history of ideas. I would particularly look for old scientific books – initially with the intention of seeing how wrong they were, but always ending up impressed by how right they were. A lot of the ideas contained in books from, say, the 1850s echo the latest findings in modern science.

As a child, Nikola Tesla, the great Serbian inventor, was one of my scientific heroes. He is best remembered today for his dispute with Edison over electricity distribution, which was in effect the first standards war. Edison fought a dirty campaign to champion his direct current over Tesla's alternating current. Tesla's own publications are few in number, but his experiments were reported in a vast number of books dating from the late 1880s – vividly illustrated books on electricity, describing how to make an earthquake, sparks the size of a house, and other experiments likely to appeal to the young reader. Tesla became quite a cult figure as a result of the dispute with Edison, and certain items, especially the reports of his lectures at the American Institute of Electrical Engineers are quite valuable today.

I'm sure you rarely come across a bookseller who didn't start life as a teacher. My only plea for originality is that I taught Physics. While I was teaching, I started doing the occasional book fair with my mother, who shared my enjoyment in handling old books. A member of the family suggested the name of Eagle Books, being the emblem of Bedford and, as my father was Polish, it also suggested the double eagle of Poland. We exhibited at modest little fairs in the area, and I soon found that I was enjoying it a lot more than lecturing on thermodynamics to sixth-formers. On my way to school, I would walk past a shop at the bottom of Magdalen Bridge. One day I noticed that it was being fitted out as a bookshop. I watched the shelves go up, and then the books come in and finally it opened as The Bookshop at The Plain. There was something about seeing someone else have a go that acted as a trigger for me, turning a dream into a real possibility.

My teaching colleagues thought I was fifty years too young to become a second hand bookseller. One colleague told me that he had never been in a second hand bookshop when there had been another customer present, and no one understood how such a venture could could possibly pay the bills. But I continued to think about what I really wanted to do with my life and, on a visit to my parents in Bedford, I noticed that this shop was for sale with a flat above it. At the time it was occupied by a remarkable set of characters, selling organic carrots under the wonderful name of The Sunflower Wholefood Cooperative. I formed a natural bond with them, and they were delighted at the prospect of selling the premises to a bookseller.

I went to my bank in Oxford, explained what I wanted to do and asked if they would lend me the money. My request was met with the usual incredulity that a mortgage could be paid off by the sale of second hand books. But they asked for my business plan, and after a few weeks it was 'goodbye' to a nice regular salary cheque and 'hello' to the world of books. My mother and I took over the premises in July 1991, and it was shelved and ready for business by the end of August. A lot of people shook their heads sadly. Bedford's reputation was not good either for sourcing or for selling books. I hope the Eagle Bookshop has done something to change this.

Over the years, as my mother's role in the shop faded, my reckless side was in danger of going unchecked. Thankfully I have a wonderful team (Tony, Jean, Andrew, Patrizia and, most recently, Vanessa) who keep both the shop and its proprietor in some sort of order. Without my mother's input in those early days, though, there would be no Eagle Bookshop.

For the first two years we received endless telephone calls about organic carrots. But the Cooperative's customers were very supportive and provided me with a ready-made customer base. There were two local dealers who were both very supportive – Aidan Mackie, who specialises in G.K. Chesterton and is now in his 80s, and Richard Wildman who had a small shop, unfairly savaged in *Driff's Guide*. Hedley Morgan is another Bedfordshire bookseller, and a most accomplished one. He is easily the shop's most frequent visitor and, over many years, his custom, advice and friendship have been invaluable. He instilled in me the importance of condition – his own books are always in superb condition.

In the early years, there was no money in the business but it was hugely exciting. I lived in the flat above the shop, and enjoyed lots of bachelor evenings, cooking sausage curries and talking philosophy long into the night. I met my wife through the shop. She was a regular customer to whom I had been giving increasingly large discounts. In the end it became cheaper to marry her! We have two young sons, both of whom like to help in the shop – Adam, I suspect, for the pocket money, but Freddie genuinely likes the books.

I have much enjoyed sharing ideas and learning from my customers who have always been very generous with their knowledge. As a scientist, literature was one of my areas of ignorance. Customers would come in and ask for a novel by the title, assuming I would know the author. I would scuttle off to my reference books, find the answer and come back looking more knowledgeable. There was a lot of bluffing at the beginning, but having a bookshop is the best university in the world.

In my wild youth, although I didn't read much literature, I was arrogant enough to enjoy writing bad poetry and scribbling down ideas for novels. Hisham Matar lived for a few years in Bedford, and we used to discuss our writing and encourage each other. A few years later his novel, *In the Country of Men* was nominated for the Man Booker Prize, and went on to win the Royal Society of Literature Ondaatje Prize. Meanwhile I'm still stuck on the thirteenth page of my novel.

I have a fondness for Percy Muir for introducing me to bibliography through his *Book Collecting as a Hobby. In a series of letters to Everyman.* It was a joy to read and filled me with enthusiasm to go out and explore the world of books. It was, of course, hopelessly out of date with its advice to look in the tuppenny baskets and pick out a few random examples of seventeenth-century books. The book itself has become a period piece but, at the same time, it contained a lot of valuable information. Seamus Stewart's *Book Collecting: a beginner's guide* is much less well known, but is also very good at communicating the excitement of book collecting.

Every book in my shop is part of my collection – albeit a dynamic one. If I didn't have this attitude to my books, it wouldn't be the wonderful job that it is. Sometimes I really fall in love with a book and then perhaps I take it home, where I have a few things that I can't see myself parting with – mainly the great landmarks in science.

It's a common pattern for booksellers to end up with too much stock and no cash to pay the bills. We all love books and naturally try to accumulate as many as possible. I ran out of space in my shop within a few years, and in 1997 my wife and I moved out of the flat, and opened the first floor as a Science Room and a room for Mathematics and other Arts – Mathematics being the supreme art. In 1998 we expanded again, this time in terms of books, by taking over the entire stock and reference library of F. E. Whiteheart, who had specialised in Mathematics. We also acquired Fred's mailing list, and started to produce our own Science catalogues.

The increased shop space and the catalogue business enabled us almost to double our turnover in the space of a few years. We also launched our website which I like to think is rather different from the general run of booksellers' websites (www. eaglebookshop.co.uk). I wanted something that would be fun to use – a virtual shop where you could just click your way around the shelves. A lot of people were involved in the project, and it was a wonderful example of a cooperative venture.

By 2004 we were running out of space again. I had just paid off the mortgage on the shop when the building next door came on to the market. I managed to persuade the bank to lend me the money for the next stage of our expansion. We were able to knock through the wall upstairs to create more space for the bookshop, and rent out the adjoining downstairs shop to pay the bills. In the event I changed my mind about the shop, and came up with the idea of opening it as a cooperative art gallery. A number of my customers were local artists who were always looking for somewhere to display their work.

The Eagle Gallery Artists was formed, and I receive a percentage of their sales to help pay the bills. This amounts to a fraction of what I could earn in rent, but the gallery brings more people into the area, and boosts our business indirectly. During the summer we have parties in the garden, and joint cultural events with the gallery, creating a little cultural centre in Bedford. It's a case of thinking slightly imaginatively.

This business is about expanding without the quality going down. It's important to keep the stock fresh. We use eBay to raise cash from old stock. Vanessa Kay is my first full-time employee and her work is largely devoted to looking after our listings on eBay – from scanning images to despatching orders. We started to experiment with eBay in 2006, and it has worked well as an exercise in cash flow management. I'm pretty ruthless about pruning the stock, and will happily reduce the price on anything that has been around for a long time. If it's a collectable book and priced over £30, we'll put it on eBay. For books in the £20 and under bracket, I'm happy to put them on our £2 shelves, or on our £1 trolleys outside.

The trolleys were quite an investment in hardware, but they sell an enormous amount of books, and encourage people to come into the shop. It's important not to worry about selling a book too cheaply. You should make it easy for people to do business with you, and be prepared for the next person to make a profit. Don't try to save money by closing one day a week or switching off the lights – give people a reason to come and visit you.

I predict that the secondhand bookshops that have survived the coming of the internet will become busier again, as people start to miss the hands-on feeling of browsing. Book collectors like the physicality of the object; they want to hunt in the corners of a bookshop, and not in the margins of a screen. It's a myth that the younger generation is not interested in books. We have pupils from the local comprehensive school visiting the shop. They always ask to see the oldest book in the shop – children are fascinated by antiquity - and to see the 'wow' factor is one of my best moments in bookselling. I consider myself supremely lucky to work in the world of books.

# A Bookseller's Guide to the Universe ∾ Alfredo Breitfeld
## Librería de Antaño, Buenos Aires

People who know nothing about this business always ask if we have read *all* our books. Of course not, I respond, but we do have to know certain things about each book that passes through our hands. When I'm researching a book, I try to make it talk to me; I hold it in my hands and this will tell me something about the quality of the binding; I open it and look for ownership marks such as an ex-libris, an author's inscriptions, provenance and suchlike, and so the process of discovery moves on with every page I turn. I look for any salient points of interest in the text which will help me assess the importance and interest of the book, and then I look for bibliography and reference material. As book dealers, we have to be informed about many areas of knowledge in order to evaluate what we have in our hands; we're not just selling books as inanimate objects.

I began my bookselling career in Uruguay, publishing and selling medical text books. I was a good salesman and enjoyed what I did. After several years, a friend, who had been working for an old established second hand book store in Montevideo, wanted to set up on his own and asked if I would put some money into the business. We opened a book store in the mid-1960s and began trading, mostly in used text books, but also in some antiquarian material. We produced catalogues and gradually began to acquire some quite interesting old books. I can vividly remember the day we received an order from the British Library. It was a fantastic moment for us.

In due course we opened a second book store, and then things started to go wrong and eventually resulted in the end of our business partnership. We had borrowed money to finance our expansion and, when we split, my partner kept the book store and I kept the debt and a huge amount of old books about which I knew very little. I had to educate myself rather quickly, and soon discovered that it was a case of *amor a prima vista*.

My wife, Susana, is from Argentina and, for various family reasons, a time came when we decided to move to Buenos Aires. We had a very good business in Montevideo, and I can only describe this decision as romantic rather than practical – it was certainly not based on sound economics. My wife had studied psychology and was working as a kindergarten teacher when we met. But she became a partner in my book business and we have worked very happily together for over forty years.

In Buenos Aires, we called our business Librería De Antaño. At first we mainly sold new books and out of print books to institutional libraries that belonged to

SALALM (Seminar on the Acquisition of Latin American Library Materials). It was largely a case of filling standing orders, and was quite a profitable business. We were also gradually developing the antiquarian side, and selling complete sets of periodicals. That particular market has completely disappeared, except for the rarest material. It's an international phenomenon, and I can only guess that it must be linked to the ease of photocopying, the coming of the internet, or simply shortage of space.

There are several universes in this business, and it is a constant challenge as one discovery leads on to the next. First you encounter the universe of 'small' books for general reading purposes, and then you move out into the rarefied world of good, very good and impossibly scarce books until you are thoroughly poisoned by the urge to explore ever further afield. We specialised at that time in rare South American material from the Independence period.

About twenty years ago, our youngest son, Gustavo, became a partner, and we have been most fortunate in this respect. It's quite unusual nowadays for children to follow their parents into the family business – I always think of the great American bookseller, Jake Zeitlin and his five sons and daughters, all of them bright and cultured, but none of whom went into the antiquarian business. I remember the exact moment when Gustavo took to the idea of becoming a bookseller. His school teacher had arranged for a group of his class mates to come and visit our book store and learn a little about the strange world of old books. I showed the children various things that might amuse them, and something in my son just clicked.

When Gustavo began working with us, I warned him that you cannot fall in love with the first book that you handle in the morning, and spend all day working on it. If you want to earn a living from books, you have to work efficiently while you're in the shop, and educate yourself in your own time – otherwise you had better be a millionaire or a collector. In the meantime, Gustavo graduated in psychology, and perhaps this helps him to work with his father! We both share an inquiring mind, and enjoy adding books to our reference library. We have an extensive collection of bibliographies on the Spanish world, and Gustavo is very skilled at describing important material.

When we acquire a rare book, we play a little 'game', testing each other about its prospective value, before looking at any online database. Our opinion almost always coincides. We complement each other very well – my experience and knowledge and his intelligence, love for the profession and understanding of modern business methods which have enabled us to bring Librería de Antaño into the twenty-first century. In 1995 Gustavo opened the Antique Book Shop, a very 'gaucho' name, in a fancy part of town, where we meet a different brand of customer.

Argentina is certainly the most bookish country in South America, even though many of the great libraries have now been dispersed. In the past it was home to many extremely important collectors, often very wealthy individuals. Nowadays there is a new generation of book collectors, highly cultured people who are not necessarily wealthy, but simply want to learn more about the history of their country. My son tends to look after this younger generation, as he is more in touch with their tastes and interests.

We began buying more international material and concentrating, within our speciality, on the better and older books in the field of Americana and, to some extent, Hispanica. We embraced the internet, of course, and both these moves were fundamental to the development of the business. I confess that my knowledge of the new technology is quite elementary, but I could not work without it. Gustavo looks after that side of the business, and the book store is now run on thoroughly modern lines.

The fashion for nineteenth-century colour-plate books of views and costumes of Argentina has almost disappeared here. The finest examples were produced by French artists. They are very beautiful books, but extremely difficult to find, and so expensive that they have priced themselves out of the local market. There are a number of foreign booksellers who visit Buenos Aires, combining business and pleasure, as it is still possible to find good books here.

We also specialise in first editions of modern literary celebrities, like Jorge Luis Borges, the great poet, essayist and short-story writer who was born in Buenos Aires in 1899. Any event to do with Borges was always a tremendous social occasion here, attracting vast crowds, journalists and photographers. I remember standing in a long queue to have my copy of his last book, *La Cifra* signed when it came out in 1981. When I finally got to the great man, I told him that I was an antiquarian bookseller, to which he replied, 'I would love to have embraced that profession when I was young, and my father too'. His father had been, amongst other things, an unsuccessful writer, and the young Borges had grown up in his father's extensive library, on the understanding that he would fulfil his father's literary ambitions. I was so nervous when I met Borges that I forgot to ask for his signature in my book. So I got back in the queue and, in due course, was amazed to find that he had remembered my name and occupation. However, he wasn't signing any more copies that day. I treasure it as one of my most famous unsigned books.

There are many collectors who are interested in the publications of the first presses in this region. The history of printing in Spanish America dates from 1539 when the first book was printed in Mexico, a hundred years before the first book was printed in America. In the early 1580s, Antonio Ricardo set up a printing office in Lima and, in 1584, the *Pragmática sobre los diez díaz del año* became the first work printed in Peru and indeed in South America. This item is of extreme rarity, not only in printing history, but also for the light it throws on the languages of Inca culture in the sixteenth century – the text is printed in Spanish, Quechua and Aymara. I have handled a few copies in my time, but not for over ten years. The dictionary sometimes referred to as the *Arte de la lengua general del Peru*, and the *Doctrina christiana y catecismos* written in Spanish, Quechua and Aymara are also very much sought after since, apart from their scarcity, they reflect the indigenous culture of sixteenth-century America.

José Toribio Medina was the greatest bibliographer of colonial Spanish America. His monumental four-volume work, *La imprenta en Lima*, was published in Santiago de Chile, 1904-7, and opens with the *Doctrina Christiana*. A Chilean lawyer and historian, Medina travelled the continent at the turn of the last century, visiting the most remote places, crossing the Mexican countryside on a donkey, discovering unknown imprints in incredible places, consulting libraries and gathering information on the history of printing in all the Spanish-speaking South American countries. If a book is described in a catalogue as 'not in Medina', you can be sure that it is a real rarity.

As an occupation, the book trade has thrived largely unchanged since the Middle Ages. Ironically it is also ideally suited to the new technology, and is one of the activities to have benefited most from the coming of the internet. As a source of information, I admire it more every day. It has certainly enabled buyers to check if a book is rare or not – I believe that many dealers have gone out of business because their definition of rarity depended on customers' inability to verify it. As a means of selling books, I have found it very useful for disposing of the odds and ends outside my specialist field – the books that we all accumulate over the years, and for which we have no particular customer. I have also benefited enormously from the ability to read catalogues online, saving a fortune in subscriptions – not to mention the frustration when the post lets me down.

Many collectors appreciate the personal relationship with their book dealer. Technology plays a very important role in our lives, but I'm not pessimistic about the future of the rare book trade. I cannot imagine a time when one of my clients will start to tremble and perspire holding in his hands a first electronic version of *Don Quijote de la Mancha*. Rare and beautiful books will disappear only if beauty itself disappears from our existence. While humanity still has a soul, the book will remain in its present physical form. Finally, I like to think that this blessed profession has enabled me to enjoy a decent standard of living surrounded by what I love most – my books and my family.

# All Things Bright And Beautiful
## ❧ Edward Bayntun-Coward

The late Pierre Berès, most eminent of French book dealers, rang up a while ago and insisted on speaking to George Bayntun. When I told him that it would not be possible, he insisted that he only dealt with the owner. 'I'm sorry, sir', I replied, 'George is dead'. 'Since when?' 'September 1940'. 'I'm so sorry. Was it sudden?' I am regularly addressed as George, who was in fact my great-grandfather. He had one child, a daughter, who married a Mr Coward. When she inherited the business, it was decided to retain the founder's name.

George Bayntun opened for business as a bookbinder and bookseller in 1894. He had served his apprenticeship with Taylor's in Bath and then set up his own bindery in Northumberland Place. Initially, he bound books and magazines for private customers and the trade, but he soon realised that it was more profitable to buy the books himself, bind or repair them and then sell them on for a profit. The American book collector, Wilmarth Lewis wrote about Bayntun, in his account of a trip to England in 1923, 'He was a binder of "standard works", which he turned out at a prodigious rate for the trade. Mr Bayntun was content with a 10 per cent profit and a turnover so rapid that the great authors galloped through his shop. In a few years I was to hear him spoken of with dispraise by bibliographers and bibliophiles as a destroyer of original boards and a perverter of history, but he was too good a businessman to destroy the valuable.'

We have always appreciated the importance of original condition, and would never destroy something valuable. If someone asked me to rebind a copy of the first edition of *The Great Gatsby* in pristine condition, in its original dust jacket, I would refuse. But I would agree to make a box to protect it. Wilmarth Lewis possessed one of Humphry Repton's gardening books, uncut in the original boards, for which Bayntun had made a box.

George had the golden touch and his business expanded rapidly, moving to larger premises in Walcot Street, and to the present shop in Manvers Street a year before his death. It was at this time that he also acquired the name and bindery of Robert Rivière, with its array of tools and brasses. Rivière had started as a binder in Bath in 1829 before moving to London where he soon reached the top of the trade. George paid £6000 for our present premises, which had been the postal sorting office. It has changed very little over the years, though we have added the old wooden dock from Bath Magistrates Court to hide the computer in the front shop.

Neither George nor my father ever threw anything away, so we have our own extensive archives, including some of Rivière's designs, though the majority of these are now in Sir Paul Getty's library at Wormsley. Queen Mary spent the war years at Badminton and would visit the shop on her regular trips into Bath. We have photographs of her taking away piles of books – she did not always pay for them, but we were awarded a royal warrant in part exchange.

After George's death, my grandmother was advised that there was no future for the business, but she stubbornly carried on, closing only for his funeral. She employed a series of managers who largely failed to manage, but kept things going until my father, Hylton, had done his National Service and took over the business in 1951. My father was not a naturally bookish person, but he was a very good businessman. When he took over, the shop was little more than a display case for the work of the bindery. He recognised that the bookselling side needed to be developed, and took the opportunity to do so in 1963, when he bought George Gregory's bookshop in Green Street. In 1981 the two businesses were brought together under one roof in Manvers Street.

My father never bought at auction; all his books came from other dealers or private sources. He had a knack for knowing the books that people wanted to buy. The 1960s were the boom years for Bayntun's, with libraries being formed throughout the United States. Three or four big American buyers from book stores such as Brentano's would come over once or twice a year and clear the shelves. They were filling American homes with beautifully bound books – the instruction to our binders was always 'put on more gold'. Dad would drive all over the country, filling the car with famous works of English literature, bring them back, bind them up and off they would go. Churchill was always bound in red morocco, with a panelled spine, a block on both covers and Cockerell endleaves. When a book sold, another copy would be taken out to the bindery and bound to replace it, like for like.

In the good old days books were regarded as part of the furniture in any self-respecting house. Dad had a couple of customers who both had three residences. In one they had a red library, in another a blue library, and the third was green. So when they ordered a book – even a set of Shakespeare – they would do so in triplicate, and have them bound accordingly. At one point my father employed over thirty people in the bindery. It was a bit of a production line, but my father refused to cut corners and everything continued to be done by hand. George Bayntun was quoted as saying, 'We work in the old way. Machine binding? Not for us'.

Of course we are more conservationally aware these days, but in every other respect we are the last of the trade binderies doing things as they were done 100 years ago. Today there are ten people working in the bindery who, between them, have clocked up 370 years in the trade – Derek Harris has been with us since 1947

– and comes in for two days a week to make our special boxes.

My father's love of books was surpassed by his interest in the book trade. He served as President of the ABA in 1980-82 and again ten years later. When he died in 2000, his memorial service in Bath Abbey was attended by almost 1000 people. The last edition of the ABA Newsletter to be published while my father was still alive told the story of the four booksellers stranded on a desert island – an Englishman, a Scotsman, an American and Japanese. They did not know each other, but they all knew my father.

When I'm asked how long I've been in the book business, I tend to reply forty-two years, as I was brought into the shop in the first week of my life. I can say honestly that I remember it in every detail, because virtually nothing has changed. From the age of eight, I would accompany my father on his annual summer buying trip, during which he would drive up the West Coast to Stockport, across to Edinburgh, and down the East coast to York and Norwich and then across southern England from Hastings to Brighton and on to Salisbury, zigzagging to and fro, visiting every secondhand bookshop in the directory. He was very gregarious and wanted someone to go with him. I'm one of four and so my mother would stay at home and look after my brother and sisters.

At my father's suggestion, I spent a few weeks working for Maggs before I went up to read Modern History at Oxford. Although he was keen to introduce me to an occupation which gave him such pleasure, he never put any pressure on me and was aware of my strongly held belief that there was more to life than bookselling. But Maggs was great fun and I subsequently spent my vacations there, working in the packing room, building shelves in the loft for Maggs's 'hospital' of defective books, and then down to the ground floor to answer the telephone. Finally I graduated to the second floor where I joined Bryan Maggs and Robert Harding and became immersed in English literature and historic bookbindings.

One of my friends at Oxford was a certain David Cameron. When I told him that I was going to be a book dealer, he replied that he was going to be Prime Minister. After graduating in 1988, I went straight back to Maggs to work with Bryan and Robert, largely on Sir Paul Getty's library. During my first year I photocopied reproductions of bookbindings in every reference book and catalogue to be found in Maggs's extensive reference library. I filled about fifty large files, with the images arranged chronologically and, in the process, I developed something of a photographic memory for bindings.

I was fortunate to join the firm at the time of Christie's sales of the Estelle Doheny Collection. On my first day at work, Maggs bought a magnificent example of English Restoration binding by the so-called 'Queens' Binder B' for Getty's library for many hundreds of thousands of pounds. I remember thinking that it was beyond belief that people called this work – buying wonderful books and selling them to extraordinary people. Within a short time, however, I began to be aware of the need to keep things in perspective. So two or three days a week I would leave Maggs at five o'clock and make my way to The Samaritans in Soho where I manned the telephones until ten o'clock, and occasionally all night. Although I take my work seriously, and it is my only source of income, bookselling hardly compares in importance to many other occupations. But we do have the opportunity to make people happy by satisfying their need for something and, in the case of some collectors, giving them their 'fix'. But it is not a harmful addiction.

Towards the end of my five years at Maggs, my father received a call from the Duchess of Bedford who wanted to dispose of 6,000 books from the basement at Woburn, which had been removed from the library a hundred years before. It was agreed that I would continue to work for Maggs part-time, while helping my father to catalogue the books from Woburn. When this was finished, I received a call from John and Myfanwy Piper's executor asking for a probate valuation of their books. I gave them a reasonable figure only to be told that it was too high for probate purposes. To prove that I was right, I offered to buy the books at that figure, and suddenly I had another 6,000 books on my hands and nowhere to store them. There is a wonderful warehouse in the middle of Berkeley Square called Maggs, and we split the collection between us. I remained on my part-time basis, before finally moving down to Bath with my wife, Laura, and our first child. My father died a couple of months later on 25 September 2000.

My father would be quite surprised to find that I have stayed put here. When I took over the ownership of George Bayntun, the building needed a lot of money spent on it, and the prospect was quite daunting. My father might have expected me to run the business from home, or to pocket the money and spend even more time on holiday than we do. Of course I do things rather differently from my father, who loved to spend time in the shop talking with customers. A lot of people regarded our shop as a club, or a waiting room because of its proximity to the railway station. Some would come in and sit down, with no intention of buying a book. Penny Cox has been with us for forty-five years and thought she had seen it all, but was taken aback when a rather shady looking character came into the shop asking for pornography. Penny's response was unequivocally negative, but he persisted and, pointing to a copy of *Moby Dick*, said, 'What's that, then?' Penny explained patiently that it was a novel about whales, to which he replied, 'Well, the Welsh are a bunch of perverts.'

I tend to hide away upstairs cataloguing my special books, a legacy no doubt from my years at Maggs. Although people associate me with fine bindings, I deal in all kinds of books which are in some way unique, and I am a fetishist about condition. My father's method was to keep selling the same book over again. I have continued this aspect of the business, but I also try to offer uniqueness in my catalogues, where you will find dedication copies, the authors' own copies, presentation copies and books in distinguished bindings.

Now that Google plans to make the text of every book ever printed accessible on the web, the market for rare books might lose some of its appeal. We will all have to learn the importance of adaptability, as demonstrated by such brilliant dealers as Sam Fogg and Colin Franklin who have moved successfully into new fields. Who would have expected them to be selling Christian icons and Buddhist artefacts? But I am quite confident that books as objects will not only survive this period of great upheaval, but be held in growing esteem. Bound by hand, a book becomes a unique object and, when done well, it becomes a work of art, or at least of ingenuity. Long after the dust jacket on a first edition of *The Great Gatsby* has perished – or been exposed as a fake – bindings bearing the name of Rivière, or even Bayntun will still be treasured.

I am blessed with a handful of private clients who are interested in buying examples of historic bookbindings or in commissioning new work. We have a stock of 15,000 finishing tools and I greatly enjoy having a certain amount of input into the design of a new binding, though I tend to look to the past for inspiration. I admire in particular the products of the English Restoration period, and Irish eighteenth-century bindings, which are superlative. I used to deride the Victorians, but have come to appreciate what bookbinders like James Hayday achieved. Howard Nixon, the great historian of bookbinding, classified his work as the 'kitchen sink school of binding'. The designs might have been over-elaborate, but technically they were most impressive and innovative.

Rivière bindings are sometimes criticised for their precision, and consequent lack of 'soul'. Faultlessness has thus become a fault. We forgive, even applaud, imperfection, so long as it is committed in the name of craft. T. J. Cobden-Sanderson could get away with all kinds of deficiencies, but I can sell his bindings, faded concave spines and all, for the price of a decent car. He has of course been given the full treatment by Marianne Tidcombe in *The Bookbindings of T. J. Cobden-Sanderson*, 1984. I would like to see a comparable history of the trade binderies, and would certainly be willing to contribute to it.

In stock at the moment I have examples of bookbinding from over twenty countries, bound in goat, calf and sheep skin, shagreen, tortoiseshell, bats' wings, ivory, silk, velvet, embroidery, gold, silver and all kinds of paper. But I am not interested in the work of binders who think it is clever to incorporate a razor blade in the binding of a book on suicide, or barbed wire on a volume of First World War poetry – you have to be able to handle a book without drawing blood. The design must work as a book.

Three years ago I bought thirty or so bindings by Roger Powell in an auction in Solihull, and most of the contents of his bindery, including ledgers, diaries, notes on various projects, correspondence, and photographs of his work and ephemera of all sorts. When times were hard, he kept himself busy by making napkin rings for Liberty's. The collection also included a number of his zinc blocks, which he made great use of in his bookbinding. Collectors of Powell's work are not always aware of this. The blocks were designed by the calligrapher and artist, Sheila Waters, who was the wife of Roger's partner, Peter Waters.

In my opinion contemporary and older bookbindings are perfectly compatible; they both employ the same techniques and materials. Obviously contemporary binders like to experiment – you cannot keep going over the same ground. I see parallels with my work as chairman of the Bath Preservation Trust, where I try to encourage modern architecture, so long as it is of a quality to be expected within a World Heritage City. I have always been very interested in architecture, and sometimes think of the bindery in terms of an architectural practice, with its aspects of design, craftsmanship and not least preservation.

Over the last few years I have been commissioning and buying a series of bindings from the likes of Glenn Bartley, James and Stuart Brockman, Jeff Clements, Flora Ginn, Jenni Grey, Bernard Middleton and Chris Shaw, and these live at home. I like to have books bound that have meant something to me – texts from school and university, but in editions printed by the likes of the Kelmscott or Doves Press. If my bindings were sold as a collection, it would be difficult for anyone else to know why this particular set of texts had been put together. Although I greatly appreciate the book as an object – a fine binding is a visual and tactile experience – I would never say that the text or edition is unimportant. Binders should concentrate their skills on books deserving of their efforts. I do not give them any specific instructions, but I do like all things bright and beautiful. I am always happy if the outcome is something that my wife and children will also enjoy. Although they are still young, my three children are showing quite an interest in books and love running wild in the shop. When customers tell them off for making a noise, I point out that this is a family business now in its fourth generation. There is nothing virtual about our bookshop, and that is so much part of the pleasure.

# The Caretaker ∾ Sabrina Izzard

Nobody grows up saying that they want to be an antiquarian bookseller. It is not one of the established career options. My father was a journalist and my mother was Molly Izzard, whose books included *A Private Life*, in which she recounts her experiences as the wife of a foreign correspondent, trying to raise a family of four children in some of the trouble spots of the world. My oldest brother was born in Delhi when my father was reporting on the partition of India, and I was born in Egypt just before the Suez Crisis. In 1958, we returned to this country and settled in Tunbridge Wells.

I spent quite a lot of my childhood at home due to ill health, and passed the time reading a huge amount. I was omnivorous in my tastes, though I always had a special interest in travel books. As a family, we were very travel-oriented and my father, who was by that stage working on adventure films, would pack us into his Land Rover and we would go off somewhere. Hall's Bookshop was an important part of my life from an early age. It was my Saturday afternoon outing to walk down into the town and buy books from Harry Pratley at Hall's. The shop is in Chapel Place behind the Church of King Charles the Martyr, and is an institution in Tunbridge Wells. Reuben Hall had opened it in 1898 in 18 Chapel Place on the site of Knight's Lending Library.

In 1919 Harry Pratley began his apprenticeship at Hall's at the age of fourteen on seven shillings a week. In 1922 he was 'sold' with the business to Charles Avery, a friend of Hall's who had a small bookshop in Maidstone. Harry completed his apprenticeship and, when Mr Avery died in 1936, was able to buy the business on the very generous terms offered to him by the family. An important tradition had begun of passing the shop on to those who had worked in it. In 1938 Hall's moved to its present location in 20 and 22 Chapel Place, where many devoted customers helped him to put up the shelves. Nothing has been changed in the appearance of the shop since that date. Elizabeth Bateman became Harry's assistant in 1955, and in turn took over the business in 1967, which she ran until her death in 1983.

My first experience of secondhand bookselling was with John Thornton in the mid-1970s. He was dealing in antiques at the time, and had The Chair Shop in Tunbridge Wells, which also had a room of secondhand books. I worked for John for around seven years, and during that time the book side of his business expanded to fill eight rooms. While John was out buying furniture, and at the same time picking up lots of books, I would spend my time in the shop, where I met all the dealers. Mr Howlett, the famous 'runner', was a regular visitor and the most wonderful person. He had had a bookshop in pre-war Bromley, where Richmal Crompton had been one of his customers. When I knew him, he was living nearby in Hildenborough, where his wife was kept busy fostering Nigerian babies for the GLC.

Elizabeth Bateman would visit John Thornton's shop almost every day. I used to put aside books that I thought would be suitable for Hall's. It was a very convenient arrangement for her – John found fantastic material on his private calls, and Elizabeth was not a driver. She was also in very poor health. One day she asked if I would come and work at Hall's. I started in 1981 on a pitiful salary, and I was only able to manage because I was living with my mother. All the books were priced in pounds, shillings and pence – Elizabeth having refused to go decimal. There were piles of books hidden under brown paper, slowly accumulating, because Elizabeth was not well enough to price them. She would rather not sell a book than make a mistake. Failure of any kind was not tolerated, and the power of her personality was such that some of her assistants were terrified of her. But essentially she was a very kind person, and felt a tremendous sense of responsibility toward the shop.

Elizabeth had recruited me with the view of training me to take over the bookshop. She had expected to have another four years of active bookselling instead of which she died within eighteen months of my joining Hall's. I was given the chance, much sooner than I might have expected, to buy the business. I bought it for £10,000, which I paid off within the first eighteen months. In the early days I deliberately copied Elizabeth's handwriting when pricing books, so that customers might not notice the change of ownership. However, word got around that Elizabeth had died, and the shop was extremely busy – no doubt some people thought that the 'apprentice' was bound to make mistakes, but most people came to show their support for the shop.

When Harry Pratley heard that I was taking over Hall's, he immediately sent me a cheque for £1000. However the ABA demanded the return of our membership plaque, which upset Harry terribly, as a former President of the Association. Actually it was one of the best things that could have happened – it made me feel determined to make it on my own. Harry used to come in to the shop every week and we would discuss what I had bought since his last visit. He kept bringing in good books for me to put in the window and sell. I resisted doing this because I was afraid that these sales would distort the true picture of how the shop was doing. It was essential for the business to be able to survive on what I was able to buy and sell. I can honestly say that I did not relax for the first ten years.

Harry Pratley died on 5 May 1987, and the residue of his fine collection of books – he had given most of them away – was sold by Sotheby's in a three-day sale in

January 1988. I spent £1000 in each day's sale, as I felt that I needed to be seen to be there and buying books. The following year the local branch manager of Lloyds Bank, which owned the premises of Hall's Bookshop, came round in person to deliver some very bad news. The bank owned the entire block in which the shop is situated, and they had plans to redevelop it. We were on very friendly terms – indeed he had lent me the money to buy the business. He explained that the decision had been made by the bank's property people and that, while he personally was on my side, there was nothing he could do to help. When a local journalist heard that Hall's Bookshop was under threat, he launched a publicity campaign which quite simply snowballed.

There was a public outcry, at first local, then national and finally international. Local people moved their bank accounts away from Lloyds. Tunbridge Wells Borough Council threatened to do the same. Finally a television crew wanted to come down, and I think it was at that stage that Lloyds Bank took an enlightened attitude and relented. The bookshop is so much part of the life of the town, as the publicity storm had so forcefully demonstrated.

In his time Harry Pratley had done an enormous amount to promote good will in the community. He was a prominent figure in the Rotary Club and a great supporter of local charities. The shop always took and continues to take advertising space in the newsletters and publications of the various local clubs, societies and places of worship, and we also display their announcements in the shop. As another gesture of good will, Harry never charged for valuations, and I have followed his example.

I rely almost entirely upon local connections for my stock. When people tell me that the shop is well stocked, I reply that it is thanks to my customers who sell me their books. It surprises me that a lot of book dealers do not like buying from the general public. The nicest part of the job for me is going out on house calls. There is something fascinating about going through someone's collection of books, and the glimpses that it offers into their life and interests. Buying privately is all about establishing a relationship of trust. I have learnt that it is important to accept the offer of tea or coffee, and to take a little time for everyone to relax. It does not always work. On one occasion I had to deal with an eccentric old lady who wanted her books valued, but would not let me in the house. She kept me standing at the back door, and showed me one book at a time.

It is very rare to go out on a completely wasted house call, although I have been known to suggest that they contact the local dump, which always prompts the response, 'we couldn't possibly throw books *away*'. I try to explain that there is nothing unique about their books, or indeed most books, and that they will not destroy civilisation by throwing them away – to which they sometimes respond that they would rather *give* them to me than dump them. I have learnt to say thank you and take them.

I depend entirely on part-time assistants to run the shop, because I cannot afford to pay a full-time salary. My best assistants tend to come in, aged fifteen or sixteen, looking for a Saturday job. I have learnt not to employ ex-librarians – they always want to impose order, when the shop requires greater flexibility. I usually hang on to my assistants until they have been through university, and perhaps for a little longer while they are looking for a full-time job. Customers are very indulgent with them if they do not know everything, as long as they show interest in their work. Harry taught me never to be frightened to ask if you do not know something – the customers will teach you, because they are steeped in their subject and like talking about it. Hall's is a very good training ground and a number of bookmen have begun their careers here. Tony Smith of Heywood Hill worked at Hall's until John Saumarez Smith spotted his talent and pinched him!

If customers ask us to look for a specific title, we record it in our book and let them know if a copy comes in. We have never advertised for books wanted. Actually I am more likely nowadays to suggest that they ask a grandchild to look for it on the internet. I am aware of a small number of people buying books from us in order to put them on the internet. In many cases I think that they misjudge the effort required in packing and processing an order, when you consider what they can add on to my perfectly good price. Sometimes people offer me a book and show me a list of eBay prices for it, completely unaware of the effect of condition, binding or even edition on the value of a book. There is also the trap of being guided by internet prices if there is only one copy listed. My mother's book, *A Private Life*, turned up at the local Oxfam shop priced at £49.50. It is not disloyal of me to say that it certainly is not worth that much. At the same time there was a single copy on ABE, and it was priced at £55. The internet has a lot to answer for in some of the mad pricing that one comes across.

In the old days, customers would come in to the shop, and you would acknowledge them and then carry on with what you were doing. Nowadays there are so few secondhand bookshops that you have to assume that it might be their first visit to such an establishment. I will now approach them, if they are new to the shop, and offer my assistance. This pro-active method seems to be working. A lot of young people have no affinity with books, referring to them as 'so last century'. I am sure that books will survive, but the next few years will be critical.

Hall's is a unique shop and it should have a future. It is firmly based in a town which has been extremely loyal to it, and the fundamentals of how the business is run are sound. When we were threatened with closure, I wondered if it would be possible to make a go of it in another location, but there is something about Hall's that simply can not be reproduced elsewhere. The shop is all-absorbing and intellectually stimulating – a lifestyle rather than an occupation. I think of myself as the caretaker. I did not create it; I just took over the responsibility for running it. The rent review came up recently and I committed myself to another three years, by which time I shall have given thirty years of my life to the shop. It is easy to stay on too long – you start to get stale, your information is out of date, your health deteriorates. Hall's deserves to be passed on in good shape. It has the potential to be the last bookshop standing.

# Between a Rock Cake and a Stone Wall ∾ Ian Marr

There are different types of calling in life. You might hear the voice of God instructing you to do something in particular, or the fates might conspire to channel you in a certain direction. I have tried to escape from the book trade more than once, but each time I am shepherded back. It's a forgiving business; and I am grateful that there is a place for me.

I was born in Windsor, educated at Eton and Edinburgh University where I read History. My father was in the City, and my mother was an artist whose artistic impulse culminated with me and my sister, who she described as her two masterpieces. I graduated in 1983 and had the idea of setting up my own company doing hedges and boundaries. I have a fascination for the outdoor world and wanted to work outside. At the time there was only one course in the entire country on dry stone walling. I applied three times, and each time the course was cancelled due to lack of interest. Finally I found an old boy on Exmoor who was willing to teach me all about hedges, while I lived down there in a borrowed caravan. Rather late in the day, I did a bit of market research and discovered that farmers were receiving grants to grub up their hedges.

My father had been quite keen for me to follow in his footsteps and, to be fair to him, I did a couple of summer jobs in the City, which only confirmed that it was not for me. My first real job was selling advertising space, which I did for two years in Covent Garden. The advertisement had promised '£££s', and I certainly did earn a lot of money, and was well trained, but it was so stressful that I spent large sums in the American Bar at the Savoy, and in the end had nothing to show for it all. After a period of unemployment, living in a flea-ridden flat in East London, my girlfriend took me off on a picnic and we discussed what I really wanted to do. It had to be some form of work from which I did not have to retire. As I did not anticipate earning a fortune, it was important to find something that would keep me ticking over into my old age.

Hence, in 1985 I applied to the four big auction houses, and got a job as a porter at Bonhams in Lots Road, and as amanuensis to Christopher Johnston, Head of Prints. His duties included cataloguing the Lots Road pictures, which I took over once he had trained me. I started on £5000 a year, which was not a living wage, but quite standard in the auction world in those days when people still tipped very generously. Lots Road was nothing like it is today. Chelsea Harbour had not been built, and the area was a wasteland of car wrecking yards. We held a general mixed sale every fortnight, with pictures, furniture, porcelain, objects and books. There was no book department, but a few plate books were simply tacked on to the end of the print sales. I knew a little bit about books and saw that they were not fetching the right money in our sales. They often came from deceased estates and just went out into the sale room in tea chests. I began to hold back the better books until I had enough to make a feature of them. In this way I built up Bonhams book department more or less from nothing.

I liked my colleagues and learnt a lot from them, and also from the buyers who were often very generous with their knowledge. We handled a vast amount of material and job lots were the order of the day. For example, I must have catalogued an average of 250,000 pictures a year. You trained your eye, got an instinct for it and watched what people were buying. We all longed to buy things for ourselves in the sales, but it was impossible on our miserly wages.

My time at Bonhams coincided with a boom in the economy, which turned into a recession shortly after I started as an independent trader in 1989. I had a business card printed by a friend, unfortunately in a very large quantity; the very bold, stark font was more apt for a funeral director. 'Black Monday' had been and gone, but its effect had yet to ripple through the market. I traded at antique fairs, book fairs and boot fairs. At first I could not buy enough stock; everything sold like hot cakes.

There was a caterer at one of the auction houses, who offered me an interesting sociological insight into the book trade. I asked her if there was any pattern in sales of refreshments to different types of dealer. Without hesitation, she replied that she sold endless chocolate cake at fine arts sales, lemon cake at picture sales, sausage rolls to dealers in general junk, but book dealers always went for the rock cakes – nothing fancy. Perhaps books are in some ways the poor relation among the Fine Arts – they are rarely the chosen vehicle for a display of conspicuous wealth.

By 1990 the trade had slowed down and a lot of fairs disappeared or struggled to survive. There was still action to be found at the boot fairs, and I did one every Sunday in Ascot. In 1993 I moved to Devon. Shortly thereafter I met my wife Anne, and moved to Germany with a sense of saying goodbye to the book trade. It had kept me going, but I would not have been able to support a family on it. My wife is American but was living with her four children in rural Bavaria. I joined her there and set about the task of learning to speak the language. Ironically, my first job did not involve having to speak. I worked as a landscape gardener and so would turn up at my language class after work covered from head to toe in mud. It did not take me long to find a secondhand bookshop and, with my labourer's wages for one week, I bought a large bundle of Penguin books that carried the official rubber stamps of some long lost POW camp. It was the stamps that interested me, and what books had passed the German censors.

The gardening work was seasonal and, anxious for work, I applied for a job as a lavatory cleaner, but did not get it. Clearly the universe was trying to tell me something. By that stage I had been in Germany for a year and had failed to learn the language adequately. Anne's children were at a stage where, for educational reasons, it made sense to settle in England. I moved back in 1994, and applied for twenty-eight jobs, one of which was a vacancy at Marlborough Rare Books. I was interviewed by Jonathan Gestetner and Mickie Brand who very kindly gave me the job, which I desperately needed. The family were still waiting in Bavaria; I found us an ex-council house in Surrey.

Alex Fotheringham and the late John Manners had left Marlborough Rare Books and, with their departure, the firm no longer had anyone to look after the subjects in which they had specialised. This left history, literature and theology wide open for me. It was an enormously sharp learning curve, although I had the benefit of Marlborough's marvellous reference library. Jonathan Gestetner was very patient, particularly as I was not a model employee – poor time-keeping, outbursts of contrariness and irrationality – and gave me a free hand, financially and intellectually, to develop my own interests. At the same time, I was also working as a book consultant for an auction house near where I lived in Haslemere. This kept me in touch with the wider market, and I had my feelers out to see what was buzzing.

John Manners described my early catalogue descriptions as 'crunchy'. I am not sure what he meant, but took it as a compliment. I like to bring out all the different angles to a book and to make connections that might not be apparent. When I am cataloguing, I become fantastically involved in the book to the exclusion of almost everything else. Metaphorically speaking you have to deconstruct a book and put it back together again to see what makes it tick, and that is how a book gently reveals itself to you. I often find that there is much more to say about something relatively humble than, for example, an expensive colour-plate book in which the illustrations speak for themselves.

When I joined Marlborough, the internet was not yet upon us, but there was already a sense of big change in the air. The profile of our customers was somewhat elderly, with no sign of their being replaced by a younger generation. As the internet began to take effect, it became clear that customer loyalty was going to be a thing of the past. The traditional hierarchy was bound to collapse. Information and expertise, experience, access to reference literature, and long-established international contacts, previously stored at the top of the trade, were increasingly open to all. Marlborough went through a period of wait-and-see. Although the idea of a website was much discussed, it was seen as time-consuming and unnecessary, and the firm was one of the last of the major dealers to go online.

I have a pattern of dramatic change every few years, as Jonathan Gestetner commented on reading my CV. However, I stayed at Marlborough Rare Books for eleven years and, when I left in 2005, it was due to a combination of circumstances not entirely of my own making: my last stepchild had flown the nest; I had come into a small inheritance, and the amalgamation of Marlborough Rare Books and Pickering & Chatto was under discussion. It was a logical stepping-off point for me. Before I went independent for the second time, I had been warned by a colleague not to be under any illusions; it would not be easy. As a result, I went in with my eyes open, and resisted the temptation to borrow from the bank. I had a strong feeling that a major recession was on the way, as had occurred during my first experience as an independent dealer.

In 2005 my wife and I moved down to Liskeard, where we are open by appointment. John Betjeman loved the town, Wilkie Collins hated it and Edward Gibbon was once the M. P. I considered having a shop with normal opening hours, as I believe that the continuity of a shop's presence is the best way to find new customers. However, I was put off by the bureaucracy of employment law and so on. We still have Wednesday early closing in the town, the people are friendly and in some respects it is like living in England thirty years ago. The Cornish are different but, as I get to know them better, my respect only increases. I had a customer recently who said that my stock gave the lie to the general belief that you could only buy mouldy books in Cornwall. There are a lot of mouldy books because of the sea air, but there are also a lot of very good books.

'What is a book worth?' That is the question I am most often asked by members of the public. It is often prompted nowadays by the internet where one finds comparable copies of the same book at very different prices – one copy at £100 might be offered for sale by someone who had paid too much for it and/or had high overheads, compared to another copy at £10, bought for virtually nothing at a boot fair by a fast turnover merchant –to mention a few of the variable factors. You might answer the question by consulting a reference database like *ABPC*, and establish a precedent, but the price might have been achieved by two people slogging it out in the auction room for reasons of their own. There are also market makers in our business – dealers who have the courage of their convictions to buy up all the books of a certain type and make the market. I am very attracted to this approach.

After I had been in Cornwall for about a year, I rang a colleague who said that he thought I was dead. Obviously I would have to improve my visibility and so, in addition to exhibiting at book fairs, I make a point of coming to London regularly. Liskeard has a railway station, and it takes three and a half hours to Paddington. I receive about a dozen visitors a year, who come down because my books are not on the internet, and you never know what you might find. I am like a magpie in my buying instincts and salting things away. I also like my books to have something unique about them. Although they are probably not talking about it, many dealers are taking this approach.

There was a time when we thought that the internet would mean the end of the bookseller's catalogue. Some dealers send their catalogues by e-mail, but I am not convinced that people like to receive them online. If you do not open the e-mail fairly immediately, it has a way of dropping out of sight. Although a hard copy may get buried under a pile of other stuff, it has a way of rising to the top. In my experience the hard copy catalogue has a longer shelf life than its online version. Interestingly, many of the giant online retailers still produce and mail out a hard copy of their catalogue, often with higher production values than in the past.

I have a rudimentary website, but do not use it for selling yet. I am fascinated by Amazon's ability to record your purchases, and then make recommendations based on them. I am not aware of any antiquarian website which is set up to do this, although it is just a question of joining up the dots. Most computer systems for booksellers already have stock, accountancy and mailing list software. If you combine these with the various key-word searches and tracking features on, for example, auction websites, and 'sniping' on eBay, your computer could go out there, buy what you need and offer it on, while you sit at home watching your bank balance fluctuate. It has not happened yet, but it is the logical conclusion to the different elements of software that are already in use. But that is not the sort of bookselling that appeals to me at all.

The *Harry Potter* phenomenon was great news for bookselling, creating a new generation of readers who might turn into collectors. As we know, book collecting very often does not come to people until later in life. At the moment I am stashing away books on folklore, legends, and fairy tales, partly in anticipation of the generation which has been reared on this genre. I do not know what effect the proliferation of electronic texts will have, but I am confident that there will always be a demand for the printed book. In one of the *Star Trek* films, I was delighted to see a shelf of old books in the Captain's Cabin. Presumably the designers of such films are futuristically-minded people, and yet they felt that there was still a place for a traditional old book.

I think many people view the secondhand book trade as a rather gentle occupation from a past age, with no idea of the work it entails. As John Bell said to me, they see the swan gliding along, but not the frantic paddling beneath. Our training should probably include hod-carrying – people think that I am joking if I tell them that I sometimes move several tons of books in a day. Oddly enough, the physical aspect of bookselling is not so very different from dry stone walling.

# Letting off steam in Britain's largest railway bookshop
## ༄ Robert Humm

I belong to the generation of post-war school boys who watched trains. None of us had any money, and train spotting was something that took you out of the house and kept you occupied at zero cost. We lived in suburban Essex and, by the age of eleven, my parents would let me wander around the London termini unattended. As we grew up many of us went into occupations in some way connected with our hobby. We became professional model makers, ran rail tour companies, worked on preserved railways or sold relevant books. We sell our products to each other in an industry, which probably occupies several thousand people.

Early railway literature tended to be aimed at the professional and technical classes. There were of course fine colour-plate books that gentlemen would want to have in their libraries, but throughout the Victorian era the emphasis was on locomotive and civil engineering, and investment literature. A whole range of weekly periodicals sprang up devoted to share issues, prices and prospectuses for new lines. There was no magazine for the non-specialist reader until 1897 when the gap was successfully filled by *The Railway Magazine*, still going today with a circulation of over 30,000 copies a month.

The publication of the *ABC of Southern Locomotives* in 1942 was a milestone in railway literature. Ian Allan had the brilliant idea of publishing cheap booklets listing locomotive numbers by region, producing a new one every six months. People were inspired all over the country to organise loco-spotter clubs, and to conform to a certain code of conduct. Allan may fairly be regarded as the father of the train spotting craze of my generation. As we have grown up, the field of railway literature has expanded with us or, I should say, exploded – 75 per cent of all the British railway books in existence have been published since I started in bookselling.

There are not many railway booksellers with shops – there never have been. Most of the people in our field trade from home, and the majority started in the business after retirement. I started bookselling while working for the Ministry of Transport. I was not a born bureaucrat, and wanted to have a second string to my bow. After some rapid early promotion rising to the rank of senior executive officer, my career reached a bit of a plateau. I decided that, if I was going to do something else, I must do it before I was forty. Bookselling has the advantage that you do not need to take the plunge all at once – the stock does not go off or go out of fashion and you can run the business at your own speed and level.

I had been collecting railway books in my youth and was familiar with the various dealers and publishers. Norman Kerr in Cumbria was the big wheel in railway literature, although I could rarely afford his prices. He started in the trade as a teenager in the 1930s, and his family are still very much in the book trade. Once I started work in 1964, I had the magnificent salary of £540 a year on which I had to survive in London. It did not leave a huge amount of spare money for buying books. But things gradually built up and within a decade I started selling books as a part-time activity.

The Civil Service was not too bothered about what you did as an outside occupation as long as there was no direct conflict of interest with the Department's business. I would come home in the evening and then get on with the night job of bookselling. I started producing catalogues, relatively modest publications aimed at private customers and fellow-enthusiasts. I fumbled ahead in a typically British approach and learnt from my mistakes. It was eleven years before I felt ready to take the plunge. My turnover had reached around £35,000 a year. I calculated that I would need to make the leap to a turnover of £60,000 to make a living comparable to my Civil Service salary in the mid-1980s. If I had the whole day at my disposal, I believed that I could make a living out of books. I took the plunge in 1985, within five months of my fortieth birthday.

My father had been a shop keeper and I knew from him what it was like to be self-employed – no staying in bed if you did not feel very well, because there was always the next slice of living to earn. If you went on holiday, you came back to a mountain of work and if you went on holiday too frequently, your competitors might have purloined part of your business. You cannot take a dilettante attitude to running a business. I had a young family to support, bills to pay and a mortgage, and I had to work out very quickly the best use of my time. In my first year of full-time bookselling the turnover hit £70,000. I knew within a couple of years that I had made the right decision.

It became obvious that the family home in West London– a six-bedroom house already bulging at the seams with books – would not be able to accommodate the growing stock which began to overflow into a lock-up garage, a garden shed and, finally, a little shop in Chiswick. Originally intended as a storeroom, we opened the shop and called it The Wyvern after the emblem of the Midland Railway. But none of these arrangements was entirely satisfactory. In the summer of 1985 an advertisement by the BR Property Board appeared in *The Railway Magazine* stating that part of the Grade II listed station house was to let at Stamford in Lincolnshire. I glanced at it and thought no more, but my wife was keen for us to go and see it.

It was a lovely former stationmaster's house in Jacobean style, built in local stone in 1848 by Sancton Wood, who built the stations for the old Syston and Peterborough Railway Company. Stamford railway station dates from the first decade of railway mania, when the system mushroomed from being a few disconnected lines to being a unified network.

The house had not been inhabited since the early 1960s, when the stationmaster fell victim to the Beeching cuts. However the station is still operational. The house was in a very poor state of repair and the Property Board offered it to us at a rent which was hard to refuse – those halcyon days are long since over. It took us two years to renovate the building, during which we discovered that it was built like a fortress. The walls are three feet thick in places, and the joists are 15-inch Baltic pine (compared with 8-inch softwood of a modern home) – I have no qualms about overloading this building with the deadweight of 40,000 or so books and periodicals.

Initially I envisaged the stationmaster's house as more of an office for our catalogue business – I certainly did not write the business plan on the basis of having to attract customers out into the sticks. However, the shop opened for business in June 1987 with no announcement, and people started walking in.

My wife Clare is the '& Co.' in Robert Humm & Co., and has combined the role with bringing up our two daughters. Clare looks after the computer side of the business, running our two websites, managing the mailing list and answering e-mails. She also does the driving, taking me to view collections and attend auctions all over the country. We have two assistants who look after the day-to-day running of the shop. What does this leave me to do? The buying and the cataloguing, meeting customers, and the general administration of running a business.

Nothing beats having a shop. We are fortunate in having very dedicated customers who travel here from all over the world. I am not saying that there is the growth in over-the-counter business that I would like, but it has held its head up and appears to continue to do so. The internet has brought us customers whom we would never have found without it, but it is a very labour-intensive way of selling a book. It requires three or four times the amount of effort compared to selling a book to a customer in the shop.

Our business is very much on the fringe of the mainstream secondhand book trade. We do not belong to a trade association or exhibit at book fairs. We restrict ourselves to two railway collectors' fairs a year, because we know that they will attract a crowd of like-minded people. I meet my friends, have a good time and the business gets done. I used to buy half of my stock at auction, but the spread of information on the internet has made it impossible to keep a good country sale secret. As time goes by, I find that I buy more and more privately.

The books from the heroic age of railway literature were overwhelmingly technical, for example Nicholas Wood's *Practical treatise on rail-roads*, 1825. It is full of algebra, and was devoured avidly by engineers anxious to learn more about this strange new phenomenon. Inevitably the railways became a prolific field for authorship in general. A vast number of guide books to the new railway lines were published – some of them no more than a recitation of what could be seen out of the window.

George Bradshaw's maps are among the nicer items from the early railway age. Bradshaw invented and published the world's first railway timetable in 1839. An edition with maps appeared in 1840, and in 1841 the first *Monthly Railway Guide,* which appeared for 120 years. A map-maker by trade, Bradshaw produced timetables as a way of selling his maps. His hand-coloured railway and canal maps are magnificent examples of cartography. I wish we could get hold of more of them.

There are comparatively few hugely valuable books in our field – the real money is to be made from scarce magazines and periodicals. A complete run of 153 volumes of *The Railway Magazine* sells for around £4000, depending on condition. I bought a fair number of sets from public libraries when they were disposing of long runs of periodicals. I understand from the publishers that they have no intention of digitising it, and this applies to a number of important periodicals in our field.

My customers are not particularly interested in railway fiction. They do not want to read Agatha Christie on the Orient Express. With very few exceptions, novelists get the railway detail wrong. John Godey's *The Taking of Pelham One Two Three* is an exception. Freeman Wills Crofts was an ex-railwayman and he gets the detail right in his novels. I also have a soft spot for L.T.C. Rolt's fiction. The great historian of engineering and biographer of George and Robert Stephenson, Rolt had served his apprenticeship with a locomotive builder.

When I put thirty or so books from my collection of railway fiction in a catalogue a few years ago, I sold two items. My customers want books on locomotive dimensions, signalling systems, diagrams of rolling stock – what the Germans call 'Fachbücher'.

I had not intended to stock new books, but they are very important in our field. As in any technical subject, new books are likely to be more accurate, and to benefit from the growing paraphernalia of academic research. They may not be as beautiful to look at or as well written as the earlier material, but the content is likely to be much more informative and reliable. Great Britain, Germany and the United States are the three main publishers of railway books and account for 85 per cent of the subject material published worldwide.

No other country has anything comparable to George Ottley's *Bibliography of*

*British railway history.* While working full time for the British Library, he embarked on this monumental project, drawing from his experience in dealing with readers' inquiries. Although he has his blind spots – he does not cover Bradshaw timetables, for example, or railway guide books or accident reports – his work remains unrivalled in railway bibliography. The first volume was published in 1966, and was followed by a Supplement in 1988, both published by Her Majesty's Stationery Office. A second Supplement appeared in 1998, with around 17,000 entries, published by the National Railway Museum and The Railway & Canal Historical Society. The premier British society for scholarly transport research, The Society became the 'keeper' of Ottley's bibliography after his death in 2006, and publishes extensive book reviews and an annual listing of British railway books and articles.

The railway industry in this country has very little glamour today. The historic stations, the marshalling yards, the locomotive depots – whole thickets of fascinating stuff – have disappeared. When I was a child, there was always something interesting to see out of the window. Nowadays, assuming that you can find a seat that lines up with a window, there is not so much to see; sometimes you cannot even admire the landscape because the railway cuttings have been allowed to grow wild. Locomotive-hauled trains have largely been replaced by look-alike multiple units of one sort or another. Today there are no young children at the end of railway platforms. If there were, they would probably be taken into care. The train spotters are in their sixties – men of my generation who never quite lost the habit of recording things of railway interest. But these days they are probably holding a £3000 camera rather than a shilling booklet.

## An Outsider's Business ❧ Peter Scupham

I like to sell books that I have read or want to read, or have in some way skirmished with. I am motivated by the desire to share a sense of literature as part of a civilised life. Education raged through my family like strong drink, to quote Philip Oakes on his childhood. My father was controller of educational broadcasting at the BBC. He had a passion for books and reciting poetry, which introduced me to the great love of my life. At school, which was a pretty blank period in my life, poetry sang its way into my bones. I went to several different schools before I was 'saved', as so many people are, by an English master who showed me that academe need not be a narrow thing. Before taking up a state scholarship to Cambridge, I did my National Service, which was alleviated by the opportunity to do a lot of reading.

When I finally got to Cambridge, I found an English Faculty riven by faction and argument. It did nothing to form my taste, and I was appalled by one of F.R. Leavis's lectures in which he held up a volume by a minor Victorian poet and said in his contemptuous way, 'I don't think we need bother with him'. I was twenty-one and had seen a bit of life; I did not want to be told by an academic what to like and dislike. He was taking away all the pleasure that I had had from the out of the way, the odd, the eccentric and the unimportant. It was too late to change subject and so I continued to read English, but I read it in my own way.

I remember being bowled over by Robert Frost's visit to Cambridge – the white-bearded grand old man of American poetry. He just threw his head back and declaimed his poems. I also heard Robert Graves deliver the Clark Lectures, in which he demolished every poet then in favour with the English Faculty, and proved that poetry was wilful and eccentric – an outsider's business. On another occasion I was smuggled into the Sheldonian, wearing a scholar's gown to which I had no right, in order to hear W.H. Auden's inaugural lecture as Professor of Poetry at Oxford.

These experiences were high points in my life. My ambition was to become a writer and a poet. I could not match these men, but would try my best to be worthy of their attention. The idea of becoming a bookseller had not yet occurred to me, though I have always believed that a good bookseller does more than a university English department for the promulgation of reading and literature.

In my generation, life was seen as a series of hoops to be jumped through. There was no such thing as a gap year or time to think. It was a quick succession of National Service, university, marriage, children, and a job with a pension. Owing to my English teacher's enthusiasm, I went into teaching, first in Skegness and then at

St Christopher's in Letchworth. It was a Quaker foundation, with no particular use for the arts but it gave its teachers enormous freedom. I taught there off and on for around thirty years, as Head of the English Department.

While I was teaching my reputation as a poet was growing. Anthony Thwaite accepted some poems for *The Listener* and the *Times Literary Supplement* when I was in my early thirties. This was the kiss of death or life – once you have published a poem in a national periodical, you do not want to stop. The best education for a poet is simply to read as much poetry of all kinds as you can, and just to work away at it. I wrote poems for ten years without writing a good one. Eventually you feel that you might have written something worth a try on the public.

I was lucky to be taken on by Oxford University Press which was very loyal to me, and published about ten collections of my poetry before its poetry list folded. Eventually I became a Fellow of the Royal Society of Literature, and part of what might be called the Establishment. Today I am that extraordinarily unfashionable creature – a 76-year-old, white, middle-class, Oxbridge-educated poet. But we had our time in our day.

Poets are very vain animals. When they start to worry about their reputations, I always murmur to myself, 'the ammonites are laughing'. They have lasted millions of years. As a poet, you're lucky if your reputation lasts twenty or thirty years. I have in spades the entertaining English habit of self-deprecation. A Hungarian friend and poet, George Szirtes, was not amused when I remarked to an American who had been talking about the importance of poetry, 'don't worry too much. It's only read by six old ladies and the clergyman'. George thought my remark devalued poetry, but it is a very English way of looking at the world.

While my friend John Mole and I were getting established as poets, we ran a private press for publishing new poetry. The Mandeville Press was named after John Mandeville the medieval traveller, as we were making our own voyages into imaginary lands. We reckoned to be tidy and clean printers of good quality pamphlets on laid paper, sewn rather than stapled. The *raison d'être* of the Mandeville Press was to publish good poetry cheaply. We published a lot of distinguished and interesting people, such as Geoffrey Grigson, R.S. Thomas, John Fuller and Anthony Hecht. For collectors, we produced signed copies, but we never set out to be a fine press. A few of our pamphlets were illustrated with original engravings by George Szirtes, and came close to achieving fine press status.

We came into the publishing business at an interesting time, just as commercial printers were getting rid of their old equipment, and moving to offset litho. It cost us less than £700 to buy a rather glamorous 1930s machine press, a flatbed press, a little treadle press and everything else that we needed to set it all whirring and clanking in the cellar of my house. John and I ran the press, with help from my wife, and Margaret Steward who was Head of Drama at St Christopher's. We were never dependent on anything except our own exertions. In 1983 the BBC made a film of us at work called 'A Dragon's Print'.

We were influenced in our printing by Roy Harley Lewis, a delightful eccentric and author of *Antiquarian Books. An Insider's Account*. Roy spent most of his working life as a journalist. He was a leader writer for *The Times*, and enjoyed telling the nation how it ought to behave and what it ought to think. I first met Roy when he asked me for some poems for the Keepsake Press, which he ran as a cure for insomnia. He published anything that took his fancy – a huge miscellany of collections and individual poems – and was a worse printer than we were. His type was jammy, his paper was not always good, his inking was all over the place and he mixed up woodcuts and lithographs and every sort of media. He was not an aesthetic printer, but wonderful in his way.

Our activities were motivated by the spirit of keeping something alive for the love of it, but all good things come to an end. After fifteen years or so of working till one in the morning, staggering around with 25lb trays of type after a day's teaching, it was getting a bit too much. When I moved with Margaret Steward to our present home, a Tudor manor house in Norfolk, we decided not to take the press with us. Most of the equipment went to Africa, where it is probably producing Marxist literature in Zaire, and the Happy Dragon's Press in Suffolk took some of our best type.

Some of your readers, looking at the photograph of our house, might be thinking, 'It's all right for that old bugger with his private means. He can *play* at bookselling.' Actually I am not a moneyed bookseller; we live here by the skin of our teeth. When we moved here in 1990, the house cost us about the same as a bungalow. It had been on the Buildings At Risk Register, and was in an appalling state of repair. We had a stroke of luck when Margaret discovered some wall paintings, and English Heritage stepped in and took an interest in the them. We have done the rest by smoke and mirrors.

We originally intended to use the house as a centre for creative writing courses. Margaret and I both had experience of teaching on Arvon Foundation courses. But health and safety legislation made it impossible to have paying guests in a house like this. We do however put on an annual play here and call it 'Shakespeare in the Garden'.

We turned to secondhand bookselling as a natural progression from the Mandeville Press. It was a congenial way to maintain the contacts which we had made, and some form of human interaction is essential when you live in a cabbage patch in the back of beyond. Margaret is a partner in Mermaid Books and, but for her, I would have gone bankrupt years ago. She tries to discourage my wilder flights of fancy. We called the business Mermaid Books after the stucco mermaids over the front door. Michael Taylor, whom we have known since he worked for The Basilisk Press Bookshop, nominated us for the PBFA, and introduced us to some very pleasant people in lots of different places.

We have been members of the PBFA for twelve years, and I can appreciate everything that is good about it as an organisation. Whether it is good for *us*, I'm not so sure. The PBFA is aimed at book collectors rather than the common reader. As a teacher and a publisher, and now as a bookseller, I have always been primarily interested in the reader. The point of our bookselling is somehow to increase the enjoyment of English literature, and I try to write entertaining catalogues introducing people to some of the overlooked or perhaps unfashionable corners in the field which I know best.

I find most of my books in shops where the bookseller does not know about literature. Very few bookshops nowadays specialise in it – in fact, the tendency is to specialise in anything but literature. Occasionally I do quite well and make some money, but then I can be tempted to spend it on something like a couple of donkeys. I bought a copy of Sir Thomas Browne's *Religio Medici* for £10 at Blickling Hall in a sale of books donated by members of the National Trust for sale in aid of the Trust. Inside the book I found a lengthy inscription by Edward Thomas to a friend. The donkeys were to be called Edward and Thomas.

When we were teaching at St Christopher's, Eric Moore was our local secondhand bookseller. We were very fond of Eric and of his shop, where my daughter now works part-time. Eric sold what Driff would have called 'roast beef' – straightforward traditional books. In this part of the world, one of the booksellers whom I very much like is Tristram Hull of Holt, whose father translated the complete works of Jung into English. Tristram ran a private press at one time, and had a bookshop in Norwich, and then managed Simon Gough's shop in Holt, which is now owned by Simon Finch.

David Ferrow of Great Yarmouth was a classic example of a certain type of bookseller – 60 years in the trade and claimed not to have read a book since leaving school at fourteen. When he invited me into his office, I saw his serried ranks of bibliographies. He liked to claim that he was as ignorant as the devil, but he knew exactly where to find out the information he needed.

In the 1960s and 1970s I used to enjoy visiting Frank Norman's marvellous bookshop in Hampstead. I would catch him when he arrived with his latest trawl of books in a Sotheby's bag, and his simple lunch of bread and cheese. I once asked him what books he kept for himself, and he replied, 'bibliography, Proust and Montaigne. The rest can come and go'.

A bookseller who wishes to make friends sells his nicest books. I tend to make friends with my customers, and give them mates' rates. Nowadays they could turn to the internet to find a particular book, but they choose to order it from my catalogue. They enjoy the serendipity of seeing what takes their fancy, or perhaps it is to do with their age and background – I don't know the explanation, and certainly have no predictions for the future of bookselling. In these days of the internet, there is nothing so common as a rare book. If you want a first edition of *The Anatomy of Melancholy*, the only thing that will stop you is not *finding* it, but paying for it.

I am aware that my style of bookselling has little to do with the reality for most booksellers. It's a hard way to make a living, and only quixotic and eccentric people, often with pensions from previous occupations, can take my attitude to the profit factor. I confess that I've always rather liked the feeling that one is doing something out of *gentillesse*.

In reality Margaret and I have been working teachers all our lives but, even as a teacher, I thought of myself as a gentleman-amateur dropping in on classes. I like the words 'courtesy', 'manners' and 'reticence', which imply a way of looking at the world which is not particularly fashionable today. They deserve to be remembered and, where one can, to be reinstated. In the words of Samuel Johnson, one reads books to enjoy life better or to endure it more. I have never varied from this in 70 years, and it has been my motto as a bookseller.

## *Irish Bookselling Uncorked* ∾ Cal Hyland

My family are from Cork, the Yorkshire of Ireland, and we believe it is the best place in the world. One of our greatest Cork men, Robert Gibbings, whose works I collect, would always insist that he was a Cork man first and an Irishman second. Cork was a great mercantile centre, providing victuals for the boats in its large and sheltered harbour. It was said that the entire British fleet could fit twice into Cork Harbour. It was also a very intellectual city in the eighteenth and early nineteenth century, with numerous educational and literary institutions. Dublin, the political centre, was always regarded as the Johnny come lately.

When I was about seven years old, I had thoughts of joining the priesthood, until it was pointed out that I could not expect to become a bishop straightaway. As I was later to discover, it is the same with the book trade; you must first acquire an education through experience. During my school years, I was rather rudderless. My father was an agricultural scientist, and wanted me to become a scientist or to join the Army. I failed to achieve either of his ambitions for me, and drifted into office work of one kind or another.

There was a considerable economic slump in Ireland during the 1950s and in 1957 I came over to London to look for work. I hitch-hiked my way to Dublin and got the boat over to Liverpool, and then down to London where I found a job on the buses. I started off as a conductor on route 31 from Chelsea to Camden Town – I can still name all the stops. By chance my driver was also from Cork. Routes 22 and 19 were good fun because they have the same journey for part of the way. We would race each other, and go twice round Piccadilly Circus and generally do things that would not be possible today.

In 1958 there was a bus strike and I found that I could not live on strike pay. I got a job in the royalties department of Chappell's the music publishers and spent a year with them. By April 1959, having been two years in England, the Queen came after me to shoulder a musket. As I explained to the recruiting sergeant, 'I came over from Ireland  looking for employment. You had jobs which you wanted filled by people like me. We are now in a state of equilibrium. If I devote two years of my life to your Army, I'll be placing you under a debt which you will never be able to repay.' I do not think he quite saw my philosophical point, but I got off  quite lightly and spent six months working on the buses in Jersey.

Back in London again, I found a job mixing Christmas puddings for Lyons tea houses. From 1959 to 1966, I worked in various capacities in the City. In my spare time I used to love dancing. I belonged to a Catholic social club in Westminster, and it was there that I met Joan, who was a nurse and also from Ireland. We got married in 1963.

All the while I had been accumulating books given to me by family and friends. I have always been a voracious reader. As a child I could not go to sleep at night without reading. I have great curiosity, and can appear to talk sense about quite a number of things. I used to spend a lot of my time at Speakers' Corner, and generally make a nuisance of myself. I do not like people with extreme views, whatever they are.

I had an Irish friend at the time who worked in Oppenheim's bookshop in South Kensington. He had gradually put together a list of Irish books, which he sent off to the trade in Dublin. His employers got wind of this and insisted on a share in his business, to which he replied, 'No thanks', contacted me and we became partners in bookselling. By that time Joan and I had our first daughter, and my mother helped us to move to our first house, which was in Belvedere, in those days a pleasant suburb of London on the south bank of the Thames. By that stage I was managing an office for a firm of steel fabricators. I would work on books from 6.30 to 9.00 in the morning, cycle to my employment, home for tea at 5.30 and then back to the books till past midnight.

At weekends I would visit somewhere like Guildford or Brighton, where there was a concentration of bookshops. Every fortnight or so, my partner and I would type up a list of twenty or thirty books, have the list xeroxed at my office and send it out to the trade in Ireland. After a while an Irish bookseller asked if he could visit us during a buying trip to the UK. This prompted Joan and me to cash in some shares in the company for which I worked and put the money into the business. I took a holiday and went on a spending spree, my partner and I setting off in opposite directions to buy stock – he went west and I went to East Anglia.

In the mid-sixties there were several secondhand bookshops in Norwich. I remember Mrs Cubitt's Westlegate Bookshop, on several floors, with notices in the upper floors warning customers not to stand in the middle of the room. The floors bowed alarmingly, but for the brave there were rewards. Derek Gibbons's shop was also rewarding, but he refused my payment by cheque – a nasty experience with a rascally Irish bookseller had coloured his view of the Irish trade.

In the event a bank strike hit Ireland and the promised bookseller did not come over. Meanwhile I had a lot of stock and an overdraft. I sent a list to a few institutions gleaned from *The World of Learning*, and the University of Texas at Austin ordered a considerable quantity – fourteen parcels to the value of £183. 10s.3d – riches untold in those days. Judge my dismay a few weeks later when I switched on the television news and saw a rifleman taking pot shots at passers by from the clock tower of the University of Texas at Austin. One of the victims was a postman… After three weeks on tenter-hooks, my nerve broke and I wrote to Austin. My books had arrived safely and un-bloodied, but I did not relax until the cheque came through.

Not long after, I had a very nice letter from Michael Walshe of Falkner Grierson in Dublin, advising me that the books they required were more specialised than I was offering, and suggesting that I sent my lists to Dr Eamon Norton of Wakefield – my first private customer. Eamon's system was to read catalogues over breakfast, and then ring booksellers between seeing his patients. I am convinced he knew the opening hours of every book cataloguer in Britain and Ireland. To sample the hospitality of Dr Norton and his wife Dorrie, and to gaze at the world of Irish books in their beautiful Tudor house in Wakefield was an experience for any bookseller who thinks he knows it all. The latter tends to know the price of everything and the value of nothing, whereas the collector knows the value, and the *why* of the value.

There was a book published in 1907, William Bulfin's *Rambles in Eirinn*, which includes a description of Gogarty and Joyce's famous stay in the Martello tower in Sandycove in 1904. Although the first edition is quite scarce, it had passed through my hands a number of times before a collector pointed out that it contained almost the identical opening, certainly in terms of atmosphere, to *Ulysses* which was published in 1922. I love these little bits of ancillary knowledge.

I was fast reaching the stage as a part-time bookseller when I was little use to my employer or myself. A board meeting with the managing *directrix* produced a decision to go full-time as a bookseller. Joan would supplement the family income with a bit of night nursing, as required. At my farewell party in 1966, my employer gave me this parting advice – always remember that stock is better than money. I have followed that dictum with ensuing tearing of hair by bank managers. By mid-1967 I had parted company with my business partner, and was working on my own from our house in Belvedere. I had no shop; all I needed was my daughter's pram in which I took parcels to the post office.

Through advertising in *The Clique* and *The Book Market*, I got to know a number of runners, who attended auctions and jumble sales and bought books with people like me in mind. One such traded under the name of Gerald Haydon from crummy Crumpsall in Manchester, as he called it. His real name was Gerald 'Hutch' Hutchinson, and he was a postman. On one occasion he offered me a copy of Yeats's *The Countess Kathleen*, one of thirty copies printed on Japan vellum for presentation to his friends. Hutch had found it at a local auction, lotted up with other volumes. As old Mr Morten of Didsbury was present, Hutch disguised his interest in the bundle – Morten would immediately check a mixed lot if another dealer showed any interest. Hutch entered a modest 'half-crown' bid which was accepted. I sold the book on his behalf and got him close to £75 for it. It's worth a bit more today…

On a trip to the West Country I met R.A. Gilbert of Bristol, who was also giving up his day job as a teacher and going full-time into books. The Gilbert/ Hyland friendship has been of great benefit to me. Bob is the most knowledgeable bookseller of our generation. He could spot an Irish book at fifty feet. Bob was a non-driver in those days, and I took him down to Barnstaple with me where we met Gerry and Sue Mosdell of the Porcupine Bookshop. Gerry joined us on a trip to an extraordinary bookshop in the old cinema at Ilfracombe. The upper floor had no lights and Mr Smith, the proprietor, would give customers a torch, but he only had one. Gerry had sufficient local knowledge to come prepared, but I had to go out and purchase a torch. In later years, there was a man who used to attend PBFA fairs in London who wore a miner's hat with a lamp on it.

I was one of the early members of the PBFA. It was Gerry Mosdell's idea – he wanted to provide a regular 'shop window' in London for provincial dealers. When he was looking for a suitable location for holding the monthly fairs, he used to stay with us in Belvedere. The PBFA did not begin officially until 1974 when we were back in Ireland. Michael Holman of Angle Books was the first Treasurer of the PBFA. We were a bunch of school boys at heart, and the early book fairs were a lot of fun. But they were also one of the biggest factors in changing the popular perception of bookselling, and the travelling book fair became a great source of education and inspiration. It brought a lot of new people into the trade, though of course not all of them have survived.

Late in 1967, I responded to the following advertisement in *The Clique*, 'Specialist Bookseller would like to meet another with own transport, with a view to sharing expenses on buying trips'. I responded and met Eric Bonner, with whom I made a number of trips in my secondhand Commer Cob van, with its back seat that folded down to make a bed. The Cob was a real go-er and 80 mph was easily done. Our first trip was to Northampton, Leicester and Nottingham. I slept in the van and Eric, who was of an older generation, stayed in hotels.

By this stage Joan and I had two daughters and began to have thoughts of raising them in Ireland. A family opportunity arose to bring us to Dublin and we made the move in 1968. I had a large book store in Dun Laoghaire, with shelves made from wood salvaged from the demolition of the old Garda headquarters at Dublin Castle. Neville Figgis of Hodges Figgis involved me in a number of large purchases, and he and his right-hand man, Padraig O'Tailliur, were an invaluable source of information.

Michael Walshe had done a lot of cataloguing for Hodges Figgis before founding Falkner Grierson. He had introduced me to Dr Norton, and was another Dublin bookseller who was very generous with his vast knowledge. The name of Michael's firm derived from George Faulkner, publisher and friend of Jonathan Swift, and Grierson, government printers in Dublin for several generations. The name therefore combined two firms famous in the Dublin book trade. Michael had a delightful sense of humour and used to produce highly comical material on his own printing press. His fictitious correspondence on the 'de Selby Codex' in Flann O'Brien's *The Third Policeman* is a real gem. The mists in Ireland encourage us to fall back on our imagination. You cannot look out of the window and see the horizon. Perhaps this has inclined us to creative writing.

Greene's Bookshop in Clare Street was the place where the Dublin literati had been gathering since the mid-nineteenth century. It was my idea of a perfect bookshop – there would always be someone there holding court, who could talk knowledgeably about books and encourage others to share their interests. We all know the story about people who would go through the new arrivals at Foyles, buy something for a couple of shillings, climb upstairs to the rare books department and make a couple of hundred pounds. To me that style of bookselling is soulless. I find most affinity with customers who read the books they buy from me, or with librarians who consider the needs of their readers.

In 1972 another daughter came on the scene and the house in Dublin was getting a bit crowded. A lovely old rectory came on the market a quarter of a mile from Joan's birthplace and eight miles from my home town of Mallow. We purchased it and moved in during the month of February 1973 – one pantechnicon a week, each with about 100 tea-chests of books. The rectory had been built by Ernest Shackleton's great-grandfather. It had twenty-two rooms, of which seven were filled with my books.

I used to produce about ten catalogues a year on books of Irish interest. It was a family affair; we printed them ourselves on a Gestetner offset litho machine. One of my daughters would watch the machine, and be ready to switch it off at the first sign of a paper jam or any other trouble. However the 'good life' became a tad less than idyllic with postage increases of 120 per cent during the Cosgrave coalition government in Ireland, and the huge increase in travelling expenses caused by the oil crisis in the second half of the 1970s.

The 1970s also saw a marked decline in my business with the north of Ireland. I used to be able to count on £20,000 a year in sales to libraries and collectors in the six counties. As a result of the political problems, money increasingly had to be spent on security arrangements. Two days before I was due to deliver a large order to Fermanagh County Library, the building was badly damaged by a car bomb.

Nowadays I consider myself lucky if I do £1500 a year in business with the north of Ireland. The mind-set has changed considerably. The old-style county librarian no longer exists, by which I mean someone who had an interest in local history and perhaps belonged to one or two antiquarian societies. The new-style librarian is likely to be trained in information technology and accountancy.

By the mid-1980s the older Miss Hylands had both returned to the land of their birth in search of work, leaving their middle-aged parents and a teenage sister in a large house with a two-acre garden in the middle of nowhere. This was no good for a teenager's social life, and none of us had much interest in gardening. We made inquiries and discovered that the economic climate for small postal businesses was more congenial in the UK. We moved to Chepstow in 1986, and spent several years there before moving to beautiful West Cork, where we had been spending family holidays since the late 1960s.

We purchased a bungalow in Rosscarbery and in 1996 we opened Pilgrim Books. The old Irish name of Rosscarbery is Ros Ailithir, which means 'The Headland of the Pilgrim'. In the summer of 1998, the eldest Miss Hyland returned from London where she had been running bars and bistros. We decided to purchase a restaurant and she joined her aged parents in running Pilgrim's Rest, a bookshop/bistro combination. Rosscarbery is a holiday resort and during the months of June, July and August, we were open seven days a week. Our daughter did the cooking, my wife did the baking and I did everything else, as well as running the bookshop. I would sit by the till with a glass of wine and, if anyone commented, I would say that it helped me to overcome my natural shyness.

After five years of hard work and good fun, we had to surrender to *anno domini*. We sold the premises and moved to a development on the outskirts of Rosscarbery. By purchasing the lower floor apartment (under two uppers), we were able to create a perfect book room, which runs the length of the properties. The books are on all aspects of Ireland, with a small selection of non-Irish material, and visitors are most welcome by appointment. I consider myself extremely fortunate. I have made a competence, raised a family of three daughters and enjoyed myself making a living of my hobby – and making friends. I would not like to re-write any of it.

©Mike Tsang

# Speculating on the Book Trade ✎ Chris Dennistoun

As a child I first became aware of books because I liked the illustrations. My father bred horses and we lived near Lambourn in a house full of books on animals. I was educated at Winchester where I did well enough to scrape a place at Exeter University to read Theology, more out of necessity than conviction. Exeter offered me a place on very easy terms, and I planned to change subject within a few weeks of going up. While this might have worked anywhere else, Exeter was desperate to keep the department open and needed to keep the student numbers up. University wasn't my finest hour.

After Exeter I came to London and found a job in publishing, reading manuscripts for Panther paperbacks. I was paid £25 a manuscript and was supposed to advise them what to publish. It was a farce; I didn't know anything but I was happy to be involved in some aspect of the book world. My next job was working for David Lichfield's *Image* magazine, an arts and photography magazine which went bust in the early 1970s.

At about this time I met David Bollam, and we opened a stall together in Portobello Road and ran it for a few years. I had inherited some money which went into starting the business. In those days you didn't need a lot of knowledge to sell books. We would go to auctions, buy them by the box and put them on the stall. We learnt what was in demand from customers' requests.

The stall coincided with the height in demand for steel-engraved plates, particularly of Switzerland and Germany – Tombleson's *Views of the Rhine*, was a perfect example. George Walford had a regular advertisement in *The Clique* asking for specific books. They put up the same books year after year; it was the booksellers' equivalent of the Ten Commandments. When the *Bookdealer* started in 1971, it quickly became the Bible of the trade. We would go through the 'Books Wanted' section, scan the titles and go out and find them. I noticed that Harold Landry was always advertising for copies of Davies, *On Dutch Waterways*. I went to see him with my copy, and we immediately struck up a rapport. Harold showed me his incredible collection of books and periodicals, which he kept on four floors in his house in Hampstead, and I realised that this was what it was like to be a real book dealer.

Harold never liked moving out of Hampstead. He didn't go much to auctions and relied on dealers to quote books to him. He had started out in Hay-on-Wye with Richard Booth, and developed a reputation for dealing in complete runs of periodicals. Fortunately for Harold, he loved packing and was very good at it. I would go to auctions and tell Harold what I had seen. It was a good system and I enjoyed the way of life – I found the material and Harold sold it. We put together a number of collections for the Japanese market when it was such a gravy train. Gymnastics was one of the more bizarre subjects for which we were asked.

When Harold started selling periodicals, national libraries and institutions were the major customers. There was no internet; microfiche was the best you could do. We developed quite a market in British parliamentary Blue Books after we bought the duplicate set – still in their distinctive wrappers – from the basement of the Peace Palace Library in The Hague. We stored them in a warehouse in Holland Park and dealers would come and buy them in the days when Blue Books were very desirable.

My two favourite bookshops in England were Tom Cherrington's in Southampton and Horace Halewood's in Preston. Tom had the most wonderful eclectic taste, and you never knew what you might find in his shop. He used to buy a lot of his books on the Isle of Wight, before there were any dealers there and the place was a kind of time warp. Horace Halewood was one of the nicest people I have ever met. He didn't like dealing with big companies, but always tried to help the small dealer. He would greet me with the words, 'Are you earnin', lad?' to which I would respond, 'Not too bad, Mr Halewood. Could be better'. He would make sure that I always made a good profit on what I bought, and liked me to go home having made at least a grand on the visit.

At the other extreme was James Stevens-Cox in Guernsey. Born in 1910, Stevens-Cox must have made a fortune from the plentiful supply of books between the wars. After his death in 1997, his collection of *STC* and Wing books went to Maggs, who put them in a catalogue in 2003. I remember one trip to Guernsey with Martin Stone – we might have been visiting the Pope, the way Stevens-Cox conducted himself. First of all, I lost £250 in the casino on the boat going over, and then Stevens-Cox would only let me buy one book for all my trouble in getting there. Martin was all right because he was buying rather obscure nineteenth- century fiction which no one knew about.

In those days the auctions were vital to the book business. I lived off books on Cyprus for a couple of years, buying everything I could find and putting them into Sotheby's, where there were two very prominent collectors who would bid against each other. I would have books to the value of £20,000 or £30,000 in every sale. Christie's South Kensington had a book sale every two weeks; there was so much material around. Hodgson's was a little before my time, but I gather it was very competitive. Ronald Gooch would not let anybody buy a  travel book. He had started at Heffers and then went on his own. When I knew him, he was working from home, selling to institutional libraries all over the world. Nobody ever got into his house in Hastings. On one occasion Bernard Shapero and I sold him some books, and he sent us a cheque for an extra £500, explaining that he had done rather well out of them. He was a clever businessman.

When Photography started as a collecting genre, there was no real distinction between photogravures and original photographs. Williams's *The Home and Haunts of Shakespeare*, with its photogravure plates, was considered the real thing. But the market has been moving away from the time when anything that had a photograph in it was considered fair game. Books like Payne Jennings's *Photographs of Norfolk Broads and Rivers*, and Howitt's *Ruined Abbeys and Castles of Great Britain* have become unsaleable as the market has moved into the twentieth century and concentrated on genuine photography books.

It was through Harold that I met Donald Heald. Don was far ahead of his time in dealing in all the big mid-Victorian colour-plate books. The books were very desirable but had been overlooked in the trade and by collectors because they were comparatively late. As copies started to be broken, complete copies became increasingly desirable, and nowadays they are very scarce and valuable. The Harringtons were also dealing in chromolithograph books and held the biggest stock in London. They were buying Count Amadeo Preziosi's views of Constantinople before anybody else in the book trade had ever dreamt of Preziosi.

I first met Bernard Shapero when he was still at school. We met at George Jeffery's barrows in Farringdon Road. He was already very determined, decisive, quite pushy and bold – always spending more than he had. On Saturdays we used to go around in my Austin 1100. I nearly killed Bernard on the way to Tom Cherrington's in Southampton, overtaking in the face of an oncoming lorry. I'm still not quite sure how we survived. When Bernard left school, we started going on trips to Paris. In the early 1980s, very few dealers went to France regularly.

On our first visit to Paul Prout, the printseller, Bernard quickly picked up that there was a market for selling views of France. We would buy as many copies as we could find of *The Rivers of France*, with its 62 plates after Turner's sketches, and started running them to Paul. We could double our money easily. In those days we travelled over on the night ferry, loaded up with our stock. We were stopped by Customs once, and 48 copies of *The Rivers of France* fell out of our bags.

Finally Paul announced that he could not buy another copy, and took us upstairs where we saw every copy he had ever bought from us. By that stage we had discovered that Paris was full of incredible books at half the price of London. You could bowl into Léonce Laget or Lolliée and just load up. The Parisian dealers would get in new stock every week from the sales at the Drouot. Everything was there – all the wonderful French view books of the Ottoman Empire. It was a licence to print money. All you had to do was get on the blower to a customer, and the book sold itself.

I have always worked from home and sold very largely to the trade. I don't have the scholarship to do catalogues, although last year Bernard published the catalogue of my collection of works on speculation, *Bubbles, Booms and Busts*, which I catalogued with Hilary Goodman. It represents a lifetime's search for the books, as well as a lifetime's reading around the subject. The collection contains over 750 titles from the seventeenth century to the mid-twentieth century, and was sold en bloc to one of the richest fund managers in the world.

There are probably only a handful of people who appreciate the importance of some of the post-1900 books, written by the men who came up with new concepts of investment theory and practice. Charles Dow's famous series of essays in 1902 appeared in the *New York Times,* but he refused offers by publisher S. A. Nelson to assemble or expand them in a book. In 1903 Nelson acted as the great man's amanuensis and expounded Dow's theories in *The A B C of stock speculation*, New York, 1903. Arguably, every work on the stock market since Dow's day has taken his theories into account.

The stock market appeals to the gambler in me. The first thing I do in the morning is switch on my computer and check stock prices. Unlike the price of rare books, they change every day. My earnings as a book dealer have always been either supplemented or often superseded by my earnings from the stock market.

I can see a time when the book trade will be reduced to a handful of big businesses in London. There are not enough books to go round, and the present hierarchy of dealers operating at different levels will ultimately disappear. The internet has made the business a level playing field. Anyone can become an expert at the press of a button. Its effect on the trade has been dramatic – the internet kills every book stone dead. The essence of collecting is the pursuit of the elusive, and then the 'wow' factor of finding it. From a collector's point of view, if there are two or more copies on the internet, the urgency goes out of it. He can buy it today, tomorrow or next year – the book is available and therefore he doesn't *need* to buy it now. The rare book business must be one of the worst trades to be in at the moment. The reason why many booksellers are still able to make a success of it is that they have very low overheads and spend nothing on themselves.

# A gentle way of doing business ❧ Elizabeth Strong

I cannot remember a time when I did not like to read. When I got into my teens I began to buy books faster than I could read them – a telltale sign of a bookseller. The first book I remember buying was a copy of Jessie King's *The Enchanted Capital of Scotland* for nine old pence in a jumble sale. I spent the first two years of my life in London, but have lived in Edinburgh ever since my father took up an Edinburgh University appointment at the Western General Hospital in the winter of 1948. I almost feel that I have become a Scot from living here for so long. I remember Grant's bookshop on the corner of George IV Bridge, and the Book Hunter's stall opposite – both had been there since the nineteenth century. In general I was a bit intimidated by antiquarian bookshops, and had the feeling that I was not sufficiently knowledgeable to go inside.

Things changed a bit in Dublin where I read English at Trinity College, and frequented the bookshops, although I was still mainly buying new books. There was George Webb on The Quays, Hanna's, Greene's and of course Hodges Figgis. Three of my grandparents were Irish and I spent a lot of childhood holidays in Ireland. Dublin was a happy place to be and a wonderful place to study literature.

After university I returned to Edinburgh to study History of Art with a vague idea of finding work in a museum or a gallery. I was afraid that it might be very competitive and, at that stage, it had not occurred to me that whatever you do in life will have some element of competition. In the event I came down to London and got a job working for the Wiener Library for eighteen months. I did some cataloguing and proof-reading, but the work was essentially secretarial. I viewed it as just a job, but I did work with and meet some very interesting people. The Wiener Library was based on the Nazi material collected by Dr Alfred Wiener, a German Jew who fled to Amsterdam in 1933, and set up the Jewish Central Information Office for the collection and dissemination of information on what was going on in Nazi Germany.

Dr Wiener managed to transfer the collection to London in 1939 and get out of Holland just in time. The collection was initially housed in Manchester Square, where its resources were made available to British intelligence workers. After the war it was extensively consulted by the United Nations War Crimes Commission. During the 1950s and 1960s, the Library embarked on the huge project of interviewing eye witnesses of Nazi activities. The transcripts of these interviews, often accompanied by photographs, were much consulted by people who suspected that a neighbour, colleague or even friend had been a collaborator.

By the time I worked for the Library, it was in Devonshire Street, and had become the Institute of Contemporary History, enlarging its scope to cover the entire field of modern European History. People would still come to the Library and go through the interview files, looking for relevant names. Some of them were Holocaust survivors; it could be very emotional, but always very interesting and I met some extraordinary people.

I was living with an aunt at the time, who one day remarked that it would be good for me to work in a more commercial environment. Meanwhile a friend from my student days told me that Mrs McNaughtan was looking for an assistant for her bookshop in Edinburgh. I was offered the job and started working for her in September 1972. Major McNaughtan was already seriously ill and died shortly after I joined the business. Sadly, I never actually met him.

It was understood that I would have the opportunity to take over the business when Mrs McNaughtan eventually retired. Meanwhile she was very much in charge, and I was the assistant in the background, which suited both our temperaments very well. Mrs McNaughtan was an excellent teacher, who appeared to have no doubts about anything. She was enthusiastic and very generous with her knowledge of books which was considerable.

John and Marjorie had begun as book collectors while he was serving as a barrister in the Army. The Major used to attend courts martial all over the country, and would always visit the local bookshops, buying law books, which he would often sell to Wildy's in Lincoln's Inn. Mrs McNaughtan meanwhile was making her own collection. When the Major retired from the Army, bookselling seemed the obvious thing to do for them to do, having accumulated enough books to launch a business. They both had Scottish forebears, and had been stationed in Edinburgh at one point, and no doubt felt that it would be a good place to open a book business.

After renting premises for a short time, the McNaughtans bought the present shop in Haddington Place on the edge of the New Town in 1957 for just under £600. The building dates from 1826, just after George IV's visit when Edinburgh was still enjoying its Enlightenment phase and was one of the great centres of the book trade. If you look at old trade directories of Edinburgh, there were bookshops on almost every street, not to mention all the publishers, stationers and printers who served the many learned societies and institutions of the capital city and its university.

The McNaughtans had good books in all sorts of subjects, in addition to the Major's special interest in law books, theology and Americana. By the time I arrived, Mrs McNaughtan had sold the law department, and most of the theology went in a huge sale shortly thereafter. While helping the late Professor Eudo Mason to build up his fine collection of children's books, now in the National Library of Scotland, Mrs McNaughtan developed her own interest in the subject which became her speciality. We used to go on an annual bookbuying tour in the autumn, closing the shop for a week or two and travelling as far south as the West Country. I would be her driver on these trips, which were a wonderful experience and a great way of learning the business. She was very particular about good book trade manners, and we always presented a business card when we went into a shop.

When VAT was introduced, Mrs McNaughtan decided that she could not be bothered with it and gave it to me to look after. She had no patience with any form of 'red tape'. I think she would have found it very difficult to run a shop today. Her attitude enabled me to learn various skills and prepare for the time when I would be running the business myself.

When Mrs McNaughtan retired in April 1979, she made it possible for me to buy the business on the most generous terms. I paid for half the business through a bank loan, and the other half over a period of ten years. I doubt if I would have got the loan if it had not been my father's bank. I had an extremely fortunate start and was able to pay off the loan within the first six months, having thought that it might take years. In buying McNaughtan's, I also took over the agency for the National Library of Scotland at a time when there were a number of important auctions. In fact I had to borrow more money to cover all their purchases in the sale of the library of the Free Church of Scotland which contained a lot of very rare material of great interest to the National Library.

The McNaughtans were proud to belong to the ABA, and were founder-members of the Scottish branch of the Association in 1972. It was not long before I realised how much benefit we derived from membership. After I had owned the business for several years, Anthony Rota, Hylton Bayntun-Coward and Ian and Senga Grant suggested that I might like to 'put something back'. I eventually succumbed to the gentle pressure, and was elected President of the ABA in 2000. It was good to keep Scottish bookselling in people's minds. My appointment coincided with the ILAB Congress and Book Fair in Edinburgh, with which I received an enormous amount of help from colleagues.

Shortly before I became President, the Committee had appointed John Critchley as Secretary, who in turn appointed Marianne Harwood, and together they transformed the day-to-day running of the Association. John was the perfect person to give me confidence, and there were so many other people working hard on the Committee that I found my role was more one of bringing things together. The setting up of the ABA website was the great issue of the day and, as I did not have the necessary expertise, I decided to serve for one year only. This decision enabled Adrian Harrington, who was next in line and had all the right expertise, to become President in 2001.

All businesses to some extent reflect their owners' interests. Although I try to maintain the McNaughtans' range of good books across most subjects, and particularly Mrs McNaughtan's children's books, the architecture and art sections have gradually expanded under my influence. If you have a shop, you need to have something for everybody. This is not a problem as I am offered books all the time in so many different subjects, and find it quite hard to say 'no'. As I am always trying to catch up with what I buy privately in the shop, I tend not to travel much – in any case, so many of the shops which I visited with Mrs McNaughtan have disappeared. Book fairs have to a certain extent replaced the old buying trips. I love buying books, researching, pricing and chatting with customers about them, but I dislike cataloguing. Perhaps it is something to do with the physical aspect of sitting in front of a computer. I have not done a catalogue since 1974, when I produced one for Mrs McNaughtan's children's books. Nowadays we have a few hundred books listed on the ILAB website, but I did not catalogue them.

I 'inherited' my first assistant from Mrs McNaughtan, who insisted that I should have one. I thought I could manage without – there is something quite nice about being in the shop on my own, but it gets a bit lonely and of course I do need some help in the shop. Shortly after I took over, Katriina Hyslop came and stayed for eighteen years before she married John Marrin. They live in Berwickshire and John runs his book business from a former gamekeeper's cottage on the Ford and Etal estate just over the border in Northumberland. Since Katriina left I have never been without an assistant, apart from a brief experiment last summer. Edinburgh Central Youth Hostel is just down the road and we sometimes get a horde of young people coming in, which is lovely, but it can be a bit overwhelming if I am on my own.

Sometimes I think that the bookshop has become a spectator sport for tourists in Edinburgh. Some visitors behave as if the shop is a museum. 'Isn't it wonderful?' they say, 'I could spend all day in here', and then promptly walk out. They like the *look* of the shop, but it would never occur to them to buy a book. Nowadays people turn to computers in the way that they would have turned to books for a lot of their needs. Quite apart from their effect on our trade, I believe that computers are actually changing the way in which people think. Everything is highly focused toward a specific goal, instead of reading around a subject and taking a more wide-ranging approach. We have to keep trying to get young people to look at books and aspire to own them. This is a role for book fairs and shops – just being there on the high street helps to remind people that books can be bought, and that we are not libraries or museums.

In recent years the West Port in the Old Town has developed into a bookselling area – I do not think there was a single bookshop there when I joined McNaughtan's. As for auctioneers in Edinburgh, a number of Phillips' senior staff left, when it was taken over by Bonhams, and joined Lyon & Turnbull. Originally established in 1826, Lyon & Turnbull is Scotland's oldest firm of auctioneers. After a long history in family hands, the business changed ownership in 1999 and is now a very lively auction house, with a marketing partnership with Freeman's in Philadelphia. Lyon & Turnbull did a marvellous job converting a redundant neo-Classical church in Broughton Place into a sale room. There are three book sales a year, and the good material is no longer creamed off and sent to London.

While Mrs McNaughtan was alive, I could not possibly have thought of changing the name of the business, nor did I particularly want to. Of course I have made certain changes and you do put your own personality on a business, for better or worse. I buy a lot of art books because of my interest in painting. I used to collect books by William Lizars, the Scottish printer and engraver, whom Audubon commissioned to produce the plates for *The Birds of America*. Work began on the first ten plates in 1827 but, before they were completed, Lizars' colourists went on strike and Audubon transferred the work to Havell & Son in London.

When I bought the premises next door, it made the shop bigger but did not improve the turnover. The extra space simply allowed me to be less disciplined about what I bought. One of my oldest customers, who first came to the shop on his tricycle, suggested that I should turn it into a gallery, and have my studio here. I have always painted a bit and, in recent years, spent some time at Leith School of Art. The school was started in 1988 by Mark and Lottie Cheverton, both artists and inspirational teachers, who were tragically killed in a car crash in 1991. Lottie was the sister of George Ramsden of Stone Trough Books, who recently published a tribute to the Chevertons' achievement in *Leith. Scotland's Independent Art School. Founders and Followers*. The school was based on Mark and Lottie's belief that anyone can paint if they are shown and encouraged properly. Leith has flourished and is a wonderfully nurturing place.

I am now getting to the age where a lot of my friends outside the book trade have retired. I would quite like to paint more and perhaps the gallery idea would enable me to do so and keep the shop going. There are a lot of aspiring artists in Edinburgh who would like to have somewhere to show their work, and it would be interesting to see if I can collaborate in some way.

I sometimes wonder if I would have been more confident if I had actually started a business from scratch; I'm never sure if the business has worked because of me or because of what I took over from the McNaughtans. My colleagues in

Edinburgh, Edward Nairn and Ian Watson of John Updike Rare Books, have a delightful trading style. They work from home, and business is always done over a cup of tea – such a gentle way of doing business. The book trade allows you to approach it in the way that suits you.

## Courting the Collector ❦ Tim Bryars

My first paid work in the antiquarian book trade was unpacking boxes in the basement of the Staffs Bookshop in my school holidays. Years later I discovered that the boxes had been packed by Ken Fuller, now my friend and neighbour in Cecil Court. My mother had worked as a cataloguer for Frank Hammond in the mid-1960s, and was responsible for many of his Voyage and Exploration catalogues. She also worked for Jim Fenning, whose business is still active. I grew up knowing the difference between sheep and calf, and how to collate a book. When my sister and I came along, my mother stopped working. We lived in Walsall, where I went to the local grammar school. In due course, my mother returned to work, and found a job with Peter Stockham in the Staffs Bookshop in Lichfield, which is about ten miles from Walsall.

It was everything that one imagines a country bookshop to be – a huge stock crammed into several rooms and the cellar, in two fifteenth-century buildings behind an eighteenth-century façade, with sloping floors and bulging ceilings. Peter Stockham had moved there in 1988, after a dozen years in Cecil Court, where he had traded as Images. The shop had been a bookshop since Peter was at school in Lichfield and had first been attracted to its warren of books. My mother was responsible for writing the series of four catalogues, which Peter issued between 1996 and 1998, entitled *For the Amusement and Instruction of Youth*. They were very highly regarded, not least for my mother's detailed notes on almost 3,500 books from Peter's astonishingly eclectic stock.

After school I read Modern History at Oxford, where the modern period is taken to begin with the division of the Roman Empire into East and West. There were still a number of rare book shops in the centre of the city, and I was a frequent visitor to the Classics Bookshop, Titles, Waterfield's and Blackwell's, although I could not possibly afford to buy anything. I was also very interested in drama, and was a member of OUDS. After graduating I performed in the Edinburgh Festival – I played Machiavelli's father-in-law in a production on Princes Street. I also won a travelling scholarship from the Rajiv Gandhi Foundation and Cambridge Commonwealth Trust to visit India to pursue my interest in the European commercial community after Independence.

In 1995 I entered the antiquarian trade, finding a job by advertising myself in the Situations Wanted column in the *Bookdealer*. It was read by Charlie Unsworth just as he was thinking of expanding his antiquarian department, specialising in early printing and the classical world, which had been and remain interests of mine since university. Charlie took me on to build up the department, giving me a pretty free rein to do it. I worked with him for four and a half years, during which time his firm became a member of the ABA. The experience gave me an excellent grounding in bookselling, and the opportunity to work with new, secondhand, remainder and antiquarian material. Charlie was experimenting with different ways of selling books, and we would cover a huge amount of ground travelling to fairs and academic conferences, trying to find out what worked best for the stock.

Meanwhile I had become friendly with Panagiotis Chantziaras and Louise Bryan of Paralos Ltd, and had been buying books from his office near Oxford Circus and his shop in Athens. Panagiotis is primarily a bookman, although he is also very knowledgeable about the golden age of cartography. We share a particular interest in early editions of the Classics – his stock of Greek material is unrivalled, which is one of the factors which brought us together.

I began to wonder if there was any possibility of working for him. It turned out that, although he was not looking for an employee, he wanted me to become a co-owner of the business. When I explained that I could not afford to buy shares in Paralos, Panagiotis lent me the money to do so. I repaid him from my dividends, and it is entirely thanks to his extraordinary generosity that I now have my own shop.

Panagiotis was living with his wife and family on Corfu, and Louise and I were based in his London office. We would meet on our frequent travels around Europe. Panagiotis hated flying, and so we would go almost everywhere by car, loaded with maps and prints relating to our destination, and then return with all kinds of material for the London trade. For example, we would track down a little gallery tucked away in northern Germany, where nobody had rifled the stock for thirty years, and find wonderful material. We worked on turnover; certain material would sell at a certain price the moment you got it back to London. On the return journey, we would telephone ahead, and dealers would be vying to help us unload the car. Although the internet was already around, it had not yet taken a firm grip on the trade. It was a very exciting time, and a style of working which probably would not be feasible today.

In 2004 we dissolved the business, though we are still great friends and work very closely together. Panagiotis and Louise now work from a magnificent gallery, also called Paralos, in Athens. In the summer of that year I opened my antiquarian and map shop at 8 Cecil Court, specialising in early printed books, classics and translations, history, literature, travel, and a range of original antique maps, topographical and natural history prints. The term 'classics' is used variously these days to cover anything from Homer to Dickens – I use the term to cover all aspects of ancient writing, including most of the arts and sciences that we know today. The distinction between disciplines was a little more blurred in the ancient world.

I do not believe that the map trade should be hived off from the rest of the book trade. A number of the most outstanding figures in the golden age of cartography would not have considered themselves purely mapmakers or publishers. John Speed is now best remembered for his county maps, but he would have regarded himself as an historian and antiquary. Similarly, Abraham Ortelius was an antiquary first and foremost, who devoted himself to gathering geographical knowledge from the corners of the known world. Both men would have been surprised to be remembered as mapmakers – because of the narrow definition.

In certain areas of the antiquarian trade, the paths are too well trodden to offer much chance of discovery. This is not the case with maps, due to the sheer range and often ephemeral nature of the material. The British Library has four and a half million maps and atlases, but there is still so much which is unknown. As a dealer, you have a very good chance of coming across something which may not be particularly rewarding financially, but will offer the potential for interesting research. Recently I sold the British Library a board game in the form of a map of India, contemporary with the Indian Mutiny. The inventor of the game had taken rooms on the Strand and was offering a guinea to anyone who could beat him at two games in a row. Given the particularly bloody nature of the Indian Mutiny, it struck me as quite extraordinary that it had inspired a board game at the time. It may be the only copy of this game still in existence; it is certainly the only one recorded. I like to make sure that this type of material ends up in institutions where it is available for public use.

People often ask the most extraordinary questions when they come into my shop. I am frequently asked if I have inherited it, or if it is a hobby, or a museum. It does not seem to occur to them that this is how I earn my living. My shop was occupied by Robert Chris for many years. His daughter-in-law came to see me soon after I moved in, and told me some stories about the old days. Bob Chris was a colourful character. He dodged military service in the First World War and went to America where he became a card sharp. He was imprisoned on his return to the UK for avoiding conscription, and later worked in this shop until a fortnight or so before his death. I gather that he was a bit of a womaniser and, to this day, women of a certain age pop in and tell me their memories of Bob Chris in his prime. I am trying to build up a collection of anecdotes about Cecil Court and am grateful for their stories.

I am Secretary of the Cecil Court Association and I want to do everything in my power to promote Cecil Court and make it the most famous street of bookshops in the world. I have heard people say, as they walk up and down, that it must be owned by a wealthy philanthropist. Actually we pay commercial rents, but the landlords are not trying to squeeze every last penny out of us. However, the government is set on clawing as much money as possible from small businesses. Last year we were hit badly by the scrapping of transitional rate relief, and an increase of 5 per cent, which amounted to our rates almost doubling. There is a possibility that rates could go up by another third again. I got in touch with our local MP and he organised a debate in Parliament in October 2009, which attracted considerable press coverage. The *Guardian*, the *Evening Standard* and the *Sunday Telegraph* all took up the cause of the little street of booksellers' attempt to challenge the policy of central Government. I have written at length elsewhere about the problems of Charing Cross Road, where there are only three rare and secondhand books left – Quinto, Any Amount of Books and Henry Pordes. It is hard to remember that it used to be called Booksellers' Row.

I believe that shops are vital to the survival of the book trade. They should not be seen as a throw-back to another age or a dinosaur business model. A few more dealers need to get the bit between their teeth and get back down to the ground floor. Of course it is very expensive to do this, especially in central London, but there is no easy way to survive in this business in 2010. We need shops to create and feed collectors. Having experienced life in an office, I know that generally speaking it is no place to make new collectors. By the time they come upstairs to your office, they already have an established interest. Similarly, by the time someone 'googles' a book online, they already know what they want.

Shops are different. They allow for browsing and face-to-face discussion, even though this can sometimes be disheartening. There are days when I despair of questions such as, 'how do you know this is old?', but there are also opportunities to foster an interest by explaining some of the surprising possibilities that exist. Few people are aware that it is still possible to buy an original 400 hundred-year-old map for under £50. I am always very welcoming to students who come into my shop and are interested in material which they cannot afford to buy. I remember my own student days and how much I enjoyed the opportunity to browse in bookshops – it is one reason why I am on the ground floor today.

I have a number of collectors whom I have encouraged over the years. I am not foolish enough to think that they are just buying from me. But I know that they were introduced to collecting by being able to walk into a shop and ask questions and handle material. Collectors tell me time and again that high-resolution scans are no substitute for the real thing. We are still coming to terms with the limitations of the internet, as well as its possibilities. The availability of information is obviously useful, but only if it is correctly interpreted. Auction records are a good example. We have all had the experience of being offered a very inferior copy of a book or a map for the same price that an excellent example fetched at auction. People come into the shop quoting auction prices, without any understanding of such factors as condition and provenance, or that a high price was simply achieved because two people were determined to fight it out in the saleroom.

I am involved with Rainer Voigt and Massimo De Martini in organising the London Map Fair. It is the largest of its kind in Europe and a wonderful opportunity for collectors to see and handle a vast variety of material. We recently moved the fair to the Royal Geographical Society, an ideal location, and their staff have been most supportive, putting on special displays and offering guided tours of the historic building. It all helps in our efforts to get people involved and attract new collectors, without whom ours is a dying trade.

Over the last three years I have been an active member of the ABA Council. My term of office is drawing to a close and I have decided not to stand again for now – as you can see I am not short of things to do – but I remain as committed as ever to the concept of a strong trade association supporting its members' interests throughout the year. I have been particularly involved with press, education and security. I think we have gone some way to raise the profile of the Association; the launch of a separate Educational Trust is imminent and the new ILAB stolen books database should become both a valuable resource (available also to non ILAB members) and a serious deterrent. But of course, there is always more that could be done, and I hope any ABA members reading this will consider standing.

At the age of thirty-six, I am aware of being one of the youngest members of the ABA – only one member is under thirty. We should be concerned about the lack of young people coming into the trade. With the disappearance of so many large firms, it has become very difficult to get a toe-hold. One-man bands like me are typical of the trade today and probably an indication of the future. To be a successful bookseller requires an unusual combination of skills. Some dealers are good on the academic side. They can do the research and write excellent catalogues, but are perhaps not as strong on such aspects as evaluating the effect of condition on the price, and actually selling the item. Other people are good at 'front of house', but have less of a grip on the stock. The ideal combination is to know and love the material, and to handle it with a decent business sense. People have joked to me that anyone capable of making a living selling old books would be able to make a very good living doing a proper job.

The codex has been around for fifteen hundred years and, although it has not necessarily reached its final form, I do not anticipate its demise any time soon. The digitisation of books will undoubtedly have an enormous impact on the new and secondhand book trade. But I do not believe that the rare book, in which so much of the interest derives from the object itself, is under threat. There is still much to be said and appreciated about seeing the book as it was intended for its original readership.

# Tea with Haile Selassie ∾ Alan Mitchell

After leaving school I joined an insurance company, and quickly discovered that I could not stand it. I had a friend who had just finished a degree in Geology, which had taken him to Africa. He had become very interested in the history of exploration, and wanted to go into the rare book trade. Within three weeks of asking me to join him in the business, he died unexpectedly. I decided that I would carry on and try to become an antiquarian bookseller although, at that stage, I probably could not spell the word. During my first year and a half in the trade, I lived off cornflakes and cheap cuts of bacon, while I slowly started to put aside books for my first catalogue.

My friend had left me a set of Kegan Paul's *African Quarterly*, an excellent series of catalogues of books on Africa, which became my reference tools. I would go around England on a motorcycle visiting bookshops, and then check what I found against the *African Quarterly*. In my first year of bookselling, I drove 48,000 miles. In those days every small town had a secondhand bookshop, and I could fill an entire car with books on a day trip to Guildford, Brighton, Hove or wherever. If I did the same trip today, I could probably hold all my purchases in one hand. Robert Sawers at Kegan Paul was extremely helpful when I was starting out, and so was Ian Hodgkins, who was a neighbour of mine in Putney. Ian taught me the intricacies of packing in the days of book post, when parcels had to be sent open-ended.

My first catalogue of books on Africa was produced on a Roneo machine which belonged to the Guildhall Bookshop of Kingston and Surbiton. I put together a mailing list by going through *The World of Learning*, looking for libraries which specialised in material on Africa, and by placing a two-line advertisement in Argus Newspapers, which was at the time South Africa's major newspaper group. My advertisement said 'African Book Catalogue Out', and gave my address. It appeared on four successive Saturdays, cost me £8, and the response was overwhelming. I was inundated with requests for my catalogue. When someone orders a book, they are confirming your judgement, which was and is very encouraging for a newcomer to the trade.

From a subsequent catalogue I sold a copy of Werne's *Expedition to Discover the Sources of the White Nile* for £25 to the Hon. Joseph Murumbi, book collector and Kenya's second Vice-President. He ignored my invoice and repeated statements, and so I wrote a letter saying that if I did not receive payment within two weeks, I would take the front page of *The Clique* to make the following announcement which would be read by a very large number of booksellers and collectors, 'If anyone would like to see Alan Mitchell's copy of Werne's *The White Nile*, they may do so in the collection of the Hon. Joseph Murumbi', and gave his address. His cheque followed very promptly.

The late 1960s and early 1970s were a good time to be selling books on Africa. Black studies were just taking off in the States and institutional libraries were keen to build up their holdings. There have always been a number of wealthy white collectors in South Africa, taking an interest in books on their country. During the oil boom, there was a certain amount of oil money in the market for books on the East African coast and the Gulf, because of Arabic trading interests and settlements in the region. If you want to have a 'comprehensive' collection of books on Africa, you need the five Bs – Burton on the Lake Regions, Barth on North and Central Africa, Burchell on Southern Africa, Bruce on Ethiopia and Captain Thomas Boteler who sailed around the entire continent.

I bought my first copy of the first edition of a *Personal Narrative of a Pilgrimage to El-Madinah and Meccah*, Sir Richard Burton's most famous book, for £30 from Maggs in 1973. I was keen to build an important Burton collection and, within a couple of years, had assembled an enormous collection which was eventually sold to Spink's. They had decided to open a book department, and regarded my Burton collection as a route into the antiquarian trade. I was paid around £27,500 for the collection which would be worth more than £1 million today. Spink's published a catalogue of the collection in 1976, which has since become quite a sought after reference work. With all the variant bindings, manuscripts and autograph letters, the collection contained around 800 items, including a great rarity – Burton's translation of *The Kama Sutra*, seven parts in the original printed wrappers, 'For Private Circulation Only', 1883. I only know of one other set, and N.M. Penzer, Burton's bibliographer, describes copies in the original parts as 'practically unobtainable'. Incidentally, I have been asked more than once to do a new edition of Penzer's bibliography, which was published in 1923. I have kept notes on a number of Burton items which are not in the bibliography, but I do not feel inclined at the moment to give away my knowledge.

While I was building up the Burton collection, I joined the campaign committee in charge of restoring the Burtons' Arab tent-styled mausoleum in Mortlake in 1974. The stone mausoleum, where Richard and Isabel are buried, had fallen into a poor state of repair over the years, and had also been vandalised in the belief that valuable items could be inside. The vandals broke down the door and in so doing dislodged two marble tablets, one of which was inscribed with Justin Huntly McCarthy's sonnet on the death of Sir Richard Burton. McCarthy had helped Isabel with her bowdlerised edition of the *Arabian Nights*.

Much of the restoration work to the mausoleum was done while I was in South America. When I returned to London, I went straight from the airport to Mortlake to look at the mausoleum, and noticed that the tablet with McCarthy's sonnet had been replaced by a new one. At the next committee meeting, I asked permission to see if I could track down the original tablet. I found it lying under a heap of rubble in the stone mason's yard in Twickenham, where the replacement had been made. The owner sold it to me for fifty pence, and I now have the original tablet in my flat.

It is interesting how people expect antiquarian booksellers to be of a certain age. I was nineteen when I was trading by appointment from home in Putney. On one occasion I opened the door to a customer who had come to look at some books, and he said, 'Is your father in?' It was Humphrey Winterton, who collected books on Kenya and also lived there. It was difficult to be taken seriously, especially as one was always meeting collectors who were extremely knowledgeable about their subject. I could not pretend to any in-depth knowledge, but I always tried to come up with an obscure fact which would demonstrate my interest. On one of Stanley's expeditions he lost a large number of porters to ill health, and was forced to abandon much of his extravagant baggage, including his travelling library. It was assumed by the Victorian public that he must have kept his copy of the Bible. He did indeed hang on to one book, but it was Burton's *The Lake Regions of Central Equatorial Africa*.

Humphrey Winterton became a great friend, and it was he who told me that Francis Edwards was up for sale. It was 1978 and I had been in the business for just over ten years. I had reached a point where I did not have to rush out every catalogue; customers knew where to find me and I was dealing in better books with a greater profit margin. I was not working terribly hard and perhaps Humphrey thought that I needed more to do. In any case he suggested that we should buy Francis Edwards. The price-tag on the stock and good will was £325,000.

Francis Edwards was the oldest purpose-built bookshop in the UK, and one of the most magnificent. It had a long history and a family member, Herbert Edwards, was still involved in the business. Humphrey and I put together a mixture of capital from what was then the ICFC and Barclays Bank. Stupidly we were not given the money to buy the building in Marylebone High Street, which would be worth millions today.

The managing director of Francis Edwards at the time was Charles Harris. When it became known that we were taking over the business, I noticed that he spent a lot of time trying to rub out handwritten calculations in the margins of his copies of Sotheby's catalogues. However, it was not easy to erase pencil annotations from glossy paper, and one could still see the evidence that he had been running a ring. When Mr Harris announced that he would like to talk to me about his redundancy and a cash payment, I picked up one of his Sotheby catalogues and said something along the lines that it might be of interest to the Fraud Squad. I did not hear another word about a cash payment.

Meanwhile we were not to know that a recession was just about to begin. When we took over Francis Edwards, the interest rate was around 10 per cent on our borrowing. Within a year, the rate had gone up to 23 per cent. Coupled with the decline in trade – people do not buy rare books in a recession – we could no longer afford the venture. The firm went into receivership in 1979, and I went back to what I had been doing before. Today the Marylebone High Street shop is occupied by Daunt Books.

In my small world of books, there will always be a market for a first edition of *How I Found Livingstone* and other classics of African adventure. A good book is always a good book, and there is something special about holding a copy of the first edition in your hand. Modern technology has been good and bad for the trade. The last time I looked there were around 740,000 books on Africa for sale on ABE. I buy a lot of books off the internet – it is astonishing how much I can look at in the course of a day – but I do not sell on the internet. After forty years in the trade, why should I give away my specialist knowledge?

At my advanced age it is very rare for me to come across a book which I have not had before. The problem today is not only finding good material but also the cost of buying it. The supply of good antiquarian books is drying up, but there are more dealers – if fewer shops – than when I started. To buy a book at auction, you really need to have a customer lined up, unless you can afford to buy a book for stock and hold it for an unknown time. Booksellers have traditionally been under-capitalised, and most cannot afford to hold on to an expensive book for several years. I started my business with one pound ten shillings. Today you would need £100,000 before even thinking of dealing in good antiquarian books.

It occurred to me the other day that this year will mark the centenary of the birth of Sir Wilfred Thesiger, the last great British traveller. Wilfred used to come to Putney to buy books from me, and I would take him home to his flat in Chelsea where he lived with his aged mother (Mrs Reginald Astley), and her even older housekeeper, Mrs Emptage. He was particularly interested in books on Africa, which had been such an important part of his life. From 1978 to 1994, he based himself in Maralal in northern Kenya, where he spent most of the year, living among the Samburu. When Maggs prepared a catalogue in 1995 of some of the books in Wilfred's library, he wrote a foreword explaining the appeal of Africa and his interest in book collecting, 'As a child, I saw sights of savagery, barbaric splendour and colourful ceremonies which affected me for the rest of my life. When I was only a few years old, either my father or my mother would read to me. One of the first books was *Jock of the Bushveld* by Sir Percy Fitzpatrick. This book, and the remoteness of our surroundings, influenced me profoundly'.

A man of action first and foremost, Thesiger had to be persuaded by his mother to write his first book, *Arabian Sands*, his desert masterpiece published in 1957. It is rare to find presentation copies of Wilfred's own books – he disliked writing inscriptions, and would just cross out his name on the title-page and write it by hand. On one occasion he came to dinner and I was determined to get him to sign my copy of *Arabian Sands* and *Marsh Arabs*. Wilfred liked his food – Eton schoolboy food – but was not interested in alcohol. He would knock back a glass of Ch.Petrus almost without comment, but he loved a dash of sherry in his favourite brown soup. I do not know if it was the effect of the sherry which my girlfriend had been pouring into his soup, but Wilfred signed both books 'With wary appreciation to Carol'.

On one occasion Wilfred bought from me a copy of Bernatz, *Scenes in Ethiopia*. When we got back to his flat, his mother noticed the book, and turned to an illustration of the mountains of central Abyssinia. Putting on her pince-nez, she announced, 'I was the first European woman to cross those mountains. I was carrying Wilfred at the time'. The eldest of four brothers, Wilfred was born on 3 June 1910, at Addis Ababa, where his father was British Minister in charge of the Legation. As Honorary Attaché to HRH The Duke of Gloucester, Wilfred attended the Emperor Haile Selassie's coronation at Addis Ababa in 1930. On one of my visits to the flat in Chelsea, I found his mother having tea with Haile Selassie. It was always one of my great ambitions to meet the Emperor of Ethiopia, and I am very proud to say that I have eaten cucumber sandwiches with Haile Selassie.

# Born (Again) in the USA ∾ John Windle

The idea that I wanted to surround myself with books seemed ridiculous to my adopted parents. They wanted me, an unwanted war baby with an unknown American father, to go into the Army, be a good soldier, kill some people and make a man of myself. I was bundled off to boarding school at seven and later to Wellington College. Luckily I had a godmother who intuited my nascent love of books and encouraged it by sending me book tokens every Christmas and birthday. Living in Suffolk, she knew a number of people in the book world including Geoffrey Keynes and Francis Meynell, who designed a bookplate for me. It was an elaborate typographic design with 'Ex Libris John Richard Windle' beautifully set in type surrounded by flowers in a Nonesuchian manner. I would take the tokens to my local bookshop in Hove, where the bookseller decided what I was allowed to buy. She started me on Sir Walter Scott, and then Conan Doyle's historical romances, and Rudyard Kipling – the edition in the limp red leather binding. By the age of eight or nine I had developed a passion for books which were the same size and colour, and took great pleasure in arranging them on my shelves.

As we lived next to the Sussex County Cricket Club I also collected cricketers' memoirs and would haunt the Club getting the players to sign my books. One sad day I came home from boarding school to discover that my mother had redecorated my room in Danish Modern and given away all my books. (Fifty years later, I have yet to find one of my books with its Meynell bookplate.) I had a tutor in Hove for the holidays to help me get through my exams, whom I recall vividly – Llewellyn Slingsby Bethell, a great scholar and eccentric whose house was crammed with books from floor to ceiling which inspired me no end. I started collecting Penguins, attracted by the different colours for the different subjects. By the time I left Wellington, I had a collection of about 1,000 Penguins beautifully colour-co-ordinated on my shelves which were the cause of much less-than-good-natured teasing from the army brats I was surrounded by.

In 1963 I went to France, partly to escape going to Sandhurst and also to pursue my love of modern French literature. I had a wonderful time at the University of Poitiers (Tours) and quickly discovered the delights of French paperbacks, unopened in their lovely cream wrappers. After a year abroad, I went to the newly-founded University of Sussex, where I had the privilege of studying with David Daiches, Asa Briggs, Tony Thorlby and David Galloway whose love of American literature opened up a whole new world.

In 1967 I moved to London and tried desperately to get a job with Jardine

Matheson. I had a romantic notion of becoming an international man of mystery, smoking Sobranie cigarettes and dealing in something exotic. When I told my best friend that Jardine's were interviewing, he also went along for an interview – and got the job. We were living in a £3-a-week flat in Islington, where I discovered the Angel Bookshop, and thought that there might be a job for me. It was run at the time by a delightful man called Hugh Crace who was very discouraging about making a living in the book trade, but suggested that I approach one of the top firms. I made an appointment at Bernard Quaritch, put on my best suit, and went along to Grafton Street looking frightfully smart. The door was opened by a man in his shirt sleeves, to whom I announced in rather an imperious way, 'I am here for an interview with Mr Dring, Managing Director', to which he replied, 'That's me'.

By sheer luck Quaritch had an opening, and I spent my first year packing books, running around the auction houses picking up purchases, and generally doing odd jobs. Quaritch did not pay me for a while – I think it was a test to see if I was serious about becoming an antiquarian bookseller. In the evenings I worked in a pub, and by my second year at Quaritch I was earning a salary of £8 a week. I was put in Modern First Editions, which was taken to mean books printed after 1700. I also had the opportunity to handle music, autograph letters, private press books, and The Blake Trust facsimiles. It was pure heaven to work for a firm of such depth and history. Occasionally I encountered 'young' Mr Newton, who was in his nineties and had worked for Mr Quaritch.

Every lunch time a particular collector would come in and go through the private press books. He was especially interested in the Daniel Press, and would pull out the slim volumes, with infinite care, examine them and make his purchase. We became friends and I went to his house in North London where he had the most wonderful book collection. He was in publishing, but on the verge of moving to the country and starting his own rare book business. This was my introduction to Colin Franklin who became my mentor. Colin taught me not to pay too much attention to the price of a book. The price is not the most important factor – it is the quality of the printing, the paper, the binding, the text and the illustrations. If they are not good, it does not matter if the price is cheap – it will never be a desirable book. A good copy of a good book will always be worth its price.

I was twenty-two when I joined Quaritch in 1967, and stayed for four years. With hindsight, I can see that I left much too soon, but I did not have the means to buy a partnership, and I would always have been an employee, and a very junior one. In England in the 1960s people rarely thought of opening their own business. America, on the other hand, seemed to be the land of opportunity. When David Magee came into Quaritch one day and invited me to visit his shop in San Francisco,

I jumped at it and left for America on a wing and a prayer. As luck would have it, David had sold his business by the time I got there but I walked into Howell's shop just as one of Warren's cataloguers was going on maternity leave. He offered me a job on the spot and I started on the following Monday. Warren liked the fact that I had worked at Quaritch and had met or at least knew of many great collectors, who were also his customers – men like Jock Abbey, Robert Honeyman, Elmer Belt, Herbert M. Evans, Raphael Esmerian, Paul Mellon, Lessing Rosenwald and the de Belder brothers, as well as the cream of the trade. Over the years I have met richer men, but not greater collectors.

I worked for Warren Howell from 1971 until late 1974, when I decided to start my own business in my bedroom in the house which I was sharing with friends in San Francisco. I had only been on my own for a few months when I received a phone call from Ron Randall who was still working at Howell's. He told me that he wanted to go into business for himself, and that his father had suggested that we form a partnership. Ron's father was David A. Randall of the Lilly Library (Indiana University), perhaps the most distinguished rare book dealer turned librarian of his or any generation.

The Lilly Library had recently bought the Ian Fleming collection of rare source material concerning Western civilisation (he was a consultant and lender to the great 'Printing and the Mind of Man' exhibition as well as the creator of James Bond) and, as a result, had a room full of duplicate copies from its own holdings. David Randall was able to arrange for the duplicates to be shipped out to San Francisco, where we catalogued and sold them, took our commission and the rest of the money went into a credit with the Lilly Library to spend with us. I did most of the cataloguing, while Ron looked after the Lilly Library business, and the collectors in his father's circle. We used to compare ourselves – ambitiously and perhaps rather pretentiously – to the New York partnership of Mike Papantonio and John S. van E. Kohn at Seven Gables Book Shop, each with our different strengths and responsibilities.

The partnership worked well until 1979 when it came unglued for personal reasons. I was going through a difficult divorce, and Ron's wife became seriously ill and died. My ex-wife and Ron's in-laws decided that their share of our book business must be incredibly valuable. Everybody in the trade knows that a business may *look* enormously valuable, but it can be extremely hard to get actual cash out of it. Ron and I decided that things were not working, ended the partnership and dealt with our family issues as best we could. Ron moved to Santa Barbara and opened Randall House where he has successfully carried on bookselling to this day, and I stayed in San Francisco for a while and did a little publishing and writing before moving to Venice Beach in Los Angeles.

At about this time it occurred to me that I could choose to do something completely different with my life. I became deeply involved in Tibetan Buddhism and joined a centre in Los Angeles, where I helped to sponsor the Dalai Lama's visit to America in 1984. When His Holiness arrived in Los Angeles, I picked him up at the airport in my VW. Things were more low-key in those days. At the end of his visit, he invited me to stay at his monastery in McLeod Ganj in the mountains above Dharamshala. I put my books in storage with Bill Dailey, moved to India, shaved my head and became the only Tibetan monk in India with an American Express Card.

I loved my new life and was quietly going about my routine in the monastery when the Bhopal tragedy occurred. In the immediate aftermath of the explosion, the tension between India and the United States was extreme. The authorities decided that Americans were no longer welcome in India. A government official arrived at the monastery, and I was given twenty-four hours to leave the country. My first thought was to contact the Dalai Lama and ask for his advice. He replied, 'Go to Los Angeles and work for peace'. And so I walked into Bill Dailey's shop in my Buddhist robes and announced that I was back.

I did some cataloguing for Bill and for Heritage Book Shop, sold some of my books, and spent time on a couple of writing projects which I had always wanted to do. Thomas Frognall Dibdin and Mary Wollstonecraft Godwin were both indirectly connected to William Blake, who has always been a special interest of mine. In my researches on Blake, I was amazed to find that no bibliography existed of Dibdin or Wollstonecraft, which was particularly ironic in the case of Dibdin, the self-proclaimed 'father of bibliomania' and founder of the Roxburghe Club. With the bravery borne of ignorance, I decided to put this right and my bibliographies were eventually published by Oak Knoll in 1999 and 2000.

Although I very much enjoyed being a researcher for a while, I did not deceive myself that I was a scholar, as my commercial instincts never died down. There is a great difference between an autodidact who dabbles in one tiny area for a certain period of time, and someone who devotes their life to its study. If I have one regret about being a bookseller, it is the loss of the ability to enjoy books as books. When I walk into some of the greatest libraries in the world, I cannot stop myself from mentally pricing every book I look at. This continual *ker-ching* taints my enjoyment of the book itself, though it has enabled me to travel the world and savour the temporary possession of some wonderful books.

In 1985, I happened to see an interview on television with David Mixner, the Los Angeles political activist. He was talking about his plans for a Great Peace March for Global Nuclear Disarmament. Remembering the advice of the Dalai Lama, I went along the next day to the office of the organisers of the march, and volunteered to help. In March 1986 I was one of the peace marchers who set off to walk across America from Los Angeles to Washington DC, a journey of nine and a half months and 3,700 miles.

In many ways it was a pure Buddhist experience, living from day to day, accepting whatever came our way, and in some ways I have never been happier in my life. After arriving in Washington I went to Florida with some friends on a second peace march down the coast to Cape Canaveral, where a Trident missile was due to be tested. We managed to delay the test, if only for a week, and all got arrested. Still, it was a symbolic gesture and one that I am proud of though it means I will never earn a Government security clearance in the USA.

It was time to sell a few books again, and put some dollars back in the bank. I asked Bill Dailey to ship some books to Florida, where I had bought an old school bus and converted it into a book-mobile, complete with shelves and a study area up front, and a comfortable bed and a shower in the back. I filled the bus with books, and began the three-month drive back to California, zigzagging across the country, stopping at bookshops on the way, and calling at all the university campuses. When I reached Texas – a very conservative state – I knew that I would be viewed as distinctly dodgy with my long hair, hippy clothes and a bus covered in peace signs. To my amazement, the head librarian of Southern Methodist University in Dallas not only came down from her office, and spent $20,000, but also told me that she admired what I was doing, saying, 'My pastor's daughter was on the Great Peace March and she knows you'.

Basically I had taken the '80s off or, as someone put it, I had my '60s in the '80s. The main thing that had changed in my absence was that my friends in the trade had made a lot of money. It had been a real boom time in the rare book business, with the Arabs and the Japanese in the market. By the end of the decade, that market had more or less collapsed. Meanwhile the internet was about to come along and kick the bottom out of the market for less expensive books. I embraced the new technology very early on. I bought my first Mac in 1986 and got on to the web as soon as I could. The internet has exposed far more people to the world of rare books, and to the kind of books in which I deal, than I ever could have reached on my own. It is a fantastic tool, but no substitute for having a bricks-and-mortar establishment. If you are thinking of spending a thousand or two thousand dollars on a book, would you like to be able to visit a dealer in a shop where he has done business for many years, and can show you different copies of a book, discuss what is available on the market, help to develop your interest in the subject and generally be available for consultation, or would you rather do business with a website that can disappear at the flick of a switch?

I moved back to San Francisco in 1989 and reopened my business full-time. Later on, my wife, Chris Loker, opened the Children's Book Gallery, our second shop in San Francisco and, within a year or two, had established herself as the leading dealer in antiquarian children's books on the West Coast. There are lots of people selling more recent children's books, but no one else currently has an antiquarian shop solely devoted to children's material from 1750 on. The traditional methods of bookselling from a bricks-and-mortar establishment can easily be combined with new technologies. In the last few years we have issued catalogues of illuminated manuscripts, children's books, and books by and about Blake and his circle, each with a CD-ROM of the catalogue included which holds the entire text and hundreds of colour images and thus serves as a fully searchable index.

Young people will be drawn into collecting by looking at books on the web, and developing a hunger for the real thing. I compare the process to watching a movie on a tiny screen on the back of an aircraft seat, and then wanting to see it at the IMAX. Areas of collecting will change. The modern firsts fad is already refining itself. For example, a new book by Stephen King no longer automatically jumps from $29.99 to $200 on publication. New subjects are emerging. I have collectors who are very interested in books on global warming. One customer collects diaries, as they frequently contain accurate observations recorded over a long period of time on the weather in a particular location. This material can be mined for priceless information on climate change. Another is fascinated by recycling and how societies have dealt with surplus and waste over the centuries. And of course, Bibles, books on food and drink, and children's literature are always in demand

As for bringing young people into the trade, I have just hired a twenty-six-year-old, who would have worked for nothing in order to get started. He is extremely well-educated and reads Greek and Latin, and two or three other languages. Nowadays there are very few occupations outside the rare book business in which someone of his abilities can feel truly valued. I would love to see every one of my colleagues bring on one young person, either as an employee or as a collector. The challenge for the book trade is to introduce young people to rare books and foster an appreciation of the importance of books as cultural artefacts. We can show them what a difference they can make to the world by what they choose to collect and treasure, to write about and share with friends. Chris and I are thinking of publishing our next ventures as apps for the iPad. If we continue to embrace technology, the future for the rare book trade is unlimited. Terry Belanger once pointed out that the less utilitarian horses became, the more highly they were valued and treasured. I'm betting the same is true of books and I hope to be selling them for many years to come.

# The Past is another Country  ∾  Paul Mills

My father was a hydrographer in the Merchant Marine, who settled in Shanghai where he met my mother amongst the émigrés who had escaped from the Russian Revolution. They retired to England in the late 1930s, and my father worked as a chart maker for the Admiralty in Bath during the Second World War. My parents had enjoyed a very different standard of living in Shanghai, and found it quite difficult to adapt to the austerity of post-war Britain. It certainly did not provide the comfortable retirement that they had hoped to enjoy. My father was not in particularly good health, and the opportunity to move to South Africa offered them a better climate and the possibility of regaining aspects of the life which they had known in China.

My father's interest in books was more or less restricted to H.G.Wells. Whenever he wanted to impress me, he would bring out his copy of *A Short History of the World* and say 'It's all in there – everything you need to know'. My Russian mother meanwhile spent a lot of her life trying to be English, and read Beverly Nichols's books for guidance on how to achieve this. She regarded *Down the Garden Path* as the acme of English literature. She rarely talked about her background, and would say that her Russia had disappeared with the Revolution.

My father was sixty when I was born, and was more like a grandfather to me. He died when I was eleven and, although I regret losing him at a young age, we had spent a lot of time together as he was already retired. By the time of my father's death, we had been living in South Africa for five years, during which the political situation was rapidly deteriorating towards Sharpeville. My mother decided to return to England, where I went to prep school and then boarding school in Dorset.

I would like to have gone to Oxford but went instead to Trinity College, a small liberal arts school in Hartford, Connecticut. My ambition at the time was to study Economics, go to Harvard Business School and rule the world. However a vocational test revealed that I was more suited to becoming a librarian. The Vietnam War was on and I would have been at risk of being drafted if I had attempted to convert my student visa to any other status. I decided to return to South Africa – more to see where I had grown up than with any intention of staying on. In the event I went back to being a student and did a History degree at the University of Cape Town. As it was my second time on campus, I was older than most of the students and not particularly interested in taking part in all the usual activities. I started to haunt the secondhand bookshops around Long Street – initially because I wanted to buy all the books that I needed for my studies, though I now see that my career as a bookseller had its origins in my student hobby.

After graduating I travelled for a couple of years in Africa and India, avoiding as long as possible doing anything more serious in life, but by the mid-1970s economic necessity forced me to turn my attention to some sort of career. Wanting to work for myself, book dealing seemed to offer an interesting opportunity and a way of turning a hobby into a business. I was introduced to Gilly Bickford-Smith of Snowden Smith Books in London, and we began producing catalogues together, which I distributed in South Africa. On one occasion Gilly drew a picture of a Cape Dutch house on the cover of the catalogue and signed it with her initials. I was inundated with telephone calls from customers wanting to buy what they assumed to be an unrecorded drawing by George Bernard Shaw, who had visited South Africa in 1932.

Although the joint venture did not last, it taught me that antiquarian bookselling required less capital to get started than publishing. Originally I thought that bookselling would supplement my earnings from publishing, but it rapidly became all consuming and profitable. I spent the next couple of years working from home, preparing catalogues, mainly of Africana, until 1978 when Tony Clarke made an offer that I could not refuse – a partnership on equal terms in his business, an old established antiquarian firm and thriving bookshop in the centre of Cape Town.

Anthony Clarke came out to Cape Town after the Second World War, in which he had served in the Royal Horse Artillery and won the Military Cross. H.V. Morton tells the story in *A Traveller in Italy* of how Tony saved Piero della Francesca's painting of 'The Resurrection' on the wall of a room in the town hall of Sansepolcro during a gun battle with the Germans. Although he had never seen the painting, he remembered that it was the subject of Aldous Huxley's essay entitled *The Best Picture*. The shelling of the town had already begun when Tony, disobeying orders, commanded his men to stop for fear of destroying the painting. His spur-of-the-moment decision could have had very serious repercussions but, as he learnt later, the Germans had already retreated. Sansepolcro and its famous fresco were saved, and today there is a Via Anthony Clarke in the town.

Tony was very much a scholar-bookseller. A correspondent of Graham Greene, who used to order steadily from his catalogues, Tony was extremely well read and ahead of his time in fields such as modern firsts and poetry. His business instincts were guided by his taste rather than by any commercial sense. It was undoubtedly a struggle for him to survive in Cape Town, where the market was dominated by Africana collecting. Tony was not particularly fond of customers, especially when they took his books away, as he described it, or – worse still – mishandled them. If he saw someone pulling a fragile binding off the shelf, he would rush up and announce that it was early closing and bundle the customer out of the shop. Five minutes later, he would look carefully up and down the street, and open the shop again.

Clarke's was a very traditional business. Tony did not allow a calculator in the shop, and of course there were no faxes or computers. We would catalogue books sitting opposite each other at the same desk. He taught me to be careful about describing a book as 'scarce' and would say that the Gutenberg Bible was scarce – everything else was relative. When we set up the partnership, Tony offered to leave his half of the business to me in his Will. He was 63 and I was 33, and so it was reasonable to expect that he would live for some considerable time. In the event I only had two years working with him before he developed pancreatic cancer and died very quickly. Tony never married and was a very private person. I think he would have been extremely surprised by how much affection for him and sadness there was from people all over the world at the news of his death. He had earned a reputation as a bookseller of great integrity, and set an example which I have tried hard to follow.

The 1980s were a time of great change in South Africa. As the country descended deeper into trouble, there was increasing demand from the outside world for books and information on South Africa's problems. It was a great opportunity for bookselling and, in 1981, I went into partnership with Henrietta Dax, whose background was in the new book business.

Clarke's catalogues of new books of South African interest began to include government reports, obscure trade union publications, pamphlets, posters and other ephemeral material that was much in demand and difficult to obtain. On our trips to London, we would visit the ANC offices and buy all their publications. These would be shipped to South Africa hidden in the bottom of boxes containing less controversial books. There was always the risk that the censor would open the boxes, and we would be summoned to his office in the port to explain ourselves. At one time it was almost enough for the book to have 'black' in the title for it to be an object of suspicion, if not actually banned. The famous example is *Black Beauty* which was on the list of prohibited books during the Apartheid regime.

The institutional libraries in South Africa were very supportive to us. We had an unofficial arrangement that if we were caught with prohibited material, one or other library would issue us with an official order for it, claiming that it was required for research purposes. It was reassuring to know that a loophole existed, although we never used it. The security police would occasionally visit the shop, instantly recognisable by their short haircuts, square shoulders and general air of never having been in a bookshop before. They would ask in rather illiterate English,

'You got Steve Biko *Student Perspectives on South Africa*?' – hardly a clever trick question – to which we would reply, 'I'm terribly sorry. It was banned years ago'.

With the release of Nelson Mandela in 1990, South Africa embarked on a decade of great hope. The first non-racial elections in 1994, and Mandela's election as President, were a time of euphoria, almost impossible to describe to anyone who did not experience it. Censorship was lifted and the country moved towards the development of a free press. Incidentally, the censor, finding himself out of a job, told Henrietta in all seriousness that he was thinking of becoming a consultant to the book trade.

In 1999 Henrietta and I decided to go in different directions, and Clarke's new and antiquarian businesses split neatly down the middle. Henrietta continues to sell new books, prints, maps and some secondhand material in Clarke's Bookshop in Long Street, while my wife, Janet, and I moved our business, Clarke's Africana & Rare Books, to our home amongst the vineyards of Constantia where our two children grew up.

Africana has undergone huge changes since the days when the market was dominated by big collectors in Johannesburg spending their mining fortunes. I am told by someone who worked for Francis Edwards that the firm was kept going during the 1930s by South African collectors. Although the collectors today tend to have smaller wallets, their range of interests has expanded enormously. Black writing, ethnography, early photography and anything to do with the natural environment – these are relatively new subjects in the field of Africana collecting. My customers have immense knowledge about their chosen subjects, and it is very enjoyable to be continually learning from them.

The biggest change of course was the coming of the internet, which we were very quick to embrace. I compare the effect to a short-sighted person wearing glasses for the first time and suddenly seeing a whole new world beyond the baffling machine on his desk. I believe that we were amongst the first ten dealers to list our books on ABE. Nowadays there are around 15,000 dealers on ABE and the inevitable has happened – the internet has called the bluff on scarcity and forced the prices down. We try to respond by only listing more unusual items, but selling on ABE is not the future. Some of the books on internet bookselling sites have been there for years. Dealers need to be more nimble and clever in how they sell their books.

One solution for booksellers is surely to hold online auctions. For the past five years we have been running AntiquarianAuctions.com as a simple and effective way to move surplus stock. I am very lucky to be working with my son, Anthony, who is an IT expert and looks after the technical side of AntiquarianAuctions.com, which is still the only dedicated online rare book auction site. We only allow bona fide booksellers to list books, which is an important difference from other online auction sites, and ensures that standards are maintained. Booksellers upload their stock to our monthly auctions under their own names and, at the end of the sale, they deal directly with the buyer. There is an 8 per cent commission charge on successful sales and no buyer's premium. Each of our sales attracts an average of 100 bidders, based in up to twenty different countries.

As the participating dealers tend to be South African, the auctions have been dominated by Africana. We believe that the future development of AntiquarianAuctions.com is likely to be regional and are seeking dealers in other countries to work in partnership with us. The cost of money in modern times means that for most businesses large holdings of stock are no longer viable economically. We must move with the times and not attempt to protect what is past. Antiquarian bookselling can be profitable with far lower costs than before – but only if we adapt to the new reality.

# A Five-Star Generalist ❧ Pom Harrington

Most booksellers are not businessmen first; they're book lovers. They trade in something they love and try to make a living at it. Being born into the trade, I was always very conscious of the business side. My father, Peter Harrington, wanted me to join the business, but nothing seemed less attractive during my years of teenage rebellion. I did however work for him on Saturdays and during the school holidays at Chelsea Antique Market, where he had a colossal back room stacked floor to ceiling with decorative bindings which I sold to interior designers. Eventually I went off to Sheffield University, where I quickly discovered that student life wasn't for me, and came down after one term with my tail between my legs. I started doing odd jobs wherever I could find them, while helping my father on a part-time basis. I was gradually beginning to appreciate the business, and to enjoy selling books. In 1994, I asked my father for a proper job, and he turned me down – for the simple reason that he thought that I wouldn't listen to him. He would have liked me to go and learn the business from someone else in the trade. We had a bit of a stand-off for a few months before my mother intervened. And that same year I joined Harrington Brothers, as it was in those days, working with my father and my uncle, Adrian.

I learnt a lot from my first few years with my father and Adrian. They had such different styles, while both being very successful booksellers. Adrian takes a more studied approach, while my father relied on his instincts. He taught me to think out of the box – to have the confidence to buy something you have never seen before and know that someone else will share your reaction and be prepared to pay more money for it. He didn't need to think about it or look it up in reference books – a nice bit of red morocco around a good book and the decision was made. I like to think that I inherited my father's instinctive approach to bookselling. We certainly found quite a lot of common ground when we worked together. In 1997, we moved out of Chelsea Antique Market and my father and Adrian went their separate ways – Adrian to a shop in Kensington Church Street, and Peter to our present location in Fulham Road. Although my father was still in charge of the business, I took over the running of the shop in 2000. When my father died in 2003, I took over his share of the business. My mother has the other half.

While my father was trading at Chelsea Antique Market, he also developed a map and print business, which was largely run by my mother. In 1989 she established Old Church Galleries with my sister Nicky in a shop in Old Church Street. The business became a thriving concern, and eventually had two branches – one at 98 Fulham Road next door to our bookshop. After thirty-five years of trading, my mother wanted to step back from the business, and last year we merged Peter Harrington Antiquarian Books and Old Church Galleries into one firm under the name of Peter Harrington, occupying a double-fronted, four-storey building, with more than 20,000 volumes and 6000 works on paper. Since my father died, my mother has been a great support. She encouraged me to spread my wings and has helped the business to succeed.

There are very few rules for running a book business. You make it work as you see fit. I employ people who bring a string of new knowledge to the business. A decade ago we didn't have anyone who knew about modern first editions. Kevin Finch joined us and introduced us to twentieth-century books, which he had been selling at the Royal National Hotel fair, where I first met him. Kevin still covers provincial book fairs for us and does all our auction viewing. We had Clive Moss with us for a while, and he introduced us to a new range of books such as the Kelmscott Chaucer and other expensive and glamorous books that he had handled while working for David Brass. My father never felt entirely comfortable with very expensive books – he would handle them occasionally, but it was not in his nature to buy them for stock. When Clive was lured by the bright lights of Los Angeles and went to work for Heritage Book Shop, I continued to buy books in new areas. I was probably a bit scatter-gun in my approach, but you learn quickly when you make an expensive mistake. In 2003 Adam Blakeney joined the firm. I would trust his knowledge of twentieth-century books over anybody else in the trade. Almost ten years on, our stock is dominated, in terms of volume, by modern first editions.

Adam Douglas is in charge of our cataloguing and we take great pride in the quality and production of our catalogues. I value them for the image that they project of our business. Hundreds of books go through our hands every month. They are all hand-picked – we rarely do house clearances – and described with great attention to accuracy. We work to a tight formula in terms of the nuts and bolts of the collation. But the tricky part is to write something concise that is entertaining, informative and captures the essence of the book. A good cataloguer will get to the point of the book – not least why it's worth the price. A lot of people don't understand why there's so much variation in prices – as a glance at ABE will demonstrate. We want our customers to trust that there's a good reason for the price of our books.

The relationship between the bookseller and the customer is based on trust. There's nothing new about this, except that the internet is changing the way in which the relationship develops. We have customers who spend a considerable amount of money with us, whom we have never met. The relationship is based entirely on e-mail, their preferred method of communication. I don't think that we have experienced the full extent of the change that technology will bring. As confidence in the internet grows, the financial threshold increases – people who were comfortable spending a few hundred pounds on our website and paying by credit card are now spending larger amounts. Our ability to describe and portray the books in ever greater detail obviously plays a large part in building this confidence. ABE allows dealers to upload several photographs of each item, so that you can present the book from different angles, which helps the customer to make a decision online. It's been very noticeable in the shop over the last couple of years that people don't come in to browse. They've already done their browsing on our website, and come into the shop to see a specific book. Of course they often browse while they're here, but they're quite focused when they arrive.

The number of bookshops will continue to decline, as people's buying habits migrate online. But I believe that it's still necessary for a business such as ours to maintain a physical presence. If you sell expensive books, you need a proper establishment in order to inspire confidence. Would you spend £50,000 on the internet with Joe Bloggs and his PO Box address? I like the ABE star-rating system, which is not only based on the fulfilment of orders, but also on orders not returned. You need to achieve a 95 per cent success rate to earn five stars, which we have had for several years. Pablo Picó is our web manager and processes internet orders, updating our online stock every day. He's immensely proud of our high order-fulfilment rate.

Collectors are learning to spot the 'chancers' on ABE – dealers with one star and a PO Box selling very expensive books. They're not so easy to spot on eBay, where rogue traders present a real problem. Forgeries are nothing new, but the problem is becoming much harder to control on the internet. I'm on the ABA's security committee, where we're doing our best to try to remove a bunch of fraudulent books from the market. There's someone at work at the moment who is responsible for hundreds, if not thousands of autograph forgeries. His style seems to be to sign reprints or undistinguished editions, which have cost him nothing if he makes a mistake. He never inscribes a book, as too much writing might give the game away. I would advise anyone to be suspicious of a cheap edition of a book by, say, Virginia Woolf, inscribed with just 'her' signature.

The internet has obviously had an enormous impact on how people are buying, but we're also seeing a huge change in what they're buying. The market is becoming much more discerning, and prepared to pay for it. We live in a time of huge prices for the right book in the right condition. For the old-style bookseller, such as my father, it was all about the book itself. If it had the dust-wrapper, so much the better, but it wasn't crucial. If the binding was unattractive, you rebound it in morocco.

Now the fashion is entirely for the unsophisticated object; the book itself is almost secondary. Last October we bought at Sotheby's a fine copy of the first edition of Thomas Hardy, *The Trumpet Major*, a three-decker in the original red cloth for £14,375. A less attractive copy sold at auction recently for a few hundred pounds.

The middle ground in bookselling has changed, but the high end has kept on selling. If I find the right book at the right price, I'll buy it, no matter how many copies I have in stock. English literature is our strongest suit and one in which we have a strong influence on the market – and in the case, for example, of *Harry Potter* – a very positive one. Over the years Adrian and I have sold a huge number of *Harry Potter* books, and tried to iron out some of the myths. There are 500 copies of the first edition of the first book in hardback, *Harry Potter and the Philosopher's Stone*, published on 30 June 1997 by Bloomsbury, who sent 300 copies to libraries. Only 200 copies went into circulation. I sold my first copy to a woman who lived around the corner and had never been in the shop before. She paid £6000, the market price, but I remember warning her that it might be worth nothing tomorrow. When the film came out in 2001, we sold six copies of the book at £15,000 each. A good copy today is now worth over £20,000. I met J.K. Rowling on one occasion and she signed a book for me. I'm sure she thought that I would sell it. She's rather suspicious of booksellers, but the trade should be grateful to her. The impulse to collect often begins with books that people enjoyed in their youth. J.K. Rowling has created a new generation of readers who may be our customers in twenty years' time.

You could spend a lot of time trying to spot the next *Harry Potter* when often it's better to wait for a book to become established and then join in. If you take the examples of Evelyn Waugh, Graham Greene and Ian Fleming, the market for good copies of their books just keeps on going. In our little world, it doesn't take many collectors to move a market. Ian Fleming is a good example – there are only fourteen books to collect; it can be done quite quickly, and there are always people wanting to do it. I collect Roald Dahl. I originally chose his books because they were cheap – you could buy a signed copy for £50. Nowadays you would have to pay around £1000, and my collection has become more of a business proposition than a hobby, as I'm spending so much more than I intended.

Book collecting is a hobby for most of our customers. As a business, we recognise this and try to make it fun. Our shop has a smart appearance, and visitors receive a warm welcome. Everything is priced, catalogued and guaranteed. I can't stand shops where the books are locked up, nothing is priced and you might just as well be in an old-fashioned library. This is not the way to attract the new generation of collectors, who expect smart presentation and full transparency. I've been involved for several years in the organisation of the London International Antiquarian Book Fair at Olympia, which increasingly faces the challenge of trying to present an old-fashioned concept to a new generation of young buyers who are more at home online. All the art and antiques fairs are facing the same challenge.

New collectors are not attracted by the image of the musty old bookshop, with a clock ticking in the corner. The Olympia fair needs to be smart and contemporary and to present book collecting in the most attractive light. I'm a strong believer in London's potential to be the centre of the world book trade – New York and Paris being the other contenders. Olympia is our big showcase and has attracted some excellent new collectors in the last few years. But we have a long way to go to catch up with the New York fair at the Park Avenue Armory – at least, in terms of number of exhibitors and quality of buyers. It must help to have a location in one of the richest parts of the world.

I'm sometimes asked if I believe in investing in books. Of course I believe in it – I've got a shop full of them, but you have to pick the right ones. In that respect they're no different to any other investment. People keep telling me that Kindle is the end of the book. It's not; it's the end of the paperback. When a new book comes out, some people will happily pay £25 for the hardback, while others prefer to wait for the paperback and they're the Kindle customers. As a result, we might find that the new trend actually increases collectability in modern books, because the print-runs will drop. Kindle doesn't change the intrinsic object. I believe the object will remain, just in smaller numbers. From our point of view, you might say that Kindle will save the book. Our business has grown year on year, and I don't see any reason for this not to continue. My children are aged six, four and one and I'd love the idea of one of them going into the business. The future of the book trade is fine.

# *Uranus Rising* ❧ Timothy d'Arch Smith

I derive my bookishness from my mother's side of the family, the Frankau gang, as I call them. They originated in the German town of Frankenau and came to this country in the 1840s as tobacco merchants. My great grandfather, Arthur, married Julia Davis, a friend of Oscar Wilde and the author of a number of 'advanced' novels under the name of Frank Danby. Their son, Gilbert Frankau, inherited and bankrupted the family business just before the First World War, having been let down by his supplier in Germany. After military service, Gilbert wrote *Peter Jackson, Cigar Merchant*, a bestselling novel of the First World War. Gilbert's sister Joan, was the only blue-stocking in the family. She went to Cambridge where she married Stanley Bennett, the Chaucerian scholar, known as 'Backstairs Bennett' for his skill in pulling strings. One of their daughters married the bibliographer Philip Gaskell. My mother, Ursula, and her sister, Pamela, both became novelists and it was through Pamela's acquaintanceship with Christina Foyle that I got my first job in the book trade.

I was born in 1936 in Farnborough. My father was an officer in the Hampshire Regiment. I hardly knew him as he was away fighting in my childhood, and then he divorced my mother. During the war we lived with my grandfather in Windsor. I had a room in the attic which had been my father's when he was a child. Above the bed there were rows of books by Edgar Rice Burroughs and I quickly developed a liking for second-rate literature and a taste in books described by my headmaster at St George's School as 'unsatisfactory'. My maternal grandfather, Gilbert Frankau, wanted me to go to Eton where he had been. It was across the river from my prep school, where I'd had quite enough of the Thames Valley. I thought that I might get out of going to school altogether if I refused to go to Eton. My plan didn't work and I was sent to Cheltenham, where my father had been. It was a good school with plenty of opportunity to express one's personality. I did a lot of acting, and began to cultivate a certain willowiness, topped with an interest in the occult.

When my friends went to Oxford, I realised that I should have worked harder at school. However, I got a job at Foyles, Pamela Frankau having eased the preliminaries, and discovered that muddling with books enabled me to pretend to be an academic. My aunt could love and hate with quixotic panache, writing scurrilous rhymes about her victims, of which Christina Foyle was one.

Poor little Christina Foyle,
She never quite comes to the boil.
She froths and she bubbles, she hisses and steams
But the kettle-lid only comes off in her dreams.

I was put in charge of the occult section as none of the other staff would touch it, having recently become evangelical Christians during Billy Graham's first crusade to London. As a boy I had been a keen conjurer and interested in all aspects of magic, much to the distaste of my aunt who sent me to be exorcised by Dom Illtud Evans, who appears in James Lees-Milne's diaries as a heavy-smoking, rather drunken priest.

After leaving Foyles, I did my National Service. While I was stationed on the east coast of Scotland, I discovered *The Quest for Corvo* in Crail public library, and was instantly hooked by A.J.A. Symons's biography of Frederick Rolfe, self-appointed Baron Corvo. I came out of the Army in August 1957 and immediately auditioned for RADA in time to start the autumn term. During my audition, I realised that I was no longer interested in the stage and that I wanted to be a bookseller. I spent most of my term at RADA in the British Library, which was just around the corner in those days. None of my family was keen on the idea of a stage career, and a sigh of relief went up, not least from the head of RADA, when I returned to the book business.

In January 1958 I joined the Times Bookshop in Wigmore Street as a general assistant. The Times Bookshop and Library had been a very grand establishment, but was beginning to lose money seriously. The combination of a bookshop and a library in the same premises wasn't working. People would find a book that they liked in the shop on the ground floor and then borrow it from the library upstairs. Harrods also combined a bookshop and a library but their customers would borrow a book and buy a grand piano on the same visit. My first job was in the basement sorting out the ex-library stock. We didn't have ladders and were expected to ascend the shelves by climbing them, removing a few books from each shelf to make space for a grip like alpine mountaineers. Within a few months a vacancy came up in the publicity department. The job involved preparing catalogues of exhibitions which were held in the shop. My first exhibition was a display of books to celebrate the Poet Laureate John Masefield's eightieth birthday.

One day there was a knock at the door and there stood Harry Pratley, President of the ABA, asking if I would do the publicity for the antiquarian book fair. I produced the catalogue and, in the process, met a great many booksellers. It was extremely helpful as I had already begun collecting books, and was gathering material for a bibliography of the works of Montague Summers. The hippies had put paid to my plans for an Aleister Crowley bibliography by seizing on his books and reprinting them in all sorts of clandestine forms that resisted researches into their origins and their print runs.

I continued to produce exhibition catalogues for the Times Bookshop with increasing extravagance. Things came to a head shortly after an exhibition of private press books, for which I had borrowed material from various sources. When my boss received the enormous bill for printing the catalogue, he took it to a board meeting where the Chairman, Hugh Astor, declared that the answer was surely to open an antiquarian department and sell the sort of book that we had been borrowing for our displays. I still have my letter of appointment as buyer of the antiquarian department from 1 January 1961 at a salary of £900 a year. I had for a long time thought of mounting an exhibition of rare books on the occult but it was not until 1965 that I persuaded the Times Bookshop to put it on. Previous exhibitions had been on the stodgy side. The directors were keen to avoid anything disreputable, especially at a time when the newspaper was initiating a series of advertisements with the slogan, 'Top People Take *The Times*'. *The Times's* chairman, John Walter, when asked at a board meeting if we might paint our name on the shop blinds so that passengers on the tops of buses would know a bookshop lay beneath them, replied, 'I wasn't aware any of our customers travelled by bus'. The directors also weren't aware that the shop had become quite well known to collectors of the arcane, not to say the improper. The astute collector could always find among the Arthur Rackhams and bound sets of Surtees some rather disreputable nugget such as Swinburne's *Whippingham Papers*.

In the event the exhibition was named 'Witchcraft' and proved quite a crowd-drawer. The Beatles came – all but Ringo, perhaps not to be accounted 'booky'. Their visit had been arranged by Paul McCartney's girlfriend Jane Asher, whose father had a distinguished collection of T.E. Lawrence which we had recently valued for quite a lot of money. I think Jane must have advised McCartney to invest some of his new-found wealth in antiquarian books. Coincidentally the Beatles' recording studio at Abbey Road has a Corvo connection in that the house once belonged to Arthur Maundy Gregory, a great Corvo collector, best remembered for selling honours under the Lloyd George government. We had Paul lined up to buy our signed copy of *Ulysses* but he didn't take the bait, telling me very sensibly that he liked to lend his books, which put him off buying anything very valuable.

On his first visit to the shop, McCartney's eye was caught by a Beardsley item. He had never heard of Aubrey Beardsley. He bought the book and shortly afterwards an art nouveau design of indisputable provenance adorned the cover of the Beatles' album 'Revolver'. The revival of interest in Beardsley was in full swing after Anthony D'Offay bought the libraries of André Raffalovich and John Gray, publishing a catalogue in 1961 of books and autograph letters mainly of the 1890s. Gray was a friend of Beardsley and the inspiration for Wilde's *Dorian Gray*

In 1964 my bibliography of Montague Summers was published by Nicholas Vane, who had published the centenary edition of the letters of Baron Corvo. Meanwhile I had started to contribute to *The Book Collector*, and the pseudo-academic in me was greatly enjoying the role of bibliographer. My first piece for the journal was an article on Edward Cracroft Lefroy for the series on 'Uncollected Authors'. Lefroy was one of the Victorian poets of homoerotic verse whose works I had been collecting for some years. Lefroy was related to Jane Austen and perhaps this connection amused the Editor of *The Book Collector*.

Shortly after joining the Times Bookshop I decided to write a book on the Uranians as I chose to call them. This was a group of minor poets active from around 1889 to 1930 who wrote homoerotic verse. Adult homosexuality has little to do with the themes of these poets, and hence the term 'Uranian' which was much used in their circles and is free from the misleading nuances of 'homosexual' and 'paederast'. The period roughly coincides with the various movements at home and abroad to change the laws regulating homosexuality. It also encompasses a change in the study of the Classics in public schools and universities, which began to concentrate on the content of the text rather than the language. I used to advertise in *The Clique* and once a runner came into the Times Bookshop shouting over the startled customers, 'Who's been advertising for homosexual poems?' There was a sinister runner called Michael O'Day, active in the 1960s, with piercing eyes, a large jewelled (probably magical) ring and a shabby but unnerving presence. He deserves to be remembered somewhere. I also put an advertisement in the *TLS* for Baron Corvo and his circle, to which Victor Hall, a bookseller in Kensington, responded very helpfully. Victor introduced me to the bookshops of Paris and taught me a tremendous amount about the business.

The acquisition of *The Times* newspaper by Lord Thomson of Fleet resulted in the shop's closure in 1968. Thereupon I entered into partnership with Jean Overton Fuller, who had been to our private press exhibition in connection with her interest in Victor Neuburg and the Vine Press. Neuburg was a disciple of Aleister Crowley and a minor poet. Jean had come into a bit of money and when she heard that I had been made redundant, she suggested that we go into business together, generously and courageously advancing a few thousand pounds of her own money to finance an enterprise of which the profitability was far from guaranteed. Jean also found wonderful premises for us in Gloucester Place where we opened Fuller d'Arch

Smith in 1970, with the reference library of the Times Bookshop which had been given to me. Within the first six months we had the good fortune to buy five tons of books from the Earl of Bradford's library at Weston Park in Staffordshire.

Jean was a writer and a poet, the author of *Madeleine,* a bestselling book on Special Operations during the Second World War. She was keen for our business to publish poetry – although not of the Uranian variety – and we held poetry days in the office, when the likes of George Macbeth and Alan Brownjohn would read their work. In the same year that Fuller d'Arch Smith opened its doors, *Love in Earnest,* my book on the Uranian poets, was published by Colin Franklin at Routledge & Kegan Paul. Colin later told me that he had sent my manuscript to a reader whose report came back with the question, 'Are you sure this man is not making the whole thing up? I've never heard of any of the poets he mentions'.

Jean's attitude to the subject was understandably unenthusiastic, and she would not have cared for the firm to issue catalogues devoted to what my grandfather Gilbert referred to as 'amatory unorthodoxy'. In 1972, by which time we had moved to 60 Oxford Street, the bookselling firm of Michael deHartington was conceived for the express purpose of jobbing off the accumulation of Uranian verse collected over the thirteen years it had taken to write *Love in Earnest.* My partner in this separate business was Michael Ayres, close friend and flat-mate, who had gained bookselling experience at Hatchard's. Michael came up with the title, a conflation of his own name, the possessive of mine and the second Christian name of the Reverend Travers Hartington Quince, MA, a mythical Uranian poet, dreamed up by our mutual friend Victor Hall.

Business hours were erratically maintained and the office was shut much of the summer while we watched cricket at Lord's. Although deHartington was only founded to dispose of my personal Uranian library, we had reckoned without the enthusiasm for the subject manifested by our fellow-booksellers – interesting from a psychological as well as a commercial viewpoint. When the business closed its doors in 1974, I continued to trade as Fuller d'Arch Smith. In due course Jean decided to move out of London. She remained a director for a few more years until around 1980 when, after my mother's death, I was finally in a position to pay back Jean's investment in the company.

I consider myself fortunate not to depend on bookselling for a living during the age of the internet. Several of my customers have given up collecting as a result of it. Quite simply they miss the thrill of the chase. A budding bookseller might launch his business by persuading his dentist to collect books on dentistry and his butcher to collect books on butchery and his solicitor to collect law books. Today my stock consists of a couple of shelves of books, and material I'm putting aside for a catalogue to mark the centenary of the death of Baron Corvo in 2013. It will be my first printed catalogue since the 1980s. Some academic kindly said that *Love in Earnest* was a pioneering study, and I would like to be remembered as a bookseller for discovering the Uranians.

# Private Passions ❧ Sophie Schneideman

I was ten years old when my father gave me an unopened set of Brontë novels. I remember being torn between wanting to read them and not wanting to cut the pages. It's my first memory of cherishing a book as a beautiful object. When I went to St Andrews to read History, I discovered many wonderful books in the university library but the idea of making a career of it hadn't yet occurred to me. I was a very keen musician and had thoughts of pursuing singing as a profession, until I realised what a hard life it would be. I left St Andrews in 1990 in the depths of a recession when accountants were the only people in demand. I didn't want to spend my time winding up companies, and thought that perhaps there might be an opening for me at Sotheby's. Although there were plenty of short internships available, they paid almost nothing. If you were sent to the Victoria & Albert Museum, for example, you had to pay your own bus fare. Just as I was deciding that I couldn't afford to work for Sotheby's, I met John Maggs who offered me a job starting the following day.

I was put in charge of answering the telephone in the front shop. At the time I found it rather boring, but didn't realise how imbued with the business I was becoming simply by all the activity going on around me. Fortunately John Collins took me under his wing quite quickly. He was a wonderful teacher and encouraged me from the start. I can't remember showing any precocious talent for the business, but he gave me the opportunity to prepare my first catalogue – a collection of books and a couple of watercolours by the rather neglected figure of Thomas Pennant.

In those days Maggs was a rather old-fashioned business. I wondered if there was a place for me in the hierarchy, and decided to study for a part-time Law degree in case I didn't find my niche. When Emma Pound left the firm, I took her place in the Bibliography Department which I found very interesting. In pre-internet days, booksellers depended on their reference books, which we sold in large quantities, especially during the June fairs when dealers from all over the world would come in and buy piles of bibliographies. Working in the department helped me to realise that bookselling wasn't beyond my capabilities as I became familiar with the tools of the trade. Catalogue descriptions had previously seemed rather opaque with their references to bibliographies by the authors' surname only, or the initials of the title with no further explanation. The feeling of knowing nothing, which had been quite oppressive for some time, began to ease.

Eventually I moved to the Modern Department with Ed Maggs, and was given complete autonomy to focus on private press books. It was a very happy time for me with a lot of material coming in and the opportunity to learn about every aspect of private press books. Only after a decade in the trade did I begin to see the big picture, and to realise that I had found the subject that excited me. Everything is so deeply felt in private press books; there's something special about owning an object created with such spirit in a world where there's so much trivia. You have such an immediate connection with the person who made a private press book, and pulled the sheet off the press, forming a connection with every single page. I compare it to having an inscribed copy of a book. In 2004 things reached a peak when a relative of Alfred Dyke Acland, St John Hornby's partner at W.H. Smith, showed me his wonderful collection of Ashendene Press books. It was a great moment and confirmed my decision that I wanted to deal in books that were beautiful and interesting, rather than just beautiful.

By that stage I was in my early thirties, I had got married and begun to find that dealers and collectors were taking me more seriously. In 2007 I decided to leave Maggs and start my own business. I had no capital and no stock, but I knew a number of very supportive dealers who let me borrow books on approval and generally encouraged me. Within a short time I found that I could earn at least as much money from 'running' books as my salary at Maggs. Before I became eligible to join the ABA, I was a member of the PBFA and exhibited at most of their fairs and loved them. I've met some of the most interesting dealers at PBFA fairs – they're often great specialists fixated on small details, or they've run a general bookshop in a provincial town, been out on extraordinary house calls and seen everything in their time.

For the first year I worked from home but it became a little unnerving with my two young children running around with sticky fingers on a Gregynog special binding saying, 'this is pretty, mummy'. My husband, Alex Schneideman, is a photographer and printer and in 2008 we opened our bookshop and gallery in Portobello Road specialising in private press, illustrated books and prints as well as books on food and drink – just after Lehmans collapsed. It wasn't perfect timing, but there comes a point when you can't expect collectors to walk up the stairs past your children's bedrooms to look at books in the attic. If you're going to set up on your own with a name that no one knows, a shop gives people confidence in your business. The gallery occupies the front of the premises, and I have my office at the back – in the best tradition of the book business where the good things are rarely on view. In 2010 we had exhibitions of John Buckland Wright and Ron King's work, and last year I curated a show of Gaylord Schanilec's wood-engravings. Bookselling is also a form of curating if you think of a catalogue as a path which you lay out for collectors to follow as they wish. The gallery and the book business complement each other, although visitors to our exhibitions tend to be focused on print collecting.

In my experience collectors of private press books are hugely knowledgeable about the people who created them and fascinated by the stories behind each press, T.J. Cobden-Sanderson and the fate of the Doves Press being perhaps the most extraordinary. For various reasons, including his refusal to have his type used for anything less than the greater cosmic being, Cobden-Sanderson threw all of it, along with the punches and matrices, into the Thames at Hammersmith. It took him a year to dispose of the type adding, by this act of madness, to the magical quality of the Doves Press whose books can never be reprinted. Like Ashendene books, the Doves Press tends to appeal to English collectors. It's also cheaper – ridiculously so – compared with the Kelmscott Press which has a more international following.

Collectors of private press books often start with the Golden Cockerel Press, which is such a wonderful introduction to the field, with its range of affordable and fine wood-engraved illustrations. My customers tend to be men, typically in their fifties and often high achievers in the legal and financial world, but they buy books because they love them and not for investment purposes. At first I found the depth of their knowledge intimidating until I learnt to listen. Some of my collectors can tell you what William Morris had for breakfast on a given day. While it's a great pleasure to sell a book to someone who is passionate about it, I find it slightly disturbing to think that this business depends on the fact that there will always be people desperate to own a Kelmscott Chaucer. Their wives often don't understand this desire to possess something – but would they prefer it to be a book or a mistress? Recently I sold a very heavy elephant folio to a collector who didn't want his wife to see it. I was asked to deliver it by car to their wonderful Elizabethan manor house in the West Country, leave the boot open, and come in for tea with his wife, while he slipped out and smuggled the book into the house. I'm sure she knew exactly what was going on. The female approach to dealing is more empathetic and less assertive and a number of my customers have become good friends. I had always assumed that bookselling was a man's world, but of course it's irrelevant to a collector whether you're a man or a woman; ultimately it's the book they're interested in.

Nowadays you can't sit on your bottom and expect business to come to you. When I first started in the trade, customers would wander into Maggs after a boozy lunch and spend the afternoon looking at books. That lifestyle hardly exists today; my customers lead very busy lives. They expect books to be brought to them, and modern technology enables this to be done very effectively. I regard being good at communication as an essential part of the job. I try to reply promptly to e-mails and always check them when I'm on holiday. My iPhone is incredibly useful when, for example, I'm at a book fair and I see something very expensive that I know a customer would like. I ask the dealer's permission to photograph it with my phone and, a couple of clicks later, I have the customer's response.

The printed catalogue is still the dealer's most important sales tool. I'm sure it's significant that huge online businesses like Boden and the White Company don't rely on e-catalogues. They still send out printed catalogues when, theoretically, they could do everything on their websites and save money. My catalogues are designed by Geoff Green, who is a book collector himself and has a tremendous feel for what I'm trying to convey. Geoff chooses what goes on the front cover, and a few years ago it resulted in my meeting two excellent customers. A copy of the catalogue, with a Gregynog special binding on the cover, was spotted on the desk of Philip Brown by a customer in Blackwell's Rare Books. Phil very kindly gave it to him and he became a great customer, introducing a friend who is also a book collector. It's hard to imagine how this could happen with an e-catalogue.

I aim to produce three or four catalogues a year and to attend all the major international book fairs. The Hong Kong fair is my favourite; it's not the most profitable, but there's a tremendous pioneering spirit amongst the exhibitors, and the visitors are very refreshing in their approach. In the English-speaking world, we've all experienced the man who collects bus tickets, or the man looking for books on swimming and resuscitation – and when you remember to bring your only book on the subject, it's always the wrong type of swimming – or the collector who tells you that he has a better copy than yours, or that yours is too expensive, and all the other comments that can make it hard to keep smiling through a book fair. The Koreans, Taiwanese and Chinese who visit the Hong Kong fair are genuinely interested to learn about books, and I'm very impressed by the breadth of their cultural vision. I can sell a lot of books under £1000 in Hong Kong, but I have no Chinese customers buying at the top level yet. Given the importance of status in Chinese society, it only takes one influential person to start collecting, and the market will take off. There's a lot of fascination with the European tradition of wood-engraving, which is so different from the Far Eastern technique of wood cuts. I'm constantly amazed by what can be done with wood as the medium, and would like to know more about Japanese woodblock printing, but am nervous about venturing into a subject where I can't read the language.

As your knowledge and experience increase, you want to buy better books, and inevitably you realise the importance of having some capital behind you. I can see that my stock has improved incrementally, but it's a slow process and I do sometimes wonder why I waited so long to start my own business. John Windle told me that by the time many of his colleagues in the States reached his age, they had inherited a wad which had given them the capital backing to buy expensive books. I have no expectations of that kind and will still be clinging to the cliff by my finger nails waiting for payments to arrive, aged 65. The book trade might have been considered genteel in the past, but it's no longer a toy occupation. I'm very ordered about the financial side of the business and know exactly what I have to achieve each month to make things add up. However, the bottom line never changes for me – it's about working with people I like and dealing in the books we love.

# A Book Room with a View ∾ Charles Cox

There was a bookshop in the small seaside town of Dawlish run by a man called Gordon Wright whom no one will remember because he never made any splash in the world. He had a few shelves of very nice books, but made his living by selling paperbacks outside the shop in the summer. It seemed to me that Gordon lived an ideal sort of life – calm, sequestered and studious, all of which I aspire to but have singularly failed to achieve.

I grew up in Perthshire and was educated at Wellington, where I had a wonderful English teacher. He gave me his copy of Robert Bridges's *The Testament of Beauty* as a prize for something that I had written. It was a 1930s edition and there was something very pleasing about it – although the book-collecting bug didn't strike until I went to university. My father was well-educated but had never been much of a reader. When it became obvious that I was interested in literature, he began to read so that he could discuss books with me, which touched me very much. He read the whole of Hakluyt's *Voyages* and Pepys's *Diary* and rejoiced in them.

In 1967 I went to the University of Exeter to read English and soon discovered the Exe Bridge Galleries, now demolished. It was a lovely tottering shop on several floors at the bottom of Fore Street by the river. As you climbed the stairs, the building became increasingly rickety and on the top floor you could see daylight through the ceiling. In retrospect it was a bit like Gormenghast. It was here that I bought the first book that really amazed me. It was a fire-and-brimstone Puritan tract. I loved it – not because of the text, but as a beautifully weathered object, with owners' names and a lovely seventeenth-century calf binding. I had in my hands what seemed to me to be a museum piece and yet I could afford to buy it.

While I was at Exeter I came across Richard Gilbertson's advertisements in the *Times Literary Supplement*. He was publishing rather cheaply produced limited editions of poetry including the work of the young Ted Hughes. Richard lived in a tiny cottage in the village of Bow in mid-Devon, where I arrived one bitterly cold day having ridden my 50cc Mobylette fifteen miles from Exeter. I was frozen to my moped and had to be thawed out with cups of tea with whisky before I was able to speak. I bought two rather battered volumes of *The Yellow Book*, which I had never seen before. As I was very interested in the 1890s, it represented the Holy Grail for me. This was the beginning of a long and difficult relationship with Richard who became something of a mentor. He had a wonderful nose for a book and over the years was extraordinarily helpful to me. I describe Richard as difficult, but I now realise that he suffered from manic depression.

After university I wrote to the main London booksellers to ask if they had a job for me. I was interviewed by Dawson's, Bernard Quaritch, Charles J. Sawyer and Bertram Rota where George Lawson offered me a job. As the position wasn't immediately vacant, Rota's arranged for me to spend three months working in Raymond Smith's bookshop in Eastbourne where I was then living with my parents. Smith was a very precise man with a neat naval officer's beard. He would tuck in his chin as a sign of disapproval, and there were many things of which he disapproved. People were chased out of the shop if they didn't put a book back on the shelf neatly or if they had a child in tow. Most of my time was spent straightening books and polishing them. The shop had a very strong smell of Backus Bookcloth Cleaner with which everything was coated – leather or cloth. I regarded my time there more as a waiting room before my proper education began at Rota's.

Bertram Rota was the most important dealer in modern firsts which, in those days, went back to around 1880. I never met the man himself but his towering presence was still very much felt. The firm had moved from Vigo Street to Savile Row where it occupied premises that had previously been a ladies' foundation garment showroom. This explained the rather precious dove grey carpet and the cherubs on the walls. Raymond Smith sold books to people who came off the pavement, but Rota's style of business was entirely different. We would reach out to the world by offering books to specific customers and doing meticulously prepared catalogues.

Rota's had a terrific reference library where I immersed myself in bibliographies such as Henry Danielson's *Bibliographies of Modern Authors*, and the works of C.B.Tinker and other scholars now considered old-fashioned. I have always been a magpie for collecting odd bits of information, although I keep very few booksellers' catalogues, George Sims's being the exception. He was a great friend of Anthony Rota's and had a way of cataloguing a book that made it immediately desirable. I extended my education by taking very long lunch 'hours' and spending them in other bookshops. Rota's were very good to me and allowed me to sell books to them from my lunchtime buying trips. I would go as far afield as Thomas Thorp in Holborn and Andrew Block in Bloomsbury where I went through the wonderful trays of ephemera. On one occasion I found a rather vulgar Victorian Easter card sent by H.P. Liddon, Church of England clergyman and biographer of Dr Pusey, to his friend and pupil Gerard Manley Hopkins just at the time of the latter's conversion to Catholicism. Liddon was trying to prevent him from taking this decision and had written a Latin verse inside the card to that effect. Meanwhile I was also putting aside material for the time when I would eventually start my own business. I had a cupboard at home in Highgate which was full of books still in their paper bags, which I didn't unwrap until that time.

While I was at Rota's I met Simon Nowell-Smith, who became my second mentor. Simon had wonderful taste and knew so much about his books and took such pleasure in them. He was a regular visitor and would be ushered into Anthony Rota's office but would always stop and chat to me at my desk in the shop. When I left to start my own business in 1974, Simon was an enormous help to me and gave me books to sell for him.

It never occurred to me that location mattered at all for a business. I planned to do everything by catalogue and wanted a nice view and lots of fields around me. My first wife and I had met at university and had Devon in common. We decided to move to Cheriton Fitzpaine in the middle of nowhere. I converted a cob barn into my book room and issued my first catalogue in 1974. It was entitled 'Some Poets of the Last Century' and Simon Nowell-Smith was my first customer, which was exciting and gratifying. It was either my first or second catalogue that Steve Weissman considered buying in its entirety. I remember thinking that everything must have been terribly underpriced.

It was a time when American universities were still building collections, and I became very involved in helping Chris Kohler to put them together, particularly one on Victorian poetry. It was a tremendous help to me as it meant that I could buy almost any verse of the nineteenth century and Chris would probably want it for his collection. I also put together a few collections myself, including one on Edwardian novels, strictly first editions, 1901-1910, which I sold to the University of Tulsa, and bought a car on the proceeds.

I did my first book fair at The Rougemont Hotel in Exeter in 1975 when the PBFA was barely off the ground. I remember lugging an enormous coffin-shaped object which was my bookcase and listening to stories of dealers who had taken £400 or £4000. I had taken £40 and didn't exhibit at another fair for over twenty-five years. Nowadays I do the Edinburgh fair, partly because it's an excuse to go to Scotland where my family comes from. In 2011 I exhibited at the Olympia ABA fair for the first time and will do so again. I don't have a website and tend not to look at other booksellers' websites. It's mostly vanity as they also list their stock in the big databases like ABE which is a much quicker way of finding a book. I list my books on ABE and on the ILAB website from which I sell something perhaps once a quarter. I'm only there out of loyalty and indolence.

There isn't enough material nowadays for me to deal exclusively in my speciality of English literature from 1780 to 1920. I have an advertisement in *Yellow Pages* and, living in the back of beyond, I have to take what comes – books on windmills, game birds and so on. It can be fun but I'm always happiest when I can get back to the nineteenth century where I feel most comfortable. I tend to be very enthusiastic about lesser known literary figures because there's more to find out about them. I still experience the thrill of the chase, but nowadays I derive as much pleasure from the research as the search.

I'm attracted to the minor late Romantics such as George Darley and Thomas Lovell Beddoes whose work gives me a lot of pleasure. Many of them were anguished and unfulfilled people who felt that they could do better. Herbert Edwin Clarke (1852-1912), a completely forgotten poet on the fringes of the Pre-Raphaelites, is a good example of a peripheral figure that deserves more attention. I bought a couple of his manuscript notebooks which I sold to the University of Birmingham. I very seldom ask a customer why they bought something – it's not good manners – but, as it was a library and I had the librarian on the telephone, I did in this case. He said that the manuscripts were ideal research material. It was very pleasing to find a librarian with the money and the enthusiasm, and I'm delighted that somebody is now working on Clarke.

Not far away from me in Devon there is a wonderful collection in private hands of the works of Henry Francis Lyte, hymn-writer, book collector and Vicar of Brixham, where he wrote 'Abide with me' in the summer of 1847. Lyte's most famous hymn was first sung (to his own tune) at his memorial service later in the same year. In the private collection there is a copy of the first printing of the hymn, as it was handed out in the church. This kind of material gives me enormous pleasure and I would love to introduce a scholar to the collection one day.

I found my most exciting archive in a sale in Exeter. It was a huge tranche of the papers of a Napoleonic officer, Lieutenant-General Baron Thiébault (1769-1846), which I bought together with Maggs Brothers. I spent the next four months burning with excitement as I found out more about Thiébault's experiences in Italy with the French army. It was such an extraordinary adventure that at first I assumed it was a novel. Thiébault fell in love with a beautiful young woman who was married to a much older Italian aristocrat. With Nelson and the British fleet in the Bay of Naples, he persuaded the Italian couple that their only chance of escape was to travel in his carriage with the retreating French army. The description of the atmosphere in the carriage is quite electric, with the presence of the secret lovers and the thoroughly suspicious husband who had been forced to accept the help of his wife's seducer. I love working with manuscript material. Of course content is terribly important, but so is the voice. I want to hear the person talking. The archive was sold in 2004 to Yale, which already had some of Thiébault's papers. The Baron's fairly rollicking memoirs were published fifty years after his death.

When Maggs acquired the enormous library of John Fowles in 2007, two years after his death, I was asked to handle the pre-twentieth-century books. We met in

Lyme Regis and it took three of us ten hours to pack the books. It was the biggest collection that I have ever moved and over the last five years I have produced three catalogues devoted to it. Fowles began his book collecting at Francis Norman's shop in Hampstead. He had a bookplate of a magpie and a blind-stamp 'John Fowles Lyme Regis', and annotated his books with much underlining of passages and scoring in margins.

Fowles was a man of extraordinarily catholic interests and a voracious reader as a stimulant to his own writing. In his diary for 1963, the year in which *The Collector* was published, Fowles noted that he collected books 'for reasons that would make most bibliophiles spit – because I want to read them'. His knowledge of English and French literature was enormous. He was fascinated by natural history, particularly pre-Darwinian geology, and ecology and conservation, and was very involved with the Lyme Regis Museum. As a writer Fowles might be considered a little unfashionable these days, but he still has his devotees who collect him keenly. Typically they were young in the 1960s and 1970s, and had grown up with *The Magus* which was very much a book of its time.

My most recent catalogue is devoted to the book collection of Jonathan Gili, distinguished film-maker and manic collector of everything small from hotel sewing kits to glass-domed snowstorms of which he had thousands. He liked association and presentation copies of novels, and had inherited a lot of books from his Catalan father Joan Gili of the Dolphin Book Company. Jonathan was married to Phillida, the daughter of Reynolds Stone, from whom more books poured into their house in Fulham. At the time of Jonathan's death, the house was so full of books that you had to walk sideways up the stairs.

All booksellers have stories of wonderful things that they have found, but I don't think that they really add much to your understanding of them as a person. It's not just a question of being good at bookselling; it has to be good for you, providing a living and a consuming interest which gets you up in the morning and probably keeps you up late at night. I'm eternally glad that I found it – or that it found me. I can think of more sensible occupations but I can't think of any more pleasurable.

## Reading Between the Lines ✒ Roger Gaskell

A book is like an archaeological site. Each layer has significance and meaning: on the substratum of paper with its inked impressions of type are deposited the evidence of the book's manufacture, of the way the book was handled and read, how it moved from place to place, how it was understood and appreciated by contemporary and later owners. The book tells the story of the text in a way that edited texts, or even a high-resolution digital copy cannot. And each one is different, and adds a little to the story. As far as possible, I like to buy and sell books which have not been restored, with signs of use and other evidence which can add to our understanding of the text. And I enjoy selling them to rare-book libraries where so much of the scholarship and resources which we depend on as booksellers is generated.

I was familiar with rare-book libraries from an early age. As a small child I was taken to swim in the open-air pool at Emmanuel College, Cambridge, where my grandfather, H.S. Bennett, author of *English Books and Readers*, was Librarian. Then in Glasgow I would visit my father, Philip Gaskell, at work in Glasgow University Library where he was Keeper of Special Collections (though it was riding up and down in the antiquated lift that I remember rather than the old books); and then back in Cambridge in the Wren Library of Trinity College. But it was printing rather than old books that I first learned from my father. In 1953 he had founded the Water Lane Press as a bibliographical teaching press and ran it for seven years. When I took up printing as a teenager we set up a  press room at home with the counterweight Albion from the Water Lane Press, a Golding table top platen and a treadle platen bought for me as my sixteenth-birthday present. We had cases of 22-point Caslon founders' type, a fount of Ehrhardt cast up in Monotype by Cambridge University Press, and some display faces. I did mostly jobbing printing but a pamphlet about Ardtornish, on the West Coast of Scotland, where we spent family holidays, exists in sheets somewhere and is the longest example of my printing.

At the grammar school in Cambridge I had an inspirational biology teacher who taught the Nuffield biology course which had recently been introduced as part of the new approach to science teaching. The aim of the Nuffield Project was to encourage curiosity and enquiry and I went on to read Biochemistry at the University of Bristol. I feel very strongly that the sciences are as good an education for life as the humanities and it irritates me that there is still something of a hierarchical relationship between them. When it became clear that I was not doing well enough to make a career in science, at least, not in the field of research,

I began to think in terms of scientific publishing or journalism. During my final year at Bristol, my father suggested that I approach Quaritch, which I dutifully did – although without much enthusiasm – and prepared by reading my father's *A New Introduction to Bibliography* and John Carter's *ABC for Book Collectors*. There was no opening at the time, but shortly before I graduated Nicholas Poole-Wilson offered me a job. I remember thinking that I would take it for a year while I worked out what I really wanted to do.

I joined Quaritch in 1973 and worked in the British Topography and Art departments before moving to Natural History, and the Science and Medicine department of which I eventually became the manager. Although I learnt a considerable amount from Howard Radcliffe in the Natural History department, there was no obvious plan on the firm's part for training me. I was fortunate to have absorbed a lot simply from my family background and being in contact with great books, booksellers and collectors. Although I had a science degree, I didn't have the type of knowledge that was relevant to the books with which I was dealing. I started to go to conferences on the history of science – not only because I was keen to learn more about the subject, but also because I was interested to discover what was going on in academic circles as this had a direct influence on institutional buying, an increasingly important part of our business which I wanted to encourage.

After eight years at Quaritch I was beginning to think about setting up on my own when Johnny Boyle suggested that I contact William Rees-Mogg, who had just bought Dawsons of Pall Mall, which had a strong reputation in the history of science. William was in the process of combining it with the English literature specialists Pickering & Chatto which he owned. The two firms were brought together in Dawsons' premises with Roger McCrow, Dawsons' manager and a specialist in books on Economics, in overall control. Johnny pointed out that William would need a specialist in the history of science and I was duly appointed to run the department, working very closely with Roger in the early days to combine the two businesses. When Roger left after a few years to set up his own business, I became managing director of Pickering & Chatto Ltd. I've always been comfortable with technology and had designed the computer system for Quaritch, although no hardware was actually installed by the time I left. At Pickering we had an IBM PC with an 8088 chip and a 10KB external hard drive; I think we were one of the first antiquarian firms to have a computer.

It was invigorating to work for William Rees-Mogg, who has an extraordinary talent for optimism and wide knowledge of books. He had very clear ideas about the business and inevitably we had our disagreements, but it was always a good working relationship. William was interested in the firm's history and wanted to revive the publishing side of William Pickering's original business. He came up with the idea of 'The Pickering Masters', a series of the collected works and correspondence of major figures in the history of ideas and literature, which has developed into one of the most important scholarly publishing ventures of recent years. William and I chose the subjects and I commissioned the editors. The works of Malthus, Babbage and Darwin were the first books in the series. In the case of Charles Babbage, the full range of his writing was not at all well known or appreciated when we published it in 1989 as the second title in 'The Pickering Masters'.

My work included liaising with academic editors, whose natural approach is textual, and to ensure that their editing was informed by knowledge of the physical books. Textual critics are not always sufficiently familiar with the conditions in which early publishing took place and how those conditions affect the texts that have come down to us. The experience was an opportunity to acquire further insight into the academic use of texts and the production side appealed to me very much – I was a printer again.

It was a heavy work-load, though we now had Melanie McGrath running the publishing business on a day-to-day basis. In the bookshop I was responsible for planning catalogue programmes, attending book fairs, managing staff as well as running my own department. Meanwhile my wife and I had moved to the country and were renovating an old house in Cambridgeshire. We had young children and I had reached a point where I wanted my work and family life to be more integrated. This was surely the point to start my own business.

I left Pickering & Chatto in 1989 and started Roger Gaskell Rare Books. I had built up almost no stock before leaving the firm to avoid any conflict of interest. I had been used to living on a good salary and knew that I had to hit the ground running. My first catalogue appeared within six months of my leaving Pickering, and contained books bought from other dealers with money borrowed from the bank, and a group of books on consignment from Richard Arkway. I think the first book I sold was a copy of Sir William Dugdale's *The History of Imbanking and Draining* that I had been allowed to buy while I was at Pickering as Engineering was not one of our subjects. It is an appropriate book for me, living on the edge of the Fens, and it is closely related to seventeenth-century English science and the Royal Society which has always fascinated me. It was bought by Alice Schreyer for the University of Delaware; I don't know if Alice knows that she was my first customer, but I am very grateful to her, and, since moving to Chicago, she has remained a loyal supporter. When a customer orders a book, they are in effect saying, 'This is interesting', validating your decision to buy it, research it and pass on the knowledge and the book.

My first and subsequent catalogues have been designed by Tony Kitzinger and working with him on catalogue layouts over the years has been one of my great pleasures. The first catalogue sold very well but there were some sticky years ahead in the early 1990s and I had to borrow more money. Despite the anxieties of sole trading, one of the joys of the book trade is the network of support. Booksellers are very collaborative and because many of us work on our own, there is always someone at the other end of the telephone to commiserate with, or who will check something in a reference book, or give advice on how to handle an awkward customer.

I joined the ABA Committee when the Code of Good Practice was being drawn up; the first point deals with the accurate bibliographical description of material offered for sale. When I said that a generally recognised vocabulary of technical terms was essential for describing books correctly, I was handed the job of compiling 'The Terms of the Trade', which first appeared in the 2000-2001 *Handbook of the Antiquarian Booksellers Association,* and has been reprinted with minor revisions in subsequent years. Voltaire's *Dictionnaire philosophique portatif* was conceived as 'propaganda by dictionary'. I was reminded of this phrase when compiling 'The Terms of the Trade' which contains some examples of a deliberately polemical nature, particularly in the sections on 'Provenance' and 'References'. Members of the trade have accused me of being idealistic, but I see no reason not to have the highest standards of bibliographical description. The ABA continues to push for this, and there is certainly a better understanding today of bibliographical and copy-specific issues.

Since the publication in 1985 of William Rees-Mogg's *How to Buy Rare Books,* to which I contributed, there have been some significant changes, particularly in terms of the very different tools available for buying, selling and researching books. But the three factors in deciding, as a dealer, whether to buy a book have not changed – the intellectual content, the copy, and the rarity. These are the elements that influence the price. Obviously an extraordinarily important work can be very common and so one has to understand the effect of rarity on the price.

Although standards of presentation and description of rare books are in general very much higher than they were, I feel that the internet is having a deleterious effect because it tends to reduce everything to the lowest common denominators, the title and the price of the book. When you compare two copies of the same book online, the most obvious point of comparison is the price. Everybody likes a bargain and the internet makes it harder for the collector or the librarian to resist the cheapest copy on offer in favour of a more expensive copy, perhaps in an unrestored contemporary binding or with other attributes that are important. Digitisation is also skewing library buying at the moment. It's particularly unfortunate in the case of British books as the vast majority printed before 1800 are available as digital surrogates from Early English Books Online, and Eighteenth Century Collections Online. Given the choice of buying a book for which there is a digitised copy – even of poor quality, as EEBO and ECCO files are, being based on old microfilm – or a book for which there is no substitute, the librarian is not unjustified in choosing the latter. This in some cases makes it harder to sell English books and will result in gaps in library collections which may be hard to fill later. When every book has been digitised, librarians who are buying for text in this way will have to stop worrying about what's online or stop buying books altogether. But in any case I believe that libraries should acquire books which have information over and above the text.

Libraries will continue to buy because since the 1980s most of the money comes from restricted endowments; but what they buy will change. We're already seeing an increased emphasis on manuscripts and archives and on libraries acquiring heavily annotated books, regardless of whether they already have a copy of the edition. In general, for printed books we will see a much greater emphasis on copy-specific features. In my vision of the future, libraries will buy multiple copies of the same book because each one has a different attribute which adds to our understanding of its intellectual content. This will also of course be good news for bibliographers, who know that you only really understand a book when you have seen at least two copies, preferably side by side.

The thrill for me is increasingly not the buying and selling of books but the books themselves. I have done some research on the printing of illustrations in books – what I call the bibliography of images – and would like to do more. It is an area that has so far been little studied. I do a small amount of teaching in Cambridge for the Department of the History and Philosophy of Science. In December I'm giving a lecture on 'Science, Illustration and the Royal Society' in the new book-collecting series organised by the Institute of English Studies (London University) and the ABA Educational Trust. Next summer I'm teaching a course on 'The Illustrated Scientific Book' at Rare Book School, University of Virginia. I enjoy sharing what I have learnt about books and using that knowledge toward a greater understanding of book history. This is what motivates me as a bookseller.

# *Going Native* ∾ Michael Graves-Johnston

People know me as Oscar – which I picked up at school in Ireland where Michael is such a common name. It was the least derogatory name that I was given and it has stuck. My mother was from Limerick and my father from Armagh, where I grew up in a large house full of books. There was no television, and radio in Ireland was very limited and so one relied on the printed word for almost everything. By the time I left prep school, I had read the works of English and Irish authors, Russian, French and even Chinese. There wasn't much else to do as a child. In the late 1960s I went to Trinity College Dublin to read Philosophy and Psychology. While I was a student I helped a friend who was selling books to customers in America. It was only a temporary job and at that stage I had no interest in books beyond reading them.

When I left university in 1970, very few of my contemporaries expected to find a job. There was a recession in Britain and a war in Ireland which had a very depressing effect upon the whole economy. I started to rebuild old cars as something to do to make money. Cars tend to rust away very quickly in Ireland because of the damp climate. Within a short time I realised how difficult it was to run a business as one after another of my suppliers in Belfast became smoking holes in the ground. On one occasion I narrowly avoided being killed when I was driving one minute behind a car that was blown up. When you're in your early twenties, you tend to think no more than a few months ahead and I wasn't particularly worried about my long-term prospects. The car-repair business eventually became impossible to run and I went to London, where my father had arranged for me to meet someone who was setting up a television channel. Nobody offered me anything and I went back to Ireland and found a job in Dublin in the fashion business, manufacturing clothing. My role was managerial and I found it quite fun for a short time.

The clothing business petered out and I came back to London in 1974 and spent a year or so driving a delivery van. My then girlfriend and I had some friends who were working in West Africa and in 1976 we went to visit them and had a very interesting time travelling around. On our second day we were arrested in the People's Republic of Benin because we didn't have the right papers. We managed to talk our way out of trouble but not without experiencing something of the extraordinary place. The republic had only recently been established and was in the grip of a Marxist regime. The only other Europeans in Benin were East Germans whose papers were in perfect order. The Chief of Police was not only very drunk but psychotic and convinced that we were intent on overthrowing his country.

One has to admire the endurance of the early explorers, who had no choice but to walk across the southern part of West Africa, unless they were carried. We travelled around in cars and lorries. Horses aren't found in the southern part along the coast because they are killed by the tsetse fly. We were in Upper Volta, or Burkina Faso as it is now called, when my girlfriend got malaria. She was turned away from the American hospital as she wasn't American. The local hospital was like something out of *Monty Python*, and she was eventually treated by an African woman who took some leaves off a tree in her compound, boiled them, rubbed them on my friend and broke the fever.

When I came back from my second trip to Africa in 1978 I decided that I wanted to deal in books. John Hewitt, an art-dealer friend, advised me that there was no money in books on philosophy and psychology and I should sell books on Africa. I advertised in the *Bookdealer* and went around London collecting material for my first catalogue of African art, archaeology and ethnography. John gave me some names for the mailing list and I found the relevant museums and libraries in *The World of Learning* and the other reference works that the trade relied on before the internet made information so accessible. Between 1970 and 1997 the British Museum's Department of Ethnography was known as the Museum of Mankind. William 'Bill' Fagg, the Keeper of the Department, had overseen the transfer of the collections from Bloomsbury to Burlington Gardens and was the author of several landmark studies on African sculpture. He regarded the term 'primitive' as pejorative in the context of his subject, and was responsible for the change of name to ethnographic or tribal art.

By the 1970s tribal art had become a recognised genre in collecting with all the major auction houses holding regular sales. There was a dealer called Michael Wimbledon who had a shop off High Street, Kensington, specialising in books on the subject. When the lease ran out he moved to private premises in Forest Hill. I briefly thought about opening a shop, but decided against it after wasting six months arguing with estate agents over premises in Pimlico. The experience taught me that the time would have been better spent buying and selling books from home. I enjoy the freedom of not having the overheads that go with a shop or employing staff. It enables me to be flexible and to alter the way I buy and sell as circumstances demand. I've never been busier than I am at the moment or perhaps I'm just not as young as I was. Whatever the reason for it, the recession hasn't noticeably upset my business. I'm still learning how to sell books and consider myself to be better at buying them. Over the years I've built up very good clients and so I must be doing something right.

Historically the market for books on Africa was dominated by South African collectors of books on big game hunting, the great Victorian explorers and the Boer

War – a market that rather petered out during the Apartheid years. The climate in South Africa is much more suitable for books than, for example, in West Africa where they don't survive unless kept in a sealed and air-conditioned environment. I can always tell if a book has been in West Africa – even if it's been well looked after. There are a few indigenous book collectors in Nigeria but almost everything is against them from the climate to the government. I spent a week showing two Nigerian librarians around London recently. They came from Kano in the north of the country and were very interested in learning about all aspects of librarianship. They are typical of the people in Nigeria who are trying to do good things but find it very difficult because of the level of corruption. It's not easy for them to communicate with us because people treat an e-mail from Nigeria with great suspicion.

Around the time of the Australian bicentenary in 1988, marking the first permanent European settlement, there was a tremendous demand for books on Australia. In many cases the prices haven't been matched since. In the 1980s books on Tibet came to the fore when Hollywood began to take an interest in Buddhism. A few years earlier they had been of no commercial value whatsoever in my experience. Now the attention is on China, but people tell me at the Hong Kong book fair that interest is limited at the moment to photograph albums and illustrated material. But if you take the example of the Japanese market, it started off quite slowly and gradually became more interested in foreign-language books on Japan and then foreign-language books *per se*. The Chinese are a learned culture with a great respect for books and will probably follow the same pattern.

Today antiquarian bookselling is about selling anything that is out of the ordinary or, in the case of a photograph album, unique. I try to sell books that are unusual in some way. Condition is also very important. First editions still have a great following but, in many cases, I slightly wonder what their purpose is. A friend told me that a gentleman always has three copies of a book – one to read, one to keep and one to lend. If you buy a first edition for a huge amount of money, you probably won't do any of those things. I have around 12,000 books in total of which 4000 are on the internet, which accounts for 10 per cent of my sales. It's a wonderful medium for buying but hopeless for selling antiquarian books. In internet bookselling, you make a sale but you don't make a customer.

The internet has made antiquarian books more valuable and secondhand books much less so. Years ago I used to sell the autobiography of Harry Hamilton Johnston, *The Story of My Life*, 1923, for £75. I bought one a couple of years ago and looked it up on ABE where there were around 200 copies ranging between $300 and £1. Harry Johnston was a very interesting man, a successful colonial administrator, a novelist and a painter who moved in influential circles and his autobiography is fascinating for many reasons apart from its African importance. But it is now worthless to me. If there are more than, say, three copies of a secondhand book on ABE, it will be difficult to sell; if there are more than thirty, you've had it.

In the mid-1980s I wrote a computer program to catalogue my books. It enabled me to replace the laborious business of typing up index cards to produce catalogues which I increased from two to six a year. I still produce a hard copy of my catalogue as a lot of people prefer to read a piece of paper than a computer screen and we are after all dealing with the printed word. I don't use new media such as Facebook. Encryption technologies on the internet are based on codes which are being broken all the time. It's better not to have too much information out there.

I was asked by Paul Minet to go on to the ABA's internet Committee as it was then called. They were having difficulties with their website which we managed to sort out and it now works very well. You can't just build a website and leave it; you have to keep fiddling with it and working on things. On the ABA Council people are constantly coming up with ideas to make things better for the members. Paul Mills, a dealer in South Africa who is a member of the ABA, runs AntiquarianAuctions. com which holds internet-based auctions every five weeks. Booksellers upload stock under their own name and deal directly with the buyer after the sale. There is a commission charge of 8 per cent on successful sales and no buyer's premium. Paul has offered to provide the software for the ABA to run something similar. I believe that it would be good for our members who are currently losing 30-40 per cent in charges when they buy and sell at auction. The annual ABA subscription is £400 and we need to ensure that it's worth everyone's while economically to be a member.

A lot of booksellers are worried by the development of e-book readers such as Kindle, but it would be far worse if people stopped reading. Printed books are only one way of disseminating knowledge and they will certainly stop being published at their present rate, which is good for our trade as antiquarian books will become more valuable. It is human nature to collect. People like to own something that is in some way different. The world population is increasing; there are fewer and fewer old books; the future of our trade has never been rosier.

## Pushing the Envelope ✑ John Martin

My wife Cathy chose the name of Mayfly for our business in ephemera, books, manuscripts, documents and autographs. The insect, whose short life shines brightly, fits well with the definition of ephemera as the minor transient documents of everyday life. There is of course a huge difference between a piece of ephemera and a piece of waste paper. In 1993 the Centre for Ephemera Studies was inaugurated at the University of Reading in the Department of Typography and Graphic Communication. It was the first of its kind in the world. Whether the study of handwritten and printed ephemera is a scholarly subject in its own right is a matter of debate. Some people argue that it's no more than an adjunct to more formal records, while others appreciate ephemeral documents as evocative reminders of the past with their own contribution to make to the study of history.

My grandfather was a freelance writer and a regular contributor of stories under the name of Radcliffe Martin to *The Boy's Own Paper*. After the First World War he became a copywriter and ultimately a director of Crawford's, the leading advertising agency of the day. My father was also in advertising and his uncle, John Percival Martin, was a Methodist minister who retired to Exmoor and, rather late in life, wrote the *Uncle the Elephant* series of children's books illustrated by Quentin Blake. He began telling the stories to entertain his children who later encouraged him to write them down. They were finally published in book form when he was 84.

My childhood was spent in Hitchin where, from about the age of eight, I frequented Eric Moore's bookshop. I liked to buy books on military history, and also collected memorabilia relating to Britain's so-called small wars of the nineteenth century. In those days Eric employed an assistant who wore a plastic overall and gave the impression that books were a bit insanitary. When the time came I could have asked Eric for a job, but I chose to read Law at university and was articled to a firm in Lincoln's Inn. I spent twenty-five years running a succession of small solicitors' practices, during which time the legal profession changed considerably. It became intensely regulated, leaving the lawyer with very little scope for imagination or creativity, at least, at the level in which I was engaged. I'm sure it's beneficial to have a variety of work experience but, with hindsight, I wish that I had read History.

In 1979 Cathy and I began dabbling in bookselling to supplement our modest incomes. There are very few ideal models for running a bookselling business, in which there is usually an inherent degree of chaos involved. We began by producing a few catalogues during the 1980s mainly containing stock that we had bought from Maurice Rickards's ephemera bazaars. Rickards had founded The Ephemera

Society in 1975 in his home in Fitzroy Square, and was in many ways quite an inspirational person through his writing and lectures. The first ephemera bazaar was held in the following year, and became a regular event, spurring many more dealers to enter the field.

Maurice Rickards was one of the first people to become interested in the idea of image banks. He recognised that there was a market, particularly amongst writers and teachers, for specific images. When I started, you had to trawl the bookshops of Cecil Court looking for illustrated ephemera, or Andrew Block's shop in Bloomsbury, the remnants of whose stock we bought in 1986. Nowadays the idea has come full circle with the huge digital picture libraries on the internet. The Look and Learn History Picture Library (www.lookandlearn.com) provides downloadable images at £2 an item, and includes the Peter Jackson collection of ephemera. Peter Jackson was a founder member of The Ephemera Society. His widow Valerie Jackson-Harris is chairman of the society and custodian of her late husband's collection.

After twenty-five years as a lawyer and my wife as a teacher, during which time we had brought up two children, the time had come to give up our day jobs. The best way for me to describe the difference between bookselling and the law is that I like 95 per cent of the people I meet in bookselling whereas I disliked 95 per cent of them in the law. Our business is run on a shoe-string. My wife looks after sales and does the book-keeping, and we employ a cataloguer. The skill of cataloguing is the ability to draw out the highlights. I'm not particularly good at it but over the years I've become pretty good at finding interesting material. We were very lucky to be left an enormous collection of ephemera by John Bramwell Taylor, who died in 2003. John had been an advertising copywriter before the Second World War when he joined the Royal East Kent Regiment and served in North Africa. On his return he suffered from post-traumatic stress disorder and spent the rest of his working life as a porter at the Travellers Club. He lived a solitary life in Spartan conditions in a rather appalling garret in Notting Hill, and spent his free time trailing around the markets in London looking for interesting items of printed ephemera. He had a deep knowledge of printing history, and was well known to the dealers and collectors in the field. Although John collected in all areas, the material that I sold to the National Fairground Archive at the University of Sheffield, including handbills and flyers for Victorian freak shows, is amongst the most important.

The thrill of the chase is undoubtedly what I enjoy best. Despite the huge amount of information available online, it's still possible to find things that have slipped through the net, so to speak. In fact the sheer volume of information makes it increasingly difficult to assimilate everything. Most booksellers don't have the staff or the time to sift through it all and, in the case of keyword searches, a simple misspelling will return the wrong result. In dealing with ephemera, you very often have to buy a large quantity of rubbish in order to acquire one item of interest. I've always been fascinated by examples of printing in unusual circumstances. A few years ago I had to buy eight boxes of rubbish in a provincial auction because one of them contained an example of a playbill for the Royal Arctic Theatre, devised by Captain Parry as a winter entertainment for his crew during his second voyage in search of the North-West passage in 1821-23. When the boxes of unwanted stuff get out of hand, I take them to the Great Southern Postcard and Paper Fairs at Tolworth Recreation Centre and price everything at £1.

This business can be so dominated by a single collector whose death, divorce or financial difficulties, for example, can cause an entire market to crumble. Steve Forbes's decision to sell his collection of letters and books related to Winston Churchill – the most comprehensive in private hands – robbed that market of its single biggest collector when it was sold by Christie's in 2010. The financial problems of one of the major collectors of English literature and poetry had a direct result on that market taking a tumble, which was perhaps inevitable after the recent death of Chris Johnson whose knowledge and expertise contributed so much to the renaissance of interest in collecting eighteenth-century poetry.

Subjects come and go and you need to be a bit flexible. Michael Portillo's BBC series on great British railway journeys, inspired by George Bradshaw who produced the first railway timetable in 1839, has resulted in a renewed interest in collecting Bradshaw's publications. We're not afraid of going off-piste, as I call it, and buying material outside our normal field. We bought a microphone that had been used by Churchill in one of his wartime broadcasts and sold it successfully. Provenance is of course the key when dealing with artefacts of this kind.

You would be foolish to purchase private papers without checking that the family is aware that they are on the market. When papers come into an estate, there is often a great temptation simply to dump them, unless they are very obviously of some significance. However, it is not uncommon for members of the family to come forward when they see the value ascribed by the market to what they previously regarded as waste paper.

The ABA security committee was successful recently in helping to convict the person responsible for a large number of autograph forgeries on eBay. Typically they would be cheap editions of a book with just a signature. I would always be wary of buying a signed copy without at least an inscription or a letter to support it. As for printed forgeries, there is very little original ephemera to be found relating to Jack the Ripper. A genuine example of the public notice produced by the police and pushed through letter boxes warning people about the murders in the East End is very difficult to find. *The Titanic* is also a subject that attracts forgery. Everything has been forged from life jackets to menus. Ian Fleming is also popular with the forgers. A colleague and I had a lucky find recently in a provincial auction where, amongst a quantity of rubbish, there was a letter written to a minor Antarctic explorer by Ian Fleming when he was working in naval intelligence during the war. It is the only known letter to survive from him at that period in his career.

In the past booksellers never quite knew what to do with ephemera apart from put it in a drawer. Since we started in the business there has been an increased awareness of the subject, partly encouraged by the huge rise in interest in family history, although it's made some people think that grandpa's ration book must be of value. We're at a stage where nostalgia plays a big part in the market. This – combined with the fact that a lot of people have very little concept of time – explains why a cornflakes packet from the 1950s can command more interest than a document of great antiquity. In the course of last week we bought a Spanish deed from 1547, a collection of letters written by a prisoner of war in a Japanese camp, and by someone who was killed in the Boer War. It's the variety of ephemera that appeals to me, and the opportunity to indulge my enjoyment in the widest sense of what has gone before.

## Managing Expectations ❧ Philip Brown

A Blackwellian is someone who might not be learned himself, but understands the traditions of academia and takes pride in them. The firm is almost like a college within Oxford University. It has given me the opportunity to meet all kinds of interesting people and opened the door to the world of learning and literature. The remarkable thing about the Blackwell family is that it produced three generations of brilliant bookmen – Benjamin Henry, who founded the firm in 1879, Sir Basil and Richard Blackwell. When I first met Sir Basil, he was in his seventies but still a regular presence in the shop. He was always addressed as 'Gaffer'. Benjamin Henry wanted his son to develop the publishing side of the firm. In 1916 Dorothy L. Sayers became Gaffer's first editorial assistant. He sensed immediately that she wouldn't stay very long, remarking that it was like harnessing a racehorse to a plough and, in 1920, she left Blackwell's to go into advertising, publishing her first novel in 1923. The firm remains in family hands and, although the publishing side has been sold, the chain of forty or so shops continues to thrive as a niche academic bookseller, with shops on several university campuses and a loyal customer base of international alumni.

President Clinton comes back to Oxford from time to time and visits us. He was in the rare books department recently and my colleague took a photograph of him holding a George Washington letter. On one occasion the President asked the deputy manager if he would like him to sign Blackwell's visitors' book. No one had any idea if we had such a thing or, if we did, where it was kept. The deputy manager, with great resourcefulness, grabbed the electrician's book, opened it at a new page and President Clinton signed it. Luckily he didn't turn back to see who else had signed the book as he would have found a lot of requests to replace light bulbs in the Norrington Room. Bill Clinton's page has now been removed and framed.

I'm only the fifth manager of Blackwell's antiquarian department since the firm's inception. Benjamin Henry originally began trading as a dealer in rare and secondhand books from a tiny room that soon expanded into the main Blackwell's shop at 48-51 Broad Street. William 'Rex' King joined the antiquarian department in the last few years of Benjamin Henry's life and, after thirty-four years, Rex was succeeded by Edward East and he, in turn, by Peter Fenemore who employed me.

I left Bicester School at the age of sixteen. It was a dreadful place in those days, but I was fortunate to have an excellent English teacher who encouraged my love of literature. I decided to look for a job at Blackwell's and joined the firm in August 1966. I enjoyed it from my first day. I started with Geoff Neill in the Wants Book department in the newly-opened Norrington Room, the largest room dedicated to bookselling in Europe. My job was to go around the various departments collecting the books for which we had received institutional orders. If the book was out of print, the details were recorded on a five-by-three-inch card, of which we had around 100,000, and advertisements were placed in the Books Wanted section of *The Clique*. When Geoff Neill retired suddenly, he was briefly succeeded by someone else and it wasn't long before I found myself running the department. There was something about the whole process that I found very exciting, not least buying something for X and selling it for Y.

In January 1968, Peter Fenemore, who was working in the antiquarian department in Ship Street, asked if I would come and work for him. Edward East was the manager at the time and had been there since 1923. It was very surprising news, as we hardly knew each other, and I shall always be grateful to Peter for giving me the opportunity to become a rare book dealer. Peter gave me an introduction to the gist of things and then I was expected to find my own way. It was a very steep learning curve, particularly as Blackwell's customers expect the best in terms of bibliographical standards and service. Peter had a particular enthusiasm at the time for private press books and modern first editions, both fields in which condition is so important. While I was learning how to catalogue them, I was also developing my own personal interest in fine printing and book illustration. A Blackwell's catalogue description should be recognisable by the amount of information it contains, particularly regarding condition. When a customer opens a parcel, the contents should match or exceed his expectations. Dealing with modern books is a good discipline for general antiquarian bookselling, because you have to concern yourself so strictly with condition. It's best to start with the highest standards; you can always adjust them accordingly.

Not long after I started, Peter became very enthusiastic about the field of transport and technology, and rapidly became a major dealer in the subject, producing a brilliant catalogue (865) in 1969. The following year John Manners joined the firm and began to develop his great expertise in eighteenth-century English literature. John had a wonderful personality and was brilliant with customers. Peter became manager of the antiquarian department in 1971, and we were joined by Derek McDonnell in 1972. Derek is the best bookseller I have ever worked with. He had the ability to take a subject, for example, antiquarian continental books, and develop it from nothing to a substantial turnover within a year. He has a good eye for a book, and can catalogue well, and played to the strengths of Blackwell's international mailing list. Derek left Blackwell's in 1976, and John in 1984, both to join Quaritch. As Peter occasionally remarked, Blackwell's had a tradition of training talented and entrepreneurial rare book dealers. Barry McKay, Simon Luterbacher, Ron Taylor and Karen Thomson have all worked here.

By the late 1970s the antiquarian department was beginning to outgrow its premises in Ship Street. Fyfield Manor near Kingston Bagpuize was purchased in 1979 to house the department, and was officially opened in October of that year with a centenary antiquarian catalogue to mark the occasion. Coincidentally, J.H. Parker, the Oxford bookseller, lived at Fyfield Manor during the late nineteenth century. Richard Blackwell was Chairman when Fyfield was purchased. He had a vision of acquiring a beautiful house, not far from where the Blackwell family lived, filling it with rare books and providing accommodation for visiting librarians. It was a wonderful idea, but in practice they tended to roam around the house setting off the alarms and, when the recession started in 1981, American librarians stopped coming over.

John Manners had been fiercely opposed to the antiquarian department's move to Fyfield, and had given Richard Blackwell a list of seventy-three objections. Meanwhile the building required endless maintenance and, when the roof had to be redone at a cost of £1 a slate, we couldn't go on throwing money at it. In 1991 we returned to Oxford to premises in Holywell Street, and to the main Broad Street shop in 1999 where the department is now located on the second floor.

Peter Fenemore retired shortly after we moved back to Oxford, and I became manager. I was confident that, with my colleague John King, we could make a success of the retail rare books business. I knew how I wanted to take the department forward but, in the environment of a large company, it was a case of educating the regional manager to the money-making possibilities of rare books. Peter Fenemore hadn't liked exhibiting at book fairs, and the firm had stopped doing them in the 1950s, although it had been a founder-member of the Antiquarian Booksellers Association and both Benjamin Henry and Sir Basil had served as President. By the 1980s I was keen that we should start again and, after a number of successful ABA fairs in London, I persuaded Blackwell's that we should exhibit at American fairs. It took three reports and the arrival of a new regional manager before I was given the go-ahead.

In 1985, the antiquarian department became the first within Blackwell's to use computers. Today 20 per cent of our business is done on the web, either via our website or, to a lesser extent, ABE. We also send out e-mail catalogues, but our hard-copy catalogue remains the most effective method of selling books. Our best-selling subjects are private press books, modern first editions and science which is Andrew Hunter's department. Andrew joined us three years ago and brought his expertise with him, and his knowledge of the institutional market. Derek Walker looks after Classics which, together with Theology, remain strong subjects for Blackwell's with its academic tradition. Derek created our website and is extremely talented in all aspects of IT.

The market for private press books is particularly strong in America, and I would always try to exhibit something special at a book fair there – for example, the Golden Cockerel edition of the *Four Gospels*, decorated by Eric Gill, or indeed anything by the Golden Cockerel Press. My own love of fine printing and book illustration began with the work of Eric Gill and David Jones. Shortly after I joined Blackwell's I began collecting St Dominic's Press. When I first started, it was possible to pick up these books, of which many are pamphlets, for as little as £2. However, the prices steadily increased and when I married and we started a family, I wasn't able to afford to add regularly to my collection. As I always tell people, you should buy books because you love them, not for investment. If you make a profit when you come to sell them, that's the cream on top.

Sir Basil Blackwell loved private press books and had a great eye for fine printing. In 1921 he rescued the Shakespeare Head Press when it was on the point of bankruptcy, recognising the potential of the typographical genius of Bernard Newdigate. Newdigate produced many beautiful editions for the press – the Froissart (1927-8), Chaucer (1928-9), Spenser (1930), Chapman's Homer (1930-1), Drayton (1941), and Malory's *Morte d'Arthur* (1935) which Blackwell considered Newdigate's greatest achievement. In 1942 the St Aldate's premises were taken over by the Americans for war purposes, and all the equipment dispersed – or quite possibly dumped in a skip – including a printing press that had belonged to the Kelmscott Press.

At times my wife Sue has regarded Blackwell's as the third person in our marriage. I am in love with this job and could have carried on until my eighties. For this reason I have chosen to make a complete break. In April I retired from bookselling after 47 years. I plan to spend my retirement pursuing other enthusiasms, including bird-watching and gardening, but I've already been approached by one or two customers who have libraries that they would like me to catalogue. I've known many of Blackwell's customers for over thirty years and friendships have developed. That's the wonderful thing about this trade; it's so much more than the simple exchange of books and money.

# Bookselling under the Microscope ❧ Jolyon Hudson

My parents were English but I was born and brought up in Scotland, where my father had a small engineering works in Lanarkshire. I went through school life in a slight daze. It transpired that I have dyslexia, and Asperger syndrome, which gives you a different way of looking at the world. People with Asperger's often have a tendency to collect things, even if it's only car registration numbers. I've been collecting 78 r.p.m records since the age of seven, and now have around 20,000. Much of this collection will eventually go to the British Library to fill gaps in their sound archive. I'm interested in the preservation and documentation of sound recording, particularly the changes in musical performance practice and our reaction to them. The question of why something is considered normal in its time but abnormal in another is something that fascinates me. This applies equally to the performance of a Beethoven string quartet and to the spoken word. Recordings of Shakespeare exist from the 1890s, and the declamatory style of the actors has changed so much in the last century that they would be laughed off the stage today.

Book collecting is also driven by fashion, apart from a certain number of key works that will always hold their own. Many of the books that I sold when I started out in the business thirty-five years ago are considered to be old dogs today, while items that were sold in bundles are now thought to be the high-water mark of saleability. As recently as the 1970s, a book in its original boards was not thought to be as desirable as a nicely rebound volume – well, in Glasgow at any rate.

Having left school in 1976 without any qualifications, I went straight to the employment bureau in Hamilton, where I was offered two jobs based on my interest in collecting. I could either work on a removal van or be a porter for the local auctioneer. I chose the porter's job with Edmiston's in Glasgow for the salary of £750 a year. There was a sale every Wednesday and the pace was relentless. The porters did everything from sweeping the floor to cataloguing the general sales. We often had to deal with the contents of whole houses and to handle the detritus of human life, which might include a bloodstained mattress from someone's death bed. It certainly gave me a vivid awareness of the cycle of life and death, and the enduring nature of objects compared to our transient existence. It gave me a feeling for the object as something that possesses its own life, in most cases considerably longer than mine. Some dealers have difficulty in parting with their books; I'm only too glad to handle them and to learn something from each item. I don't need to possess the object itself (excepting records of course).

The books would arrive in tea chests and I was given the job of putting them out on trestle tables for Charlie Douglas to go through them. Charles Edmiston Douglas was the owner of the company and a descendant of one of the founders. It was very much a local sale room. Most of the dealers came from Glasgow or Edinburgh – Mrs McNaughtan, or young Miss Strong, Cooper Hay for John Smith, James Thin, Ian and Senga Grant and Bruce Marshall were all regulars at our sales. Some of the dealers were very elderly and a few had been to the final sale of the contents of Hamilton Palace sold by Christie's in the palace itself in 1919. I remember one old boy, who had been paid off by the Army after the First World War, spent all his money on a lot containing silver plate. It's incredible to think that Hamilton Palace plate was being sold from a barrow in the  streets of Glasgow.

A couple of years after I joined, the firm was taken over by Christie's and was re-named Christie's & Edmiston's. The first time that I took a sale I was so nervous that I had to go to the doctor for some kaolin and morphine, a bucket kindly placed under the rostrum stool by my colleagues. Although I have a near-photographic memory for books and can remember something from thirty years ago in minute detail, I have no memory for names. Before the paddle bidding system was introduced, I would make a diagram of where people were sitting, and then they would move somewhere else and I had no idea who they were.

We worked closely with the book department in London, and Hans Fellner would come up to Scotland when we had an entry to an important library. Hans Fellner had run his own book business in Museum Street for twenty years before joining Christie's in 1976. He had suffered a heart attack and it was thought that a regular salary might be less stressful for him than self employment. Hans was my mentor. I owe him an enormous debt of gratitude for all that he taught me. Everything I learnt from my time as an auctioneer fitted me for that task only, but it did not prepare me for the book trade. Auctioneering is a much more rough-and-ready approach; you learn an enormous amount from the quantity and variety of material that passes through your hands, but you don't learn much finesse. Bookselling is all about finesse. Hans Fellner taught me how to *look* at a book. If you have seen a copy a hundred times before, you should look at it again and never think that you know everything about it. He had enormous humility and was always ready to listen to the opinions of less experienced booksellers who might have noticed something that he had missed.

In 1983 we had an entry to the library of Sir Ivar Colquhoun of Luss. The books were in exceptionally fine condition, kept in Chippendale-style bookcases in a room that had never been gas-lit. Candles were used at Rossdhu House until the installation of electricity. The library had been virtually untouched since the eighteenth century, although a few books had found their way on to the market. The Rothschild collection of eighteenth-century printed books and manuscripts contains volumes from the library of Sir James Colquhoun (1741-1805). When the Colquhoun library was sold on 22 March 1984, it was the biggest book sale in Scotland up to that date.

The library at Andrew Carnegie's Skibo Castle was another time capsule in the Highlands. I was asked to do the valuation. Carnegie did not believe in inherited wealth and on his death in 1919, his 30,000-acre estate in Sutherland was left in trust for his daughter to be sold once she had no need for it. It was used occasionally for only a few week at a time over the next sixty years. Meanwhile the house was kept immaculate and heated all year round. Carnegie asked Lord Acton, who had recently been appointed Regius Professor of Modern History at Cambridge, to choose the books which were purchased for the library at Skibo by Hew Morrison, head of the Carnegie Library in Edinburgh. Carnegie wanted to have the best, not necessarily the first, edition of the books recommended by Lord Acton, and to have used copies to give the impression of a working library. He was very disappointed to find that the books on his shelves had been rebound by Henderson & Bisset of Edinburgh in leather on the instructions of Morrison, to whom Carnegie wrote a wonderfully acrid note: 'I asked you to get the best editions of a list of books Lord Acton would furnish you. I never said one word to you about changing the bindings of these gems, never. I now learn that you have spent more money on bindings than the precious gems cost.'

I went to view Skibo in midwinter. I had come by train from Glasgow and the train deposited me at the wrong station so I had to walk, or rather crawl, in the pitch-black darkness along the tracks to the modest little hotel at Invershin. Major Spowers, who had come up from Christie's in London for no good reason but to have a look, arrived in style by plane and taxi from Inverness. To the surprise of the management and the handful of guests, the Major came down to dinner wearing dinner jacket and dress medals. He spoke very loudly and drank copiously thus finishing off my very modest budget for the trip. He was an impressive figure and it's easy to see that many clients would have loved his manner.

At the time of the recession in 1991, Christie's reduced its staff in the Scottish office by almost half. I was given the option of moving to London where I joined the general valuation department and also worked in the book department. It took me many years to come to terms with London after my little Glasgow world. In 1992 it was suggested that I might be the person to run Pickering & Chatto for its new owner. Bill Lese, a retired American businessman, had bought the company from William Rees-Mogg. I consulted Hans Fellner who advised me not to take the job, as he believed that the stock had little value and that the overheads of a big shop in Pall Mall would be crippling. When Lionel and Philip Robinson moved into the same premises in 1930, they did so not for selling, but principally for buying; the shop was in the right location to meet owners of country houses as they came and went from their clubs in St James's. I knew that the great days of Pall Mall as a centre of the book trade had long gone but, typically enough, I believed that everything would be fine and took the job.

Bill Lese liked the idea of a big shop and was prepared to put a certain amount of money into the business. The staff worked their guts out but the overheads were just too high and the company almost went bankrupt. My colleagues had had enough and quite rightly too. Susanne Schulz-Falster, Amanda Hall and Becky Hardie all left Pickering & Chatto to set up their own book businesses. The time had come to leave Pall Mall and move into office premises. I looked at a map and decided that I should try to find somewhere in Conduit Street, as it was ideally situated in relation to Maggs and Quaritch, Sotheby's and Christie's, and Bernard Shapero. Together with my colleagues Ed Smith and Deborah Coltham, we got Pickering & Chatto back on its feet again. And then one day in 1998 in walked Percy Barnevik.

Percy Barnevik, the Swedish businessman, was putting together a library in Stockholm and had the vision and the wealth to pursue it. Barnevik was like a whirlwind going through the London antiquarian trade. He was a man in a hurry and you had to be able to convey information very quickly. He would ask, 'Why should I buy this book?' and you had to give the answer in a few persuasive words. It reminded me of Edwin Wolf's biography of Dr Rosenbach in which there are many wonderful examples of Rosenbach's ability to persuade others to share his enthusiasm for great books. Pickering mainly bought incunabula for Barnevik's collection. The business that we did with him helped us to strengthen our core areas of social sciences, the humanities, medicine, English literature and to develop in other directions.

I think of Pickering & Chatto as dealing in books without pictures, and Marlborough Rare Books as a business of books with pictures. It was therefore a logical move when the opportunity arose in 2005 for the two firms to come together. Bill Lese wanted to retire from the business and Jonathan Gestetner was looking for ways to develop Marlborough Rare Books. When Mickie Brand retired and Ian Marr left in 2005 to set up his own business, Marlborough was rather short of staff. As Jonathan is a great salesman and Pickering had plenty of cataloguers, the two firms could make a perfect fit. I remember walking along New Bond Street with Jonathan discussing how to join the two companies when we spotted a twopence coin on the ground. When we both reached for it, I knew that we could work together.

It was agreed to keep the two trading names of Marlborough Rare Books and Pickering & Chatto, but we are in fact one company – rather like so many businesses today which own a number of different brands. I became manager of both companies, and Pickering moved in 2006 from Conduit Street into Marlborough's premises in New Bond Street. We have retained the identity of the two companies with their different cataloguing styles and subjects. Pickering has been selling to institutional libraries since the nineteenth century and now it's a question of finding the gap on the shelf. This is aggravated by the fact that many libraries are combining their resources and won't buy a book if a copy is available in another library in their geographical area.

The heyday of the bookshop was not in the distant past, but in the 1950s, 1960s and 1970s during the displenishing of the great country-house libraries. Those books have gone into institutional and private collections and we have to make money from an ever-decreasing amount of 'fresh' material. Dealers are now looking at books more in the round, and seeing how they link with other subjects and their place in the society that produced them. We have to be more speculative in what we buy and perhaps, in this process, lift a book from one category to another. Booksellers at the top of their game create new markets and then move on. It's important to develop your interests and to avoid selling the same material, as your descriptions will inevitably be copied in the race to the bottom on the internet.

In the days when J.R. Hartley was telephoning bookshops in *Yellow Pages* looking for his book on fly-fishing, he had to buy the first copy that he found as the search might have gone on for twenty years. Nowadays the search takes twenty seconds. All the J.R. Hartleys have found their books and much of what is left is almost unsaleable. Therefore we have to pay much more attention to what makes a particular copy stand out. Today it's the minutiae that will sell your copy, and the microscope's magnification is getting larger.

# A *Feeling for Books* ~ William Poole

Although I know of people who have continued to be booksellers when their sight has deteriorated or even gone completely, I don't know anyone who has become a bookseller having always been blind. I was born in Malta in 1935 where I lived with my parents until I was sent to England at the age of three to be educated at special schools for the blind. My mother was very reluctant to let me go, but I wouldn't have received a proper education in Valletta and my father's decision prevailed. I have grounds for believing that it was a very traumatic experience for me, because a huge amount of memory regarding the time I spent in Malta before I came to England and my first year at school has been obliterated. The separation from my parents had been so absolute that, when they came to claim me back at the age of nine, they could have been complete strangers. I didn't recognise their speech mannerisms or tone of voice and had no memory of their having been people with whom I had interacted. My father must have sensed that the conversation wasn't going well as I heard my mother say, 'It's all right. He does know who we are.' This wasn't something that had been bargained for in the plan.

My father was in operational charge of the Malta dockyard during the war. The school tried to censor news of what was going on, but inevitably it filtered through and I knew that my father had an important and dangerous job to do. There were a few other children in the school who were for one reason or another separated from their families. Everyone said that it would be a marvellous time when our parents came back, but it didn't work out that way for me. However, I had school friends and there were some teachers, mostly women, who took an interest in me beyond what was required by their work for which I was very grateful. I learnt Braille when I was six and found it absolutely fascinating. Some blind people don't have an aptitude for it and the proportion who learn Braille is comparatively small, but it's very important to those who do. At the age of eight I learnt Braille music notation and thought it was quite magical that you could anatomise music into its constituent parts and write it down.

One of the earliest dreams that I can remember concerns reading Braille. At primary school we were normally given vocabulary lists and excerpts from stories to read but, in my dream, I had a proper book. I looked through it and, although there were signs that I didn't understand, I was making progress. Suddenly, as I ran my fingers over the dots, they started to turn to sugar-like granules and slide off the page making it impossible to read. I woke up with a terrible sense of loss unlike anything that I had experienced before. It was absolutely devastating and for a few days I couldn't get it out of my mind. Fortunately the dream wasn't fulfilled in real life. My parents gave me books as presents and I spent school prizes on buying many more for myself. I was wrapped up in gaining knowledge from reading a very wide range of books, though of course I didn't have the choice available to sighted children. I didn't start buying printed books until I went to university.

A blind person can learn that the grass is green, and some effort was made to teach us at school to appreciate natural phenomena, but it's impossible to convey any idea of the sensation that goes with that knowledge. However, I had no difficulty coping with intellectual ideas, and was very good at mathematics. When I was still at primary school, I was given a book of Greek myths and it determined me to learn about the ancient world, which was later to become my speciality both as a collector and a dealer.

I went up to Oxford, to Lincoln College, in 1954 to read Classical Mods for the first part of my degree and then changed to English. I chose to do a combination of subjects because I thought that there might be a shortage of appropriate texts in Braille for the study of ancient history in which, in any case, I wasn't as interested as I later became. Meanwhile English gave me the opportunity to learn Anglo-Saxon, Middle English and Old Norse which I enjoyed, and also introduced me to the study of bibliography. Oxford had a procedure which made it possible in the days before computer technology for a blind student with an amanuensis to take examinations under the same conditions as a sighted student. Some of my school friends didn't find Oxford congenial but I settled in quite quickly. Of course you had to deal with people's assumptions about what you could or couldn't do. In my first term a student knocked on the door one evening and I opened it without switching on the light. She assumed that she had called at a bad time and started apologising for disturbing me. I replied that now that she had disturbed me, she should tell me what she had wanted to say. She seemed embarrassed and said that she had been going to persuade me to see an undergraduate production of a play by Ibsen. I told her that I had just discovered Ibsen and thought him a very important writer, and why shouldn't I go to the production? Her assumption was that, if you can't see, you can't go to the theatre.

After coming down from Oxford, there was a problem as to what I should do, although it was very clear to me that I shouldn't stay at home with my parents who were then living in a village in Buckinghamshire. There were tensions between us and so I decided that I would take the first job I could find. Eventually I went into Braille publishing and became an editor for the RNIB in London. I enjoyed the work because I believed that providing books for blind students was a good thing to be doing. I also spent some time working on a PhD at UCL, where I am now an honorary research fellow, on the reconstruction of lost works of classical literature, particularly lost Greek plays. In addition to the complete Greek plays that have survived, there are a large number of fragments in existence, which lead you to speculate how the plot might have worked out. The reconstruction of these lost works is the aspect of classical literature that has most captivated me, and I sometimes wonder if it relates in some way to my childhood dream.

While I was at Oxford I had often consulted books from the eighteenth and nineteenth centuries. I didn't realise at the time that they could be bought on the open market and, in due course, the idea of collecting came naturally to me. By that time I was working in London, sharing a flat with Patrick Pollard who was an academic librarian at The Warburg Institute and later became a Professor of French at Birkbeck. I had first met Patrick when he was selected to read to me during the holidays. My father had advertised at the local school for someone who could read Greek and Latin to me in the holidays, and Patrick was chosen. He went on to study French and spend some time in France, but we remained in touch as friends, and in 1962 we decided to live together.

Frank Norman, who had a shop in Hampstead with a certain amount of classical books, gave us a directory of book dealers, and we began to visit shops outside London, travelling by train and bus. In the late 1960s and early 1970s, there were still enough bookshops for it to be worthwhile. We gradually progressed to taking an interest in book sales, attending auctions at Sotheby's, Christie's, Phillips and Hodgson's, learning how to operate in them by watching the dealers. I aim to have in my collection a decent copy, by which I mean a textually sound copy, of every literary text from pagan antiquity. I also include texts from the early Christian period up to about AD 600. By the end of the 1970s the idea of becoming a bookseller was beginning to take root, but no one would have employed me as a trainee bookseller. And why should they? In any case, the point of being one was precisely to become independent. And so I built up a scheme for running a bookselling business by catalogue. I had accumulated quite a lot of books, inherited a bit of money from my mother and received an interest-free loan from the RNIB, all of which enabled me to get started. I left my job at the end of 1978, and we sent out our first catalogue in 1979.

Having Patrick to help me has obviously been indispensable. When we were getting started, Patrick was teaching at Birkbeck, which meant that it was convenient for us to go to auctions together during the day. He reads the catalogues, collates the books and describes their physical condition, and I know about the history of the texts and which scholars and editors are important, and other details that are likely to affect their value. I'm interested in books for their intellectual content and, because of my academic training, I tend to regard them as more valuable to me if they are the best text of a work, rather than the first. Of course I recognise the value of its first appearance and the valid reasons for people wanting to pay more money for it, just as I recognise that aesthetic considerations make a difference to the value. I keep a record in Braille of all the books in our stock, which acts as my primary reference source. Patrick dictates the details to me for the stock register and I use that information as the basis for my catalogue descriptions.

When Patrick reads an auction catalogue to me, he has a very good idea of what I'm looking for. He doesn't read it from cover to cover as we would never get anything done. There was a blind Law don at Oxford who was known to be rather quick-tempered with his readers. On one occasion someone was reading a law case when he interrupted and said, 'Held?' The reader didn't understand and carried on until he interrupted with the same question. He didn't want to hear the facts of the case; he wanted to know the judge's decision.

If Patrick is unable to bid with me at a sale, I do the bidding on the telephone. I like to engage with the person who is my 'minder' on the other end of the line, as it gives me an awareness of what's going on in the room. For example they might tell me that there are a lot of foreign dealers in the room and other bits of information that will have an effect on what I decide to bid. I recently bought a copy of Velleius Paterculus, a first-century AD Roman historian, of which the book is not only the first printing of the Latin text, but is also the substantive source for our knowledge of the text, as the manuscripts from which it was printed have disappeared. There are a number of texts to which this has happened, often due to the practice in the sixteenth century of printing a book and then using the manuscript for binders' waste. The manuscript of the last book of Pliny the Younger's letters containing his correspondence with the Emperor Trajan has been lost, and so we only have the printed text to rely on. Among other things, they discussed the problem of how to treat the large population of Christians in Bithynia where Pliny was Governor.

It's surprising how often we've managed to find books in mixed lots that were unnamed but very important. We came across a copy of the works of Sir William Davenant, published in 1673, which is not in itself very rare, but we discovered during viewing that it had belonged to Herman Melville. Davenant was Shakespeare's godson and, although my knowledge of Herman Melville is fairly limited, I couldn't fit this book into what I knew of him. We put it in our catalogue and received a telephone call from someone on behalf of an American university who was collecting books that had belonged to Herman Melville. He had traced the copy of Davenant through sales up to 1951, when it had disappeared from the market. We put him in touch with the auctioneers in the hope that they might have been able to give him some details of earlier provenance. In another mixed lot, in which the lead item was quite an important sixteenth-century book, we found the first translation into Italian of the Koran dating from 1547. It didn't take any special skill to realise that it was extremely rare. The first complete English translation of the Koran did not appear until 1649.

I'm always more disappointed when I fail to get a lot that I would have kept for my own collection than one that I would have sold. I'm aware that many dealers don't collect books because of this conflict, but for me to stop collecting would be a terrible self-inflicted wound. We try to do two catalogues a year, one on the history of classical scholarship to the present day, and an early printed catalogue which includes, among other subjects, books on linguistics, philosophy and the history of ideas. We aren't online people and, although many customers order by e-mail, our catalogues are only available in hard copy. There is a note on the front cover asking customers to circulate the catalogue among their friends and colleagues, and we have found word-of-mouth to be more successful for us than advertising.

We'll have to think about winding down before too long, although I've never thought about retirement as such. I'm very much in favour of the relaxation of the compulsory retirement age. People are living longer and are healthier on average and I see no reason why you shouldn't go on for as long as you are capable of working. I appreciate that I've never been forced to do work that I don't enjoy for any length of time, and so I've never regarded work as a burden.

In my lifetime there will always be collectors who like books in the way that I do, but we're on a downward track. It's idle to deny the direction of travel. The development of electronic texts is going to affect the demand for hard-copy books, but you shouldn't assume that a book has become worthless just because it has been digitised. We don't know how long these technologies will last or how stable they are compared to what we know about parchment and paper. Traditional books will cease to be produced in their present quantity and will become less valued until people find that digital texts are no longer readable for whatever reason. I shan't live to see that day but of course it brings me back to my dream which has coloured the way that I think about things.

# All Roads lead to Italy ∾ William Ward

My family went to Ireland in 1570 and bought the Castle Ward estate from the Earls of Kildare in County Down, on which, in 1610, Nicholas Ward built one of the so-called 'ten pound houses'. This was a scheme dating from the time of King Henry IV whereby a subsidy was given to enable people to build a fortified house. Eventually it was replaced by a very pretty Queen Anne house, which was destroyed when my ancestors built Castle Ward. My father, Edward Ward, seventh Viscount Bangor – pronounced 'anger' with a 'b' on the front to distinguish it from a sausage or an old car – was a war correspondent and journalist. He sold Castle Ward to the government in 1950 in lieu of death duties, and the government endowed it to the National Trust. We have the right to stay there for one month each year. Unfortunately the sale included the library and a fabulous archive of over 3000 documents dating from 1604 to 1950. The Ward Papers are now in the Public Record Office of Northern Ireland, and include such wonderful material as Lady Franklin's papers relating to the search for the remains of her husband and his expedition in search of the North-West Passage.

I was educated at St Edward's, a school in Oxford which I disliked intensely, and which my great-aunt thought resembled an enormous public lavatory. From there I went to University College London, where I read Economics for my sins. It was a crazy choice as Greek and Latin had been my subjects at school, and Classics would have been so much more useful for the sort of books that interest me. When I left university without knowing what I wanted to do, a friendly master at my old school put me in touch with Westminster Abbey library. I was paid £7 a week, which, in 1970, got me through Friday evening and a bit of Saturday. I was given some pink treasury tape and told to tie up books with detached covers, and generally left to get on with things. Although the work wasn't very demanding, it did stimulate my interest in books. After a while I helped in the Muniment Room in the gallery above the east cloister, where the medieval and early modern archives of the Abbey are kept in surroundings that are pure Richard II, with the wonderful painting of his white hart on the wall. The muniments are stored in chests made from timber felled in the twelfth century from trees that had begun to grow, according to dendrochronologists, in the early eighth century.

After a couple of years I decided that I could no longer afford to work at Westminster Abbey. Someone introduced me to Michael Heseltine who gave me a job in Sotheby's book department at Chancery Lane, where my colleagues were David Stagg, Paul Quarrie and Robert Hesketh, the second son of Christian, Lady

Hesketh. Bobby was a great friend who was later to become my partner in Hesketh & Ward. The idea for our future business came to us on Bobby's twenty-first birthday in 1972 when we got frightfully drunk and ended up in a candy-striped telephone engineer's tent in Chancery Lane. My first job was to catalogue a huge collection of the Nonesuch Press. Private press books are very beautiful (but not the Nonesuch Press), but I do tend to think of them as 'whited sepulchres'. After the catalogue was finished, I moved on with a sense of relief to working with proper books, and enjoyed myself enormously during my three years at Chancery Lane.

Meanwhile Toby Rodgers, another close friend, was head of the book department at Christie's where I went to work in 1975. Within a few months of my joining, Toby left and I suddenly found myself running the department, aged twenty-seven. I was required to report to Jo Floyd, Chairman of Christie's, every morning for the first fortnight, an experience that I found nerve-wracking but perhaps he thought he was putting a fatherly hand round my shoulders. My immediate boss, Major Bill Spowers, whose name was pronounced, in his words, 'power' with an 's' on both ends, thought that I needed some help and brought in Hans Fellner. Technically, I was senior to Hans within the organisation but, in reality, Hans had forgotten more about books and manuscripts than I would ever know. It was during my time at Christie's that I was bitten by the Italian bug. Soon after my arrival, Toby Rodgers had sent me to look at some books in Italy. In due course I started doing all the sales for Christie's in Rome. I remember taking my first sale in Italian, after a good shot of brandy. I also met my wife at Christie's, Sarah Bradford, the historian and biographer, who was working in the manuscript department. It was an office romance and we were married in 1976.

The sale of the Evelyn library in 1977-8 was an extremely busy time, during which Bill Spowers went slightly crazy for a while. We were all working flat out except for one person in the department whose idea of a weekend was Thursday to Tuesday. It got to the point where I couldn't put up with it anymore and complained to Jo Floyd who simply said that I had better leave. The circumstances were slightly more complicated than I've described but, basically, Bill Spowers had arranged things to get me out. Perhaps he felt that I was a threat to him; I was rather more ambitious in those days than I am now.

In November 1978 I returned to Sotheby's book department which had moved to New Bond Street where my colleagues were John Collins and David Park. My first job was to catalogue the late Solomon Pottesman's collection of incunabula and sixteenth-century printed books. Potty, as he was always known, had been a familiar figure in the trade, carrying books in paper parcels, often suspended from his little finger with a piece of string. When Michael Morton-Smith, my boss at

Chancery Lane, went to value Potty's books at his flat in Bloomsbury, he was offered a cup of tea, while Potty drank out of an empty milk bottle because he didn't have two cups.

Potty's ambition had been to represent, with as early a book as possible, every town in which incunabula had been printed. The result was a poor man's Broxbourne Library, as Potty had often had to settle for imperfect copies. However, he did have one wonderful book, in which material printed by the prototypographers at Westminster, London and Oxford were combined in a single volume. It was a copy of John Lathbury, *Liber moralium super threnis Ieremiae*, printed at Oxford by Theodoricus Rood, 31 July 1482. The vellum sewing guards, inserted in the middle of each quire, include printed fragments by William Caxton and John Lettou.

I took the last book sale held in Sotheby's Bond Street before the department moved across the road to Bloomfield Place. The last item sold at Chancery Lane had made a lot of money out of nostalgia, but there was no such feeling when I sold the final lot in Bond Street. I remember being quite rude to the people in the room for not rising to the occasion. Basically the auctioneer is only a conduit between the seller and the buyer, and the quicker and more efficiently that you can do it – and ideally with a bit of humour – the better. You could have a bit of fun in those days, especially before the introduction of the paddle bidding system. We would invent names of fictitious purchasers for lots that were bought in. During a sale of Russian Futurist books, there was a long period of about thirty lots that were all bought in, and so I started saying, 'Lenin', 'Stalin', 'Khrushchev' and so on. I remember David Temperley calling out, 'You haven't said Ustinov yet'. And so I did. We also had a lot of fun in Monaco where I did all Sotheby's book sales. I shall never forget the warehouse which was stocked with beer in the fridge and a wind-up gramophone with a selection of records from the 1930s of Ambrose & His Orchestra.

In 1983 I fell out with Roy Davids, who was head of the book department and marketing director. Roy wanted me and H.A. 'Feisy' Feisenberger to catalogue Nicholas Tzakas's library. I didn't like Tzakas's method as a collector, which was to buy books in England, sell them at auction in Germany, buy books there and sell them in France, and so they would go round in a triangle. When I said as much during a meeting at Sotheby's, Roy objected strongly to what he saw as my disloyalty. There came a point a couple of years later when Roy was so annoyed with me that he wanted to exile me to Sotheby's book department in Paris. Meanwhile I had already mentioned to Bobby Hesketh that I had had enough of things and that I was going to set up my own business – at which point he reminded me that we had planned to do this together. And so in March 1985 I resigned in front of five senior directors of Sotheby's, which was incredibly pleasing. Hesketh & Ward was founded in our house in Fulham on April Fool's Day 1985, twelve and a half years after my drunken night with Bobby in the telephone engineer's tent.

After leaving Chancery Lane, Bobby had gone to work for Gabriel Austin at Sotheby's in New York. When he came back to England, he had a few business interests but didn't need to work for a living. Our business plan for Hesketh & Ward, inasmuch as we had one, was that I would do everything. Bobby provided the initial funds for the business, which was going to be quite high-value and small-volume. We never considered having a shop; there's not much passing trade for sixteenth-century Italian books. It seems to happen to most dealers that, in their first year, God smiles on them. In my first year I bought some fantastically nice books. My first catalogue went out in November 1985 and was devoted to fifteenth- and sixteenth-century books. Bobby came here and we sat in the kitchen sticking stamps on envelopes. The catalogue went out to Sotheby's mailing list, which included such unpromising addresses as Unit 4, Milton Keynes, before the list was whittled down. I have always tried to make my catalogues quite light-hearted, and am very interested in their design. From Catalogue 5 onward, I did all my own paste-ups, and I'm happier with the result than with the printer's designs for my first four catalogues. My second catalogue didn't appear until March 1987 after which I aimed to do two a year, which I have more or less achieved.

From 1991 to 2004 I went to Italy on buying trips twice a year with Paul Grinke, and more recently with Bogislav Winner. Turin has more bookshops than any other city in Italy. Cesare Birocco of Libreria Antiquaria Bourlot eventually became my main supplier. On my first buying trip with Paul, we started in Bologna, stupidly hiring a car, and made our way to Turin where we kept taking the wrong turn. When I told Paul that we were looking at a map of Padua, he claimed that it didn't matter as, according to him, all Italian cities had a Via Garibaldi, a Via Mazzini, a Via Cavour and so on. We travelled by train in future, sometimes going as far south as Bari to visit Mario Somma of the Bottega Apulia from whom I used to buy a lot of books. He had the annoying habit of making you look at a drawer of unpriced catalogue cards from which you selected what you wanted to see. He would go to the back of the shop and fetch them, and the pile of books would slowly reduce as he told you the prices. I bought my best ever book in a shop near Naples for €450. Described rather unpromisingly as a law book, it turned out to be the regulations for Venetian gondolas in 1570, with the penalties for failing to observe them. It was an extremely ephemeral publication and, although it stated that there would be one published every year, I have only been able to trace another example for the year 1576.

Bobby Hesketh was killed by a drink-driver in California in 1997. Although it made no difference to the business, it was a terrible loss from a personal point of view, and marked the start of a year in which I lost three other close friends in the space of a couple of months. Alvise di Robilant, a former head of Sotheby's in Florence, Toby Falk who was Sotheby's Oriental miniatures and manuscripts consultant, and Toby Rodgers all died within weeks of each other. Toby had recently established himself in Charlotte Street and issued his catalogue of '100 Rare Books on 100 Different Subjects', to which Bernard Levin had devoted an entire column in *The Times*. His business was doing very well at the time of his tragic death.

I have been more or less retired since 2010, largely as a result of a couple of setbacks which killed the business for me. My main supplier, Cesare Birocco, died, and my best customer in America, the Beinecke Library – particularly in Bob Babcock's time – stopped buying early Italian books because of the problem of theft in that field. I used to buy thirty or forty books a year from Birocco and, although Libreria Antiquaria Bourlot continues, his son has different interests. I could have survived one of these setbacks, but not both. I would like to be remembered for doing amusing and interesting catalogues. At least I got to Catalogue 44 as Hesketh & Ward. That's mildly respectable.

# APPENDIX

In 1991 Barry Shaw, the editor of the *Bookdealer* magazine, for whom I had been writing a weekly column, invited me to contribute an autobiographical piece for inclusion in a series of articles to celebrate the 1000th edition of his magazine. Entitled 'A Foot on the Ladder', it describes my experience of working for Marlborough Rare Books during the 1980s. It was my first job in the antiquarian book trade in which I had the great good fortune to work for Michael Brand and Alex Fotheringham, both highly respected and well-liked booksellers in their very different ways.

It was while working at Marlborough that I first met the book dealers and collectors whose passion, eccentricity, expertise and occasional roguery inspired the idea that perhaps I would one day write about them. I am very grateful to Barry Shaw for giving me the opportunity to do so by commissioning a series of profiles for his magazine, of which many were included in *A Book of Booksellers*, the first volume of my conversations with the antiquarian book trade, published in 2004.

I have chosen this occasion to reprint 'A Foot on the Ladder' as a tribute to Michael Brand and Alex Fotheringham who both died in 2012.

Mickie Brand                    Alex Fotheringham

# A Foot on the Ladder ∾ Sheila Markham

'I'd like you to have the job, but I only hope you're strong enough.' No would have been the truth, but there it was – a foot on the ladder. It was strange to think that twenty-two years of sustained indolence had ill-prepared me in mind and body for the business of finding gainful employment. And here I was embarked on a career in antiquarian bookselling for which, apparently, I was seriously under-size. I suppose it was my fault – I had drifted into and, more seriously, out of education without the slightest ambition beyond a Mercedes 280 SL. Someone had suggested university and I chose to read the Ancient Near East with as much thought as that. It was all of a deadness to rival the dodo, with nothing to disturb the peace of my ivory tower beyond the religious crises of Akhenaton.

In my studied ignorance, I thought antiquarian bookselling might be the sort of backwater to ensure a regular afternoon sleep. Anyway, it seemed the least uncongenial method of getting on with this tiresome project of earning a living. Years later, catching my breath after a full afternoon's packing, I reflected wistfully, as Akhenaton might have, on the extreme deception of appearances. So it was that I came to work for Michael Brand and Alex Fotheringham at Marlborough Rare Books in Old Bond Street. And there was good reason for being strong – in fact, a well-developed gorilla might have served them better. They had an international reputation for books of quite outrageous size, which, when packed, resembled nothing so much as a concrete paving stone. I had never packed anything larger than a Christmas present, and came to the job with strong misgivings, if not muscles. I knew I was not good with my hands, and feared I might not master an effective slip-knot. My predecessor, with whom I coincided just long enough to learn the tricks of the trade, worked swiftly with a proper respect for getting things right. Under her critical eye, my nervous fingers fumbled the knot. It took me back years to the unforgettable horror of needlework classes, and having to unpick tacking on a blood-stained garment that had to be wearable on the last day of term.

Standards in the packing room were high, with no shortcuts like the contemptible use of padded bags or, worse still, shoe-boxes rattling with those infernal plastic beans. Our American visitors regarded the packing room much as they would an old craft museum. We had an antique pair of scales that weighed in regardless at one kilo, and an extraordinary Heath-Robinson device for gumming labels. Like all good ideas, it was really very simple – a rusting tray of stagnant water and a sponge, over which the label passed. Sadly, times move on and the modern typewriter ink cannot withstand such a soaking, the labels emerging with half the address gone. And the Americans just stood and watched, much as they might have watched me shoeing a horse. They told stories of the wonderful machines back home that packed books in polystyrene moulds, some sort of spin-off from the silicone-implant business. It is strange to think that we have Hollywood wives to thank for the safe arrival of our books.

The next stage was the post office run, with the somewhat doubtful assistance of a trolley ordered from a glossy catalogue. I must say I was completely taken in by the picture of a rather petite secretary manoeuvring an awkward load with absolute confidence across her shag-pile carpet. When the beastly thing arrived, it seemed unsuited to holding an even load at any angle. I persevered for a bit, thinking it might just be a knack of sensible loading or steering, as it resisted my directions with the same will as a supermarket trolley. The real stumbling-block, however, was the kerb outside the post office, where the load invariably shifted to an unhealthy angle before the final spurt to the counter. I think I finally gave up on it after running aground outside one of those striped tents to the vast amusement of the telephone engineers inside.

The entire business of posting a parcel was fraught with complication. These were the days before the compulsory enrolment at charm school, and the counter clerks were allowed to resist any attempt to post anything. They would query every aspect of each parcel before sending it on its way with a flick of the ankle down the ten-foot shaft into the loading bay. If one had the temerity to point out it was fragile, the clerk grabbed his rubber stamp and banged the parcel with FRAGILE FRAGILE FRAGILE. And so it was launched on a journey that would involve many such pitfalls, ending, as often as not, in the New York postal system which specialised in pulverising parcels at point of entry. Many a customer's long-awaited purchase came to grief under the remorseless wheels of a 747 reversing into the infamous loading bays at JFK.

The Compendium of Postal Services is an extraordinary document, and every packer's vade-mecum. It is about the size of a telephone book, and seeks to encompass the world in a network of sealing wax and blue crayon, with the cautionary note that neither is to be used in the despatch of livestock. An eminently practical book, it warns against expecting a full range of counter services in Upper Volta or New Guinea. In the case of Japan, it points out the reduction in maximum parcel weight to allow for the smaller postmen. One memorable afternoon, Alex caught me emerging from a roll of corrugated to ask if I enjoyed packing. The merciful upshot to this was the arrival of an outside packer and life took on a different aspect.

It was extremely pleasant to work in a particularly select stretch of Bond Street. The office was on an upper floor and somewhat isolated, so I soon befriended Ken, the security guard who was paid to take a nominal interest in the welfare of the tenants upstairs. He seemed equally unsuited to his job – overweight and suffering from a heart condition aggravated by surprises. We got on very well, despite a shaky start and his unexplained insistence on calling me the Duchess. Almost on my first day, the pair of us got stuck in the lift, and he discovered at once that I was not much of a good-time girl. I can vividly remember telling him to keep as still as possible to conserve oxygen, which did not suit his plans. We eventually plummeted to the ground floor and shot out into the perennial squalor of the entrance hall. This was still Ken's patch, but he chose to turn a severely blind eye to the mounting pile of discarded newspapers and assorted rubbish that blew in from the street, all lightly washed with a faint but stubborn stain. The story goes that the building, situated between two busy pubs and boasting a concealed entrance and large letterbox, made a perfect latrine for passing revellers. And complications really only arose when the postman put the box to its legitimate use.

Upstairs, our office was largely furnished from skips with which Mayfair was littered as leases ran out and the developers moved in. The general feeling was that, while I might have liked to call in Colefax & Fowler, a bit of chintz about the place did not actually increase sales. This did not deter me from the considerable entertainment of reading office furniture catalogues. Were there really offices with stunning models in skimpy beachwear reclining on immaculate desks, and getting a quite unaccountable pleasure from a new range of shorthand pads? And what disappointment there must have been when the desk arrived minus the girl, and the regular secretary, sensibly dressed in Damart's latest, set about applying a liberal coating of Tipp-Ex to the 'Teakolene' finish.

It was sheer bad luck that a leaking radiator had ruined a perfectly good carpet, leaving my desk all but afloat in a ten-foot oil slick. Mr Brand regularly stood in it dictating letters and grinding his cigarette ash into the explosive pile. I feared the place would blow up one day, and the insurance man, picking amongst the wreckage, would come across an oil-soaked carpet. Still, one must not be too anxious and I had no desire to build on my reputation for over-reacting after a premature bulk purchase of mineral water against the threat of a water shortage. It did not happen, and we all had to live with the considerable obstacle of a 120 unwanted bottles.

The desk furniture had an unpremeditated but quite distinct seashore theme. Mr Brand had a beaker for his pencils, heavily coated with varnished shells and made by one of his children. One of Alex's daughters gave him a quite remarkable plastic crab that doubled as an all-purpose desk-tidy. The back removed to store paper-clips, while elastic bands strung conveniently between the claws, in which messages could be poked. It always excited comment from disbelieving visitors and, with practice, I managed to say, 'That's Alex's crab' in a tone of stating a self-evident fact. Another unique fitting must have been Mr Brand's angle-poise lamp. From a distance, it just looked grubby, but on closer inspection it was exquisitely mottled to resemble lizard skin. It was the last thing one would expect of Mr Brand, with its air of something Liberace had slung in the attic.

Mrs Brown, the cleaning lady, had to do battle with all this, coming in before the office opened. On the rare occasions that I surprised her, she would be comfortably seated at my desk half-way through the crossword with a duster hanging limply at her side. Actually, surprise is the wrong word, and I admired her complete composure. Presumably she thought we were all employees together and what the hell anyway? But work she could – and with a vengeance, knocking the spines right off some of the weaker bindings in her determination to keep abreast of the infernal dust-traps that they were. It was suggested that she might be less dangerous with a feather duster. I rather jibbed at the prospect of travelling in from the suburbs with one, but feather dusters are not for sale in Bond Street. Mrs Brown insisted, quite rightly, that she needed a six-foot cane to reach the top shelves. My heart sank at the thought of manoeuvring something that length, not to mention the feathers, on a packed commuter train. I finally hit on the idea of disguising the feathers inside an empty kitchen roll, but then it looked like an overgrown firework, and quite as idiotic as ever. Fortunately, my mother, whose embarrassment threshold is considerably higher than mine, agreed to bring it up when she next came to town. Mrs Brown made good use of it, and the occasional orange feather sticking out of a book marked her path across the stock.

And over all this, Mr Brand presided with unruffled courtesy. In the early days, we were constantly having bomb scares, the police wanting the building evacuated and most people did not argue. Mr Brand, however, sat unflustered against a backdrop of windows and glass bookcases, saying, 'By all means go if you like, but I can't be bothered'. His nerve was almost infectious, and I resolved to sit tight, though white with anxiety, thinking of running a roll of brown tape over the windows. He was the sort of man that if anyone knew where Lord Lucan was, he did. He moved in the most exotic circles with all the understatement and perfect ease of his class. I think he disliked dictating letters which, in any case, he had reduced to four-line models of clipped elision, relieving the tedium by playing with cigarettes and jingling coins in his pocket. I played my own games in between each perfectly balanced sentence, trying to guess the exact wording of the next line. He would sometimes ask me the word he was looking for, and, after several years of ruminating together, we often had a combined shot at the *mot juste*.

Monday mornings were sometimes a struggle for Mr Brand. The dictation of letters was often reduced to the vague instruction that I write to Miss What-Not at the What's It Library to tell her that whatever she ordered was or was not available and would be sent in the usual way or not, and that we much looked forward to her visit in April or May, or just say forthcoming. Meanwhile, we hoped she was well – oh dear, hadn't she just died? – better leave that out, and I'll sign it, no, you sign it ...

At one period that I cannot quite tie in with the general economy, we received a flood of CVs from would-be booksellers, one of whom I could personally have shot for her irresponsible suggestion that she start on a low wage. Mr Brand always read the CVs, although it was my job to send the disappointing reply. If he commented at all, it might be to say that so-and-so sounded fearfully bright – not a compliment, as Mr Brand personified the aristocratic disdain for middle-class endeavour. If one had some learning, that couldn't be helped, but it certainly wasn't something for public parade. It was altogether more becoming to be quietly smart, and Mr Brand affected this easy nonchalance.

I never understood why he went into old books in the first place, with their tendency to attract an earnest clientèle. Mr Brand's cousin, speaking from an acquaintance with collectors in all fields, pronounced bibliophiles lunatics and I cannot believe that Mr Brand disagreed. For a long time, the stock resembled the library of an English country house, and scholarly books were discouraged on the grounds of their ugliness and tendency to attract impecunious collectors with some madcap scheme of reading the wretched things.

For all his low profile, Mr Brand enjoyed an international reputation for his expertise and strict code of honour. He did things his way, which did not necessarily include accepting an invitation to address a party of Japanese booksellers. In Bond Street, we applauded his steadfast resolve, though in Tokyo it no doubt activated a chain of humiliated suicides. However, it did not in any way affect our thriving Japanese trade. There was still the steady stream of visitors, always men and usually in pairs, cameras loaded for the compulsory shot of Mr Brand pressed up against a selection from stock. They bought heavily, paid promptly and usually presented me with a delicately-printed handkerchief with cranes flying across a gold and silver sky.

Alex Fotheringham was Mr Brand's business partner with qualities that made for an unlikely but successful pair. He was through-and-through a northerner, and in my imagination I always pictured him striding across Brontë Country with a dead rabbit or two over his shoulder. He was frugal to the point that I was sure he could have run a business out of a tea chest, and not feel the want of anything. For a man in his early forties, he had a curious dislike for modern gadgetry. Old ways were best, with no machines welcomed, and in this environment very few machines survived. A classic victim was a rather silly pencil sharpener that I bought on a whim. According to the box, it simply battened down to the edge of the desk with something that I had last seen on the end of a table-tennis net. To demonstrate its absurdity, Alex shoved in his pencil somewhat unsympathetically and the whole thing collapsed with its dinky tray of shavings all over the floor. Alex immediately sharpened his pencil to a diamond point with his pocket knife or something equally primordial.

He had an enviable capacity for hard work, which he fuelled by regular attention to his blood-sugar. It was an agony to walk past his desk without dipping into an extensive assortment of confectionery. On a Friday, the St James's Market sold old-fashioned sweets by the quarter in candy-striped paper bags, and Alex bought without hint of stint. I must confess I pinched the odd one when the office positively stank of aniseed twists, but I was deterred from serious theft by the awful thought that Alex might actually count his supplies and notice at a glance the decimation of his jelly babies.

One Friday afternoon, our munching was interrupted by a visit from a regular customer. I did not notice his unusual colour or that he was slumped in his chair until his head banged the desk with a fearful crash from which the deepest sleeper would have recoiled. Instead, his head just rested immobile on the book. Horrid thoughts of heart attacks and first aid rushed through my head. The great thing was, as I recalled, not to disturb the patient. I decided to get a second opinion from Alex whose diagnosis was swift if surprising – a simple case of being 'pissed as a newt'. He lifted the inert customer off the book which he stuffed into a bag on the assumption that he was more dead-set than most on a purchase. With all the advantage of his height and strength, Alex gathered up the man and his luggage and humped the lot to the door with the air of an exhausted ventriloquist. I think I remember saying feebly, 'Where are you going?' 'Comes from the North, doesn't he? – I'll get him in a cab to Euston'. A few minutes later, Alex returned with the situation clearly in hand. I started on the invoice with some misgivings about this style of salesmanship. Some time later, a cheque arrived with a tragic note about the dangers of missing a dose of insulin.

As Alex was indisputably a man of action, it seemed inevitable that the office routine would fall under his scrutiny. It was a great relief to discover that he saw my function as a general 'facilitator' – a job description that I enjoyed – not least for its decidedly American ring. I had visions of large advertisements in bold type in *The Wall Street Journal*: 'Facilitator Required – Salary Substantial'. Anyway, it seemed considerable promotion on 'secretary', or even 'secretart' as so much post was addressed.

In my job as facilitator, I was greatly assisted, though some thought hampered, by the dominating presence of Erica Spender. When we first met, Erica had nominally retired, but it must have been hard for her to break a life-time's habit of feverish work. She was of decidedly foreign extraction on whom fifty years in this country had left not a trace. She was without doubt the greatest eccentric I have ever had the pleasure to meet. Highly cultured and erudite, Erica was at her happiest doing the menial chores I delighted in saving for her. I always felt there was something of Laurel and Hardy about our relationship, my loyalty and affection quite unbending beneath the weight of Erica's colourful abuse. Once I suggested it would be fun to write a novel about her, at which she snorted, 'Darling, you haven't the stamina. A book's hard work and you're such a lazy little cow'. She brought out all that was silliest in me and I loved her for it. I played up to her like a naughty school girl, responding strongly to her delinquent streak that just stopped short of being criminal. It was astonishing to think of the fifty-year gap between us, though Erica was extraordinarily young in mind and body, and thought nothing of running up Bond Street with an IBM typewriter under her arm.

She had wild mood swings in her attitude towards me – one minute I was 'little rabbit' and the next 'loathsome child'. Her command of obscene language was, I believe, unrivalled outside the armed forces. She had no concern for the petty hypocrisies of social intercourse. No subject was taboo, and I can still hear her shouting over a customer, 'Darling, how's your sex life?' – and, not waiting for the answer, which was not on the tip of my tongue anyway, she continued, 'Dear God, I couldn't stomach a wedding just yet. It would be too up-feeding to have a think of a present at the moment'. Any discussion on the subject of men usually ended in furious disagreement. Our tastes, it seemed, did not coincide and Erica expressed grave concern at what she saw as my inexplicable penchant for 'blackamoors'. It all started with an innocent enough holiday snap on which Erica pounced, shrieking, 'Darling, I don't know how your mother can bear it – with you going off to horrid places to sit on the first camel you see. There you are looking so demure, sandwiched between two blackamoors you say you don't even know'.

Erica combined racial prejudice, which, by the way, she could defend on the most involved anthropological grounds, with an equally strong religious intolerance. The Sisters of Mercy had a particularly hard time of it, coming to the door one Christmas collecting for the sick and needy. There they were, three nuns with a large black sandal wedged in the door to prolong almsgiving – and Erica's iron fist on the petty cash. It was a potentially explosive situation:

'Darling, would you give me five pounds if I knocked on your door?'
'Probably not.'

'Well then, tell the rosary-clinking scroungers to push off.'

I feared the nun in the door might have heard the glad tidings, but decided to report something other than the authorised version. The only thing was to buy them off from my own pocket, which earned me the promise of eternal peace, though I do not remember it lasting the afternoon with Erica aroused on the detestable subject of charity.

All this was child's play compared to the wrath Erica reserved for the doorman of a smart shoe shop opposite us. Many years ago, Erica had had a difference of opinion with the doorman and her revenge was both monstrous and on-going. As ammunition, she drew on my enormous collection of empty milk bottles. From time to time, she loaded a plastic bag and clinked down to the street where she would lie in wait for the doorman to slip off for another sort of pint. On his return, he was naturally astonished to find his entrance littered with evil-smelling bottles and the elegant clientèle of Brooks-Brothered men and Chanel-suited wives picking their way through the glass like guests at a Jewish wedding gone mad.

But Erica really came into her own in the month of August, traditionally reserved for tidying the mailing list – a terrible job like playing Happy Families with a pack of three thousand. The Laborious Twelfth signalled the start of the mailing season. By the end of the month, we were both reduced to a myopic state of post-code-induced dyslexia. There was always a fearful rumpus over American institutions, and whether to file them under name, town or state. I stuck Harvard in H, Erica insisted on C for Cambridge, and it invariably surfaced somewhere in M for Massachusetts. And so it went on throughout the world of learning. Whole campuses went missing simply because no one knew their American geography. The most intractable problem of all was the persistence on a worldwide scale of the habit of moving and dying. Clearly, the dead do outnumber the living, and it was hell's own job to keep up with them. I did sympathise with the regular stream of distressed widows, traumatised by the relentless plop of yet another mailing for their dearly departed. Perhaps we should have invited them to find their dead in the mailing list – they might have accepted the challenge with more zeal.

Although a number of people had worked on the mailing list, I was responsible for one huge error that permeated the system. In a fit of misplaced etiquette, I decided to style all male Americans Esq., only to discover that by so doing I had elevated them to some high rank in their legal profession. To keep up morale as we sloshed on the Tipp-Ex, Erica and I amused ourselves with the wilder spelling mistakes. Lurking in the section for private American customers, we found two ladies, lost and no doubt far from home, the Misses Ann Arbor and Iniv Muchigan.

In Erica's time, she had also done the book-keeping. I reluctantly inherited care of the petty cash, but the serious work was now in the hands of a professional accountant, Mr Maxwell. I liked him enormously, even though his monthly visits generated the most ghastly amount of paperwork. I think we were a part-time diversion for his retirement. His visits noticeably coincided with bad weather that might have spoilt his eighteen holes. I marvelled at his capacity for concentration, seated at an overcrowded desk with Erica crashing around him, determined to empty all bins every hour on the hour. While I tried to type over the noise of Erica cursing in the packing room, Mr Maxwell tapped his calculator with an unerring finger. I think our behaviour must have resembled the only joke I know about two fishwives – shouting at each other across the street and a passer-by remarks, 'They'll never agree, they're arguing from different premises'.

One thing did unnerve Mr Maxwell, and that was a tiny plastic spool for the calculator paper. He was convinced it would break and prove obsolete. It was a very curious anxiety in one so solid. I was driven to distraction by the other hazards of this machine, for example, the regularity with which the plug fell out leaving a faint trace of a lost total. But the fragile spool had never occurred to me in a thousand nightmares. Every time the paper ran out, we relived this trauma, calling the roll doll's house loo paper to ease the tension of the moment.

It was office policy that Mr Maxwell should see all bumf, into which category fell anything in a brown envelope or with a window. Correspondence from the Inland Revenue went into a special file where Mr Maxwell kept his arcane tax tables giving details of pay and, more curiously, maternity benefit for merchant seamen. The bills file was in itself a liability, nicknamed the rat-trap for its alarming habit of slamming shut when least expected. Inside, there was a theoretical division of Inland and Overseas creditors, who were paid with so cavalier an attitude that we called it the lucky dip. Through it all, Mr Maxwell soldiered on with amazing fortitude when a lesser man might well have gone for early retirement. The bills were the lucky ones with a fire-proof cabinet of their own. Other documents took their chance on the window sills, an integral part of the filing system. It worked with remarkable ease until the monthly upheaval of the window cleaner's visit. If anything went missing, Mr Brand's first question was, 'Has that damn window cleaner been?'. My job was to circle discreetly while he hung out of the windows, Erica having said rather darkly that he had been 'inside'. And I frequently caught him leafing through papers on Mr Brand's desk. I never knew quite what to do except to mark my presence with a tight little cough.

Once a year, the Department of Health and Social Security, or maybe Employment, sent an unreadable booklet for the attention of all shop workers, outlining conditions of work and minimum wages. I would have stuffed it in Mr

Maxwell's drawer but for the capital-lettered instruction to post it prominently for the benefit of all employees. Every year I posted it with due solemnity behind the central heating pipe, and felt there was something vaguely Lutheran about sticking up these edicts. Perhaps the religious mood was coming upon me.

And it came to pass in the seventh year of my sojourn in the camp of the booksellers, and lo, I felt unto myself the shelf-life expire. Marlborough Rare Books had given me an education from which this time I emerged – with ambition. I wanted to discover that America was more than a troublesome section of the mailing list, and I would go back and back until I found those dear pen friends of mine, little Ann Arbor and Iniv Muchigan. Meanwhile, the writing was on the wall, as it usually is for students of the Ancient Near East: 'May he who sits in the place of clerkly lore shine like the sun'.

# Epilogue

*I would like to give the last word to Michael Silverman, to whom this book is dedicated, and only regret that it takes the form of his obituary. It was written for the ABA Newsletter with the help of his childhood friend, Robert Bartfield, and first published in July 2011.*

With the untimely death of Michael Silverman, the world of literary and historical manuscripts has lost one of its most respected dealers, and the antiquarian trade in general a much loved and popular colleague. Internationally acknowledged as a dealer of great integrity and expertise, Michael wore his knowledge lightly. He liked to affect an air of mild indifference to the exceptional material that often passed through his hands. His self-deprecating style, so far removed from that of the hustling businessman, was much appreciated by the many collectors, private and institutional, who responded to the good manners that informed his dealings as a whole. In 2008 Michael was justly proud to be elected a Fellow of the Society of Antiquaries. Earlier this year he was honoured to be invited by Michael Meredith to talk about manuscript-collecting to the boys at Eton, to whom he gave a characteristic piece of advice not to bother with Keats unless they had a lot of pocket money.

Regarded as a model of their kind, Michael's catalogues contained fastidious descriptions of thoughtfully chosen material, meticulously researched, and beautifully presented. Published in 2010, Catalogue 28, entitled *One hundred Select Manuscripts*, was to be his last catalogue. Full of original and engaging material, it is a perfect illustration of his interests and expertise. The descriptions reveal his ability to evaluate the significance of a letter and to place it in its proper context – a skill which depended on the patient accumulation of biographical, historical and miscellaneous information, in order to arrive at an informed appreciation of the material. Michael combined formidable scholarship with a sound financial grasp which enabled him to strike the difficult balance between competing factors such as rarity, interest of contents, and the many other considerations that ultimately determine commercial value. Described by James Fergusson as 'a catalogue to read and keep', Catalogue 28 has been widely acknowledged as the high-point in his achievement as a dealer in literary and historical manuscripts.

Michael Silverman was born in Leeds in 1949, and grew up in the leafy suburb of Alwoodley. His father owned a wholesale cloth business in North Street. Michael was educated at Leeds Grammar School where he excelled academically.

A considerable classical scholar, Michael was also a keen sportsman. He liked to play football wearing Pelé's number 10 shirt, and cricket with his shirt carefully buttoned at the sleeve in imitation of his other sporting hero, Geoffrey Boycott.

To the intense pride of his parents, Michael went up to Oxford to read Law, which he disliked, and then to York where he studied Anglo-Saxon poetry, followed by an MA at Leeds. His student years were intermingled with many happy times as a star performer in the Jewish social scene in Leeds, where he resumed his cricketing career. Playing for the aptly-named Jesters, he never hit a boundary but was always able to ensure that the match continued until after tea. The Jesters competed in the Barkston Ash League and were famous for their consistent performance at the bottom of the lowest of the leagues, suffering notable defeats by the Inland Revenue 'B' Team and the equally dangerous Post Office 'C' team.

Well-educated, personable and with a striking resemblance to Bob Dylan, Michael finally embarked on an unconventional path to finding his vocation. While his childhood friends applied themselves to the traditional professions, Michael supervised a a Coca-Cola bottling plant, managed a roller-skating rink, put up tents for holidaymakers in the South of France, and sold encyclopaedias in Australia, with many a picaresque adventure along the way. There was also a short spell at Hambros, where he found the work boring but greatly enjoyed long City lunches.

Walking down Sackville Street one day in 1984, Michael's eye was caught by the enticing window display of Sotheran's. Although there was no situation vacant, Robert Kirkman immediately recognised Michael's potential and took him on to develop an autograph letter department. Within a short time Michael had not only made a success of it, but also met his life-partner, Dorothy Lothian, who was running the print department.

In 1989 Michael left Sotheran's to start his own business in literary and historical manuscripts, supported by his childhood friend Ian Montrose. Michael rapidly became a respected and hugely popular figure on the international stage with regular appearances at book fairs in Paris, New York, Los Angeles and San Francisco. He relished book fairs as social occasions as much as business opportunities, and was always ready to leave his stand for a cup of tea and a chat. As he would say, 'we didn't have wine in Leeds'. Michael adored his trips to the States where he felt very much at home and had many friends and family. He found New York particularly stimulating, and sometimes wondered if he could have moved his business there. He was a member of the Grolier Club and, in recent years, had formed an important friendship with Declan Kiely, head of literary and historical manuscripts at the Morgan Library.

In 1992 Michael joined the ABA and became a member of the General

Committee in 1998. It was the start of his long association with and distinguished contribution to the work of the Committee where his gift for turning a heated debate into a shared experience of laughter was much appreciated. Within a year he became editor of the *Newsletter*, and of the *Handbook*, introducing the current format and producing seven editions of a publication which is widely regarded as a model of design and a pleasure to consult. He served as a member of the Export of Books and Manuscripts Committee from 1999, and Chairman of the Trustees of the ABA Educational Trust from its inception in 2010 until his death.

Although Michael made a success of running his own business, he was not temperamentally suited to the isolation of working from home. It might come as a surprise to those who only knew him from the sober prose of his catalogues that he was highly gregarious and a born entertainer. Almost every weekend he hosted a 'gala night' for his close friends at his home in Blackheath, when he would slip into his stage persona of Johnny Paris and sing (very badly) a medley of first lines – he could never remember the second line of any song. Stylistically Johnny Paris was somewhere between Frank Sinatra and the Black and White Minstrels.

Michael would have made a wonderful stand-up comedian, or possibly more of a sit-down one. He was not so much lazy as a martyr to chronic lethargy. He could quickly descend into a state of near-bedridden boredom from which, however, he would just as easily recover at the prospect of some slightly eccentric escapade. Few activities gave him more pleasure than 'styling' in town, when he would saunter along Jermyn Street admiring the window displays of quilted smoking jackets and brocade dressing gowns and other essential items of clothing which, to his frustration, he could never find in TK Maxx. Michael would love to have been a gentleman of leisure with sufficient private income to indulge his dilettanti interests and expensive tastes. Not long ago he bought a pair of exquisite lemon-yellow chamois-leather gloves, of the kind that Horace Walpole might have owned. He was not at all pleased to discover a few days later that Halfords sold an almost identical pair at a fraction of the cost for shampooing the car.

Born in the wrong age, Michael identified closely with the eponymous hero of Ivan Goncharov's tragicomic masterpiece *Oblomov*, which was one of his favourite nineteenth-century novels. The description of Oblomov's daily struggle to get out of bed is worth quoting as it could equally have been written of Michael:

> As soon as he woke he made up his mind to get up, wash, and, after he had had breakfast, think things over thoroughly, come to some sort of decision, put it down on paper, and, generally, make a good job of it. He lay for half an hour, tormented by this decision; but afterwards it occurred to him that he would have plenty of time to

do it after breakfast, which he could have in bed as usual, particularly as there was nothing to prevent him from thinking while lying down.

'That was what he did. After breakfast he sat up and nearly got out of bed; glancing at his slippers, he even lowered one foot from the bed, but immediately put it back again. It struck half-past nine. Oblomov gave a start.

'What am I doing?' he said aloud in a vexed voice. 'This is awful! I must set to work! *

When the decision had finally been made, Michael would apply himself to his work with great mental stamina and, like Oblomov, make a good job of it. He took an equally determined approach to his leisure pursuits which included classical Chinese, Albanian and chess. He collected celadon ware and had become quite knowledgeable about Chinese ceramics, attending handling sessions at the British Museum – no doubt stressful occasions for the curators as Michael was notoriously clumsy, frequently smashing more than one utensil at a time in Dorothy's kitchen. His interest in Albanian was inspired by Lord Byron's travels, and by his admiration for the work of Ismail Kadare, the Albanian novelist and first international Booker Prize winner. Kadare was born in Gjirokastra, the UNESCO World Heritage site in Southern Albania, where Michael was seriously thinking of buying property. In preparation for this somewhat fanciful move to Gjirokastra, Michael attended an Albanian evening class at Morley College. After a term of hard work and much homework, he had strung together enough vocabulary to compose a violent short story on the theme of Balkan blood feuds. Hoping perhaps to have left all this behind her, the Kosovo-born tutor gave Michael a respectable mark before disappearing on mysterious sick leave. And so ended Michael's Albanian experiment, and with it the dream of spending his retirement, smoking a delicious Turkish cigarette within the ancient walls of a beautiful Ottoman town, dressed in Byron's famous Albanian costume or as close an approximation to it as could be achieved from TK Maxx Tirana.

In reality Silverman belonged to Leeds. It was his spiritual home to which he made regular visits. Many of his closest friends live there, and he had recently taken enormous pleasure in becoming a surrogate father to Lucy, the teenage daughter of his life-long friend, Alan Brown, who died in 2007. Michael was fortunate to have his sister, Louise, living closer to home in London, and he was a devoted uncle to her son, Charles.

Michael Silverman is survived by Dorothy Lothian who enabled him with quiet devotion over many years to keep his unique show on the road. He died rich in friendships and leaves a legacy of wonderful memories.

---

* Ivan Goncharov, *Oblomov*, translated by David Magarshack, Penguin, London, 1954.

# Abbreviations

ABA          Antiquarian Booksellers Association

ABE          AbeBooks, an online marketplace for books

ESTC         English Short-Title Catalogue, a database of books, pamphlets and other ephemeral material, mainly published in the British Isles and North America between 1473 and 1800, and mainly, but not exclusively, in English

ILAB         International League of Antiquarian Booksellers

PBFA        Provincial Booksellers Fairs Association

STC          *Short-Title Catalogue of Books printed in England, Scotland and Ireland, and of English books printed Abroad, 1475-1640*

TLS          *Times Literary Supplement*

Driff         B.C.M. Driffield, author of *Driff's guide to all the secondhand & antiquarian bookshops in Britain,* London, 1984

The Ring: an illegal auction practice in which two or more people agree in advance not to bid against each other, in order to reduce the competition and thereby depress the hammer price. The lot is purchased by one member of the ring, and subsequently re-auctioned in private amongst his fellow ringers. The difference between the price fetched in the official and the unofficial auction is shared between members of the ring.

Runner       A travelling (book) salesman

# INDEX